The Complete Prenuptial Agreement Kit

(+ CD-ROM)

The Complete Prenuptial Agreement Kit

(+ CD-ROM)

Edward A. Haman

Attorney at Law

SPHINX® PUBLISHING
AN IMPRINT OF SOURCEBOOKS, INC.®
NAPERVILLE, ILLINOIS
www.SphinxLegal.com

First Edition, 2006

Published by: Sphinx® Publishing, An Imprint of Sourcebooks, Inc.®

<u>Naperville Office</u>
P.O. Box 4410
Naperville, Illinois 60567-4410
630-961-3900
Fax: 630-961-2168
www.sourcebooks.com
www.sphinxlegal.com

This publication is designed to provide accurate and authoritative information in regard to the subject matter covered. It is sold with the understanding that the publisher is not engaged in rendering legal, accounting, or other professional service. If legal advice or other expert assistance is required, the services of a competent professional person should be sought.
From a Declaration of Principles Jointly Adopted by a Committee of the
American Bar Association and a Committee of Publishers and Associations

This product is not a substitute for legal advice.

Disclaimer required by Texas statutes.

Library of Congress Cataloging-in-Publication Data
Haman, Edward A.
  The complete prenuptial agreement kit / by Edward A. Haman. -- 1st ed.
     p. cm.
  Includes index.
  ISBN-13: 978-1-57248-534-1 (pbk. : alk. paper)
  ISBN-10: 1-57248-534-5 (pbk. : alk. paper)
 1. Antenuptial contracts--United States--Popular works. 2. Husband and wife--United States--Popular works. 3. Marital property--United States--Popular works. I. Title.

KF529.Z9.H355 2006
346.7301'662--dc22
                                                                                    2006018567

Printed and bound in the United States of America.
SB — 10 9 8 7 6 5 4 3 2 1

Contents

How to Use the CD-ROM

Thank you for purchasing *The Complete Prenuptial Agreement Kit*. In this book, we have worked hard to compile exactly what you need to customize and complete your own prenuptial agreement. To make this material even more useful, we have included every document in the book on the CD-ROM in the back of the book.

You can use these forms just as you would the forms in the book. Print them out, fill them in, and use them however you need. You can also fill in the forms directly on your computer. Just identify the form you need, open it, click on the space where the information should go, and input your information. Customize each form for your particular needs. Use them over and over again.

The CD-ROM is compatible with both PC and Mac operating systems. (While it should work with either operating system, we cannot guarantee that it will work with your particular system and we cannot provide technical assistance.) To use the forms on your computer, you will need to use Microsoft Word or another word processing program that can read Word files. The CD-ROM does not contain any such program.

Insert the CD-ROM into your computer. Double-click on the icon representing the disc on your desktop or go through your hard drive to identify the drive that contains the disc and click on it.

Once opened, you will see the files contained on the CD-ROM listed as "Form #: [Form Title]." Open the file you need. You may print the form to fill it out manually at this point, or you can click on the appropriate line to fill it in using your computer.

* * * * *

Purchasers of this book are granted a license to use the forms contained in it for their own personal use. By purchasing this book, you have also purchased a limited license to use all forms on the accompanying CD-ROM. The license limits you to personal use only and all other copyright laws must be adhered to. No claim of copyright is made in any government form reproduced in the book or on the CD-ROM. You are free to modify the forms and tailor them to your specific situation.

The author and publisher have attempted to provide the most current and up-to-date information available. However, the courts, Congress, and your state's legislatures review, modify, and change laws on an ongoing basis, as well as create new laws from time to time. Due to the very nature of the information and the continual changes in our legal system, to be sure that you have the current and best information for your situation, you should consult a local attorney or research the current laws yourself.

This publication is designed to provide accurate and authoritative information in regard to the subject matter covered. It is sold with the understanding that the publisher is not engaged in rendering legal, accounting, or other professional service. If legal advice or other expert assistance is required, the services of a competent professional person should be sought.

> —*From a Declaration of Principles Jointly Adopted by a Committee of the American Bar Association and a Committee of Publishers and Associations*

This product is not a substitute for legal advice.
> —*Disclaimer required by Texas statutes*

Using Self-Help Law Books

Before using a self-help law book, you should realize the advantages and disadvantages of doing your own legal work and understand the challenges and diligence that this requires.

The Growing Trend

Rest assured that you will not be the first or only person handling your own legal matter. For example, in some states, more than 75% of the people in divorces and other cases represent themselves. Because of the high cost of legal services, this is a major trend, and many courts are struggling to make it easier for people to represent themselves. However, some courts are not happy with people who do not use attorneys and refuse to help them in any way. For some, the attitude is, "Go to the law library and figure it out for yourself."

We write and publish self-help law books to give people an alternative to the often complicated and confusing legal books found in most law libraries. We have made the explanations of the law as simple and easy to understand as possible. Of course, unlike an attorney advising an individual client, we cannot cover every conceivable possibility.

Cost/Value Analysis

Whenever you shop for a product or service, you are faced with various levels of quality and price. In deciding what product or service to buy, you make a cost/value analysis on the basis of your willingness to pay and the quality you desire.

When buying a car, you decide whether you want transportation, comfort, status, or sex appeal. Accordingly, you decide among choices such as a Neon, a Lincoln, a Rolls Royce, or a Porsche. Before making a decision, you usually weigh the merits of each option against the cost.

When you get a headache, you can take a pain reliever (such as aspirin) or visit a medical specialist for a neurological examination. Given this choice, most people, of course, take a pain reliever, since it costs only pennies; whereas a medical examination costs hundreds of dollars and takes a lot of time. This is usually a logical choice because it is rare to need anything more than a pain reliever for a headache. But in some cases, a headache may indicate a brain tumor, and failing to see a specialist right away can result in complications. Should everyone with a headache go to a specialist? Of course not, but people treating their own illnesses must realize that they are betting, on the basis of their cost/value analysis of the situation, that they are taking the most logical option.

The same cost/value analysis must be made when deciding to do one's own legal work. Many legal situations are very straightforward, requiring a simple form and no complicated analysis. Anyone with a little intelligence and a book of instructions can handle the matter without outside help.

But there is always the chance that complications are involved that only an attorney would notice. To simplify the law into a book like this, several legal cases often must be condensed into a single sentence or paragraph. Otherwise, the book would be several hundred pages long and too complicated for most people. However, this simplification necessarily leaves out many details and nuances that would apply to special or unusual situations. Also, there are many ways to interpret most legal questions. Your case may come before a judge who disagrees with the analysis of our authors.

Therefore, in deciding to use a self-help law book and to do your own legal work, you must realize that you are making a cost/value analysis. You have decided that the money you will save in doing it yourself outweighs the chance that your case will not turn out to your satisfaction. Most people handling their own simple legal matters never have a problem, but occasionally people find that it ended up costing them more to have an attorney straighten out the situation than it would have if they had hired an attorney in the beginning. Keep this in mind while handling your case, and be sure to consult an attorney if you feel you might need further guidance.

Local Rules

The next thing to remember is that a book which covers the law for the entire nation, or even for an entire state, cannot possibly include every procedural difference of every jurisdiction. Whenever possible, we provide the exact form needed; however, in some areas, each county, or even each judge, may require unique forms and procedures. In our state books, our forms usually cover the majority of counties in the state or provide examples of the type of form that will be required. In our national books, our forms are sometimes even more general in nature but are designed to give a good idea of the type of form that will be needed in most locations. Nonetheless, keep in mind that your state, county, or judge may have a requirement, or use a form, that is not included in this book.

You should not necessarily expect to be able to get all of the information and resources you need solely from within the pages of this book. This book will serve as your guide, giving you specific information whenever possible and helping you to find out what else you will need to know. This is just like if you decided to build your own backyard deck. You might purchase a book on how to build decks. However, such a book would not include the building codes and permit requirements of every city, town, county, and township in the nation; nor would it include the lumber, nails, saws, hammers, and other materials and tools you would need to actually build the deck. You would use the book as your guide, and then do some work and research involving such matters as whether you need a permit of some kind, what type and grade of wood is available in your area, whether to use hand tools or power tools, and how to use those tools.

Before using the forms in a book like this, you should check with your court clerk to see if there are any local rules of which you should be aware or local forms you will need to use. Often, such forms will require the same information as the forms in the book but are merely laid out differently or use slightly different language. They will sometimes require additional information.

Changes in the Law

Besides being subject to local rules and practices, the law is subject to change at any time. The courts and the legislatures of all fifty states are constantly revising the laws. It is possible that while you are reading this book, some aspect of the law is being changed.

In most cases, the change will be of minimal significance. A form will be redesigned, additional information will be required, or a waiting period will be extended. As a result, you might need to revise a form, file an extra form, or wait out a longer time period. These types of changes will not usually affect the outcome of your case. On the other hand, sometimes a major part of the law is changed, the entire law in a particular area is rewritten, or a case that was the basis of a central legal point is overruled. In such instances, your entire ability to pursue your case may be impaired.

Introduction

Dividing property in the event of death or divorce can be a hassle and can cost a small fortune in legal fees if a battle develops. If you have children from a previous marriage, the divorce laws of your state may deny them the share of your property you would like them to have. The probate laws may deny them everything in the event of your death. If you are getting married late in life, and have built a successful business, the divorce or probate laws of your state may give a large share of your business to your spouse (or even force the sale of the business), even if the marriage was only for a short time. If your fiancé is wealthy, he or she (or his or her family) may be questioning your true intentions. These and many other problems connected with marriage can be solved by a contract known as a prenuptial agreement. Prenuptial agreements are also known as premarital agreements, especially in legal language. However, this book will primarily use the term "prenuptial agreement."

Even if you are already married, it is possible to enter into the same type of agreement with your spouse. In such a case it is called a *postmarital* or *postnuptial* agreement, but almost everything else will be similar.

This book explains what a prenuptial agreement is, help you decide if you need one, and show you how to prepare one. By preparing your own agreement, you can save the cost of a lawyer. Even if you decide to have a lawyer prepare an agreement for you, this book helps you understand prenuptial agreements and work more effectively with your attorney.

This is not a law school course, but a practical guide to enable you to draft a legal contract without a lawyer. Legal jargon has been kept to a minimum. The emphasis is on practical advice in plain English. The terms *fiancé* and *fiancée* are used interchangeably.

Chapters 1 through 5 give you information you need to understand prenuptial agreements. Chapters 6 and 7 give you detailed instructions for preparing and customizing your own prenuptial agreement. Chapter 8 guides you through creating a postnuptial agreement. Additional forms that are important to the process are explained in Chapter 9. Chapter 10 tells you how to change or cancel your prenuptial agreement. Next, there is a glossary of terms that you may see or hear in connection with prenuptial agreements. Appendix A gives information about the law relating to prenuptial agreements in each state. Appendix B contains the *Uniform Premarital Agreement Act*, which has been adopted by several states. Appendix C gives you some prenuptial agreement forms to use as models for preparing your own prenuptial agreement.

Chapter 1: Prenuptial Agreement Overview

A *prenuptial agreement* is a contract between two persons planning to marry that determines the rights they have to each other's property. You may also see them called *antenuptial* agreements, or *premarital* agreements. Prenuptial agreements are used to control how property will be divided in the event of divorce or the death of one of the spouses.

Marriage contracts are nothing new. For hundreds or even thousands of years, marriages have been based upon agreements between families and nations. Marriages were arranged by the parents in order to enhance family fortunes and keep peace between families and countries.

Most people do not fully appreciate the legal rights and obligations that are created when they marry. The legal aspects are often overlooked until it comes time for divorce. Then they find out that marriage is easy to get into, but difficult to get out of. The death of a spouse can also cause various problems with the couple's property.

When you get married, the law gives you and your spouse certain rights in each other's property. This includes property you acquire during your marriage, and may include property you acquired before you got married. The law also has provisions for how this property is handled in the event of divorce or death.

A prenuptial agreement might be considered a will for the death of a marriage (either due to actual death or to divorce). Just as a will can be used to avoid some of the hassles of probate, a prenuptial agreement can be used to avoid some of the hassles of divorce (and probate). Actually, everyone already has a will and a prenuptial agreement through the law. These are the probate and divorce laws, which can be viewed as the will and prenuptial agreement the state writes for you if you do not write your own. The divorce laws and the probate laws of your state give guidelines for the judge to follow in determining how property should be divided or distributed. By using a prenuptial agreement, you and your spouse can write your own guidelines to be used instead of your state's laws.

For a long time, many courts would not enforce prenuptial agreements. The law has traditionally favored marriage. In the minds of lawmakers and judges, a prenuptial agreement seemed to encourage divorce, so the lawmakers would not approve them and the judges would not enforce them. However, with the simplified divorce procedures and high divorce rate in more modern times, lawmakers and judges finally came to accept reality. Every state's laws now allow for prenuptial agreements.

Some people even include non-financial rights and responsibilities, as specific as who takes out the garbage and who does the dishes. However, since these types of agreements will not be enforced by the courts, they are better left out of the prenuptial agreement. If desired, these types of provisions should be part of a separate agreement that is just used to remind the husband and wife of their rights and responsibilities when disagreements arise.

Divorce Situations

When a couple gets divorced, the parties are required to divide up their property. If they cannot reach an agreement, the judge must decide who gets what. Most states have guidelines that the judge must apply in making this decision. Although the exact wording is different in each state, the general ideas are the same and the following factors are typically considered:

- ◆ whether the property belonged to one of the spouses before they were married;
- ◆ whether the property acquired during the marriage was a gift to one spouse;
- ◆ whether the property was inherited by one spouse during the marriage;
- ◆ whether the property was acquired by exchanging one of the types of property mentioned above;
- ◆ the length of the parties' marriage;
- ◆ each party's age and health;
- ◆ each party's financial circumstances, including income, occupation, education and training, and employability; and,
- ◆ each party's contribution to the acquisition, preservation, or appreciation of property.

The following is just one example of the type of problems that may occur in the event of a divorce.

Example: *When Joe and Maggie decided to get married, both of them were 38 years of age. Joe had opened his own business a year before and was still struggling to see his first profit. Maggie had no desire to help Joe in his business. Maggie had* *a home, with a mortgage that would be paid off in six years, although it was a real struggle for her to keep up the payments and make necessary repairs. She was depending on having the house paid off as part of her retirement nest egg. After they got married, they pooled their money for their living expenses, including the mortgage payments and house repairs. Joe also did some repair and improvement work on the house. Joe continued with his business.*

Three years later, they have decided to divorce. According to the divorce laws of their state, Maggie can claim part of Joe's business and Joe can claim part of Maggie's house. If Joe's business is highly successful, he may have to borrow money to pay off Maggie's interest. This may get him in debt over his head and cause him to lose his business, or he may have to sell the business to settle the divorce case. On the other hand, Maggie may need to refinance the house if she wants to buy out Joe's interest and keep her home. She may not be able to handle the new payments, and therefore, may have to sell the house. Even if she can make the new payments, it will take much longer than six years to pay off the mortgage, which will destroy her retirement plans.

A prenuptial agreement could have avoided such problems. Joe had a potentially profitable business, but Maggie had no interest in his business and there was no assurance that it would become profitable. Maggie had some degree of security in her home, and Joe would have no interest in her home if they were not married. A prenuptial agreement could have been written where Maggie would give up all rights to Joe's business in the event of divorce, and Joe would give up all rights to Maggie's home. This would preserve Maggie's retirement security and Joe's profits from his business.

Probate Situations

When one spouse dies, either the state's probate laws or the person's will determines how property is distributed. This generally depends upon how the property was titled. Property may be *titled*, or held, in one of four ways.

1. *Sole ownership*—All of the pieces of property are titled to one person.
2. *Tenants in common*—Two or more people hold title together. If one owner dies, his or her share of the property goes to his or her beneficiaries (by state law or will), and not automatically to the other owners.
3. *Joint tenants*—Again, two or more people hold title together. However, if one owner dies, his or her share automatically goes to the other owners. To make certain there is

no room for debate, you will often see this stated as "joint tenants with rights of survivorship."

4. *Tenants by the entirety*—this is basically the same as joint tenants, except that it can only exist between a husband and wife. Tenancy by the entirety is not available in all states. In states that do not have this type of tenancy, it is typical for spouses to hold property as joint tenants.

Property held in both spouses' names either as tenants by the entirety or joint tenants automatically becomes the sole property of the surviving spouse. What happens to other property (held by one spouse alone or by both as tenants in common) depends upon whether there was a will.

If there was no will, the other property will generally go to the surviving spouse, unless there are children. Then it is typical for a portion to be given to the spouse and a portion to be given to the children.

If there is a will, the other property will be distributed as directed in the will. However, most states make it impossible to deny property to the surviving spouse. In most states, the surviving spouse is entitled to a certain share of the property—regardless of what the will says. This is called the surviving spouse's *elective share* or *forced share*.

Example: *Frank is divorced and has a son from his first marriage. Frank and Lois have been married for one year, and they do not have any children together. Lois is financially independent, as she has a large trust fund set up by her wealthy parents. Frank dies, leaving a will that gives $10,000 to Lois and the balance of his estate (his business worth $800,000) to his son, who helped him in his business for fifteen years.*

Under the laws of their state, Lois can claim one-half of Frank's estate, or $405,000. The main asset in Frank's estate is his business. This leaves Frank's son with a sad choice: either borrow $405,000 to pay off Lois' claim, take on Lois as a business partner, or sell the business to pay off Lois' claim. This is certainly not the situation Frank desired, and it could have been avoided with a prenuptial agreement.

There are numerous situations where a prenuptial agreement could be of help. Chapter 2 discusses this idea more, and helps you decide if you can benefit from a prenuptial agreement.

Chapter 2:
Deciding on a Prenuptial Agreement

Your state government has created a plan for how your property will be divided in the event of divorce or death. Ask yourself if you are satisfied with the state's plan or if you want your own plan. Think about all of the laws your state legislature has passed. Then, ask yourself if you like any plan the legislature came up with on any subject.

Most state laws regarding the distribution of property after death or in the event of divorce leave plenty of room for a judge's interpretation. Therefore, you can never be sure what a judge will decide is really your property after a marriage. The only way to possibly avoid this is with a prenuptial agreement.

The need to have a prenuptial agreement often does not become apparent until there is a divorce or a death, which is when problems you never thought of tend to emerge. Divorce is more common than most want to believe. Some statistics suggest the divorce rate is even higher in second marriages than in first marriages.

Do not forget that prenuptial agreements can be useful in the event of death, which is a subject even fewer people seem comfortable thinking about. It is always strange to hear insurance salesmen talking about "in the event of death," as if some people escape it altogether.

Most people think that a prenuptial agreement is what rich people use to protect their property in the event of divorce from their less wealthy spouse. Actually, there are many more reasons to use a prenuptial agreement.

First Marriages

Even if you and your partner are a young couple with no significant property and typical jobs, and this is the first marriage for both of you, there is some evidence to indicate that prenuptial agreements actually promote stability in a marriage. This is because preparing one gives you a chance to carefully think about the significance of marriage, to clearly understand each other's financial situation, and to consider how you see your financial futures (individually and together). Discussing a prenuptial agreement, even if one is never finalized, will make you realize that by getting married, you are entering into a legally binding contract with financial rights and obligations. This side of marriage is usually totally overshadowed by the romantic and religious aspects, and by the ceremony and honeymoon planning.

Many spouses do not know any of the details of the other's finances. Since one of the requirements of a prenuptial agreement is fully disclosing each party's financial situation, preparing one will help the couple get a clearer understanding of their total financial health. This can be very helpful in making financial decisions. If more couples had worked together on such things as purchasing decisions and monthly budgeting, perhaps the bankruptcy and divorce courts would not be as crowded as they are today.

It is also good for a couple to share common dreams and goals. Focusing on a prenuptial agreement can help the couple discuss their career and economic goals in life. Especially with the common two-career couple, it is important to share thoughts on where each person intends his or her career to head. If each person is intent on developing his or her career, it might be a good idea for the couple to sign a prenuptial agreement giving up rights in each other's income or business (especially if they have a fairly equivalent earning potential and they are just starting out in their careers). On the other hand, if they are in business together, a prenuptial agreement could outline how the business will be divided in the event of divorce. This document would avoid expensive attorneys' fees later, and prevent a fight over the business in the divorce proceeding.

Children of Prior Marriages

One of the main circumstances for a prenuptial agreement is when one or both of the parties have children from a prior marriage or relationship. In such cases, a prenuptial agreement may be the only way to assure that the children are protected in the event of divorce or death. Otherwise, all of your property may go to your second spouse, with your children getting nothing.

Example: *Rob and Rita are married and have no children together, but Rob has two adult children from his former marriage. If Rob dies without leaving a will, under the laws of their state, all of Rob's property goes to Rita. Rob's children will receive nothing.*

A prenuptial agreement can help assure that children from a prior marriage will be provided for as intended by their parent. Your future spouse should have no objection to you wanting to take care of your children.

Business or Investment Partners

If you have business partners, especially if they are family members, you should have a prenuptial agreement to prevent disruption of the business in the event of divorce or death. Otherwise, you or your partners may end up with your spouse as a business partner, and that can cause all kinds of problems.

This caution also applies if the business is a privately held corporation. Many problems have occurred when a spouse inherits stock or receives stock as part of a divorce judgment.

Example: *Mark and his brother Jim each hold 50% of the stock in a small restaurant business started by their father. Mark married Jane, and several years later Mark died, leaving Jane his half of the stock. Jane was then the business partner of her brother-in-law. Jane then married Fred. When she and Fred divorced two years later, she gave Fred the stock in the restaurant as part of the property settlement. Now Jim has Fred for a partner. Is this what Mark would have wanted? Is this what Mark and Jim's father intended to happen to his family business?*

Suppose Mark and Jane had divorced. A judge might have divided the stock between them. Now Jim would have 50%, and Mark and Jane would each have 25% percent. Now Mark has his ex-wife as a business partner. Mark and Jim together could out-vote Jane, but what might happen if the relationship between Mark and Jim was strained to begin with? Now Jim and Jane might join forces to out-vote Mark.

Your Situation

Most states first divide property into two categories: *marital property* and *nonmarital property*. Generally, nonmarital property includes what each of you had before your marriage. If you are like most people, you would both want to keep what was yours before you got together, in the event you split up. This sometimes becomes a problem if you cannot prove what was yours before. In a prenuptial agreement, you can write down what these nonmarital items are for each of you. That way, there is no arguing later.

You may have family heirlooms or other special items that you would like to stay in your family when you pass away.

Example: *Diane has a diamond pendant that belonged to her great-grandmother. In the event of her death, Diane would want it to go to her sister. However, if she died without a will, the pendant would go to her husband. Even if she left the pendant to her sister in a will, her husband might have the right to the pendant if it was so valuable that it is a substantial portion of Diane's estate. Diane's husband might then marry, have a daughter with his new wife, and give the pendant to his daughter.*

This type of situation is common in countless families, quite possibly including yours. In such cases, a prenuptial agreement might avoid undesirable results. You should consider a prenuptial agreement if any of the following situations apply:

◆ you and your fiancé want to review your financial situation and plans for the future;

◆ one or both of you own a business;

◆ one or both of you are starting out in a career or in a business with potential for substantial financial growth;

◆ one or both of you have significant property (including cash) that you want to preserve for yourself in the event of divorce; or,

◆ one or both of you have certain items you want to preserve for someone else (such as a family member) in the event of divorce or death.

In addition to these situations, you need to examine your financial circumstances (including future plans for your career, business, or investments) and think about how they might be affected by a divorce or death.

Chapter 3:
Hiring a Lawyer

Whether you need an attorney will depend upon several factors, such as how comfortable you feel handling the matter yourself, whether your financial situation is extremely complicated, and whether you have a very large estate to protect. If a lot of money is involved, you should hire a lawyer. As you will see in the next chapter, if your fiancé will be giving up a substantial amount, it may be best if he or she sees a lawyer before signing anything.

One of the first questions you will want to consider (and most likely the reason you are reading this book) is *how much will an attorney cost?* Attorneys come in all price ranges. Fees will also depend on how complicated your prenuptial agreement needs to be.

Selecting an attorney is not easy. It is difficult to know whether you are selecting an attorney you will be happy with. Most have probably never prepared a prenuptial agreement. This chapter details the best ways to find a lawyer, how to work with the one you hire, and what to do if that lawyer does not work out.

Selecting a Lawyer

Selecting a lawyer is a two-step process. First, you need to decide which attorney to make an appointment with. Then, you need to decide if you want to hire that attorney.

Finding Lawyers

The following suggestions will help you identify a few lawyers you may want to consider hiring.

Ask a Friend

A common, and frequently the best, way to find a lawyer is to ask someone you know to recommend one. This is especially helpful if the lawyer prepared a prenuptial agreement for your friend, or represented your friend in some other family law or probate matter.

Lawyer Referral Service

You can find a referral service by looking in the Yellow Pages under "Attorney Referral Services" or "Attorneys." This is a service, usually operated by a bar association, that is designed to match a client with an attorney handling cases in the area of law the client needs. A bar association referral service does not guarantee the quality of work, the level of experience, or the ability of the attorney. Some private referral services may offer some additional protections or guarantees. Finding a lawyer this way will at least connect you with one who is interested in family law matters and probably has some experience in this area.

Yellow Pages

Check the Yellow Pages under the heading for "Attorneys." Many lawyers and law firms will place display ads here indicating their areas of practice and educational backgrounds. Look for firms or lawyers that indicate they practice in areas such as divorce, family law, domestic relations, probate, or estate planning.

Ask a Lawyer

If you have used the services of an attorney in the past for some other matter (for example, a real estate closing, a traffic ticket, or a will), you may want to call and ask if he or she handles prenuptial agreements or could refer you to an attorney whose ability in this area is respected.

The Internet

There are listings of attorneys and their primary practice areas on the Internet. Try **www.lawyers.com** or **www.martindale.com**.

Evaluating Lawyers

From your search, you should select three to five lawyers worthy of further consideration. Your first step will be to call each attorney's office, explain that you are interested in having a prenuptial agreement prepared, and ask the following questions.

- ◆ Does the attorney (or firm) handle prenuptial agreements?
- ◆ How much can you expect it to cost?
- ◆ How soon can you get an appointment?

If you like the answers you get, ask if you can speak to the attorney. Some offices will permit this, but others will require you to make an appointment. Make the appointment if necessary. Once you get in contact with the attorney (either on the phone or at the appointment), ask the following questions.

♦ Has the attorney prepared prenuptial agreements before?

♦ How much will it cost?

♦ How long will it take?

♦ How long has the attorney been in practice?

♦ How long has the attorney been in practice in your state?

If you get acceptable answers to those questions, it is time to ask yourself the following questions about the lawyer.

♦ Do you feel comfortable talking to the lawyer?

♦ Is the lawyer friendly toward you?

♦ Does the lawyer seem confident in him- or herself?

♦ Does the lawyer seem to be straightforward with you and is he or she able to explain things so you understand?

♦ Can you afford the fees?

If you get satisfactory answers to all of these questions and feel comfortable with the lawyer, you probably have a lawyer you will be able to work with.

Working with a Lawyer

In general, you will work best with your attorney if you keep an open, honest, and friendly attitude. You should also consider the following suggestions.

Clear Agreement

Most attorneys ask for money up front. Your attorney should clearly tell you what will be done for this fee. Horror stories abound of attorneys using up $500 or $1,000 with nothing to show for it. Be sure that for the fee, you are going to get a prenuptial agreement prepared in a format ready to be signed.

Questions

If you want to know something or if you do not understand something, ask your attorney. If you do not understand the answer, tell your attorney and ask him or her to explain it again. There are many points of law that even many lawyers do not fully understand, so you should not be embarrassed to ask questions. Many people who say they had a bad experience with a lawyer either did not ask enough questions or had a lawyer who would not take the time to explain things to them. If your lawyer is not taking the time to explain what he or she is doing, it may be time to look for a new lawyer.

Complete Information

Anything you tell your attorney is confidential. An attorney can lose his or her license to practice if he or she reveals information to a third party without your permission, so do not hold back. However, one of the basic principals of prenuptial agreements is *full disclosure*. This means you will need to tell your fiancé about all of your property. If you hide anything, it can be grounds for a court to refuse to enforce the prenuptial agreement.

Reality

Listen to what your lawyer tells you about the law, and accept it. It will do you no good to argue, because the law does not work the way you think it should. By refusing to accept reality, you are only setting yourself up for disappointment. Remember, it is not your attorney's fault that the system is not perfect or that the law does not say what you would like it to say.

Patience

Do not expect your lawyer to return your phone call within an hour. He or she may not be able to return it the same day, either. Most lawyers are very busy and overworked. It is rare that an attorney can maintain a full caseload and still make each client feel as if he or she is the attorney's only client.

Your Lawyer's Secretary

Your lawyer's secretary can be a valuable source of information. Be friendly and get to know him or her. Often the secretary will be able to answer your questions, and you will not get a bill for the time you talk to the secretary.

Keeping Things Moving

Many lawyers operate on the old principle that *the squeaking wheel gets the oil*. Work on a case tends to get put off until a deadline is near, an emergency develops, or the client calls. This is because in order to make the income they desire, many lawyers take more cases than can be effectively handled. Your task is to become a squeaking wheel that gets attention but does not squeak so much that your attorney and his or her staff want to avoid you. Whenever you talk to your lawyer, ask the following questions.

♦ What is the next step?
♦ When do you expect it to be done?
♦ When should I talk to you next?

If you do not hear from the lawyer when you expect, call him or her the following day. Do not remind your attorney that he or she did not call—just ask how things are going.

Money

Of course, you do not want to spend unnecessary money for an attorney. The following are a few things you can do to avoid excess legal fees.

 ◆ Do not make unnecessary phone calls to your lawyer.
 ◆ Give information to the secretary whenever possible.
 ◆ Direct your question to the secretary first. Your question will be referred to the attorney if necessary.
 ◆ Plan your phone calls so you can get to the point and take less of your attorney's time. Make notes or an outline if it will help.
 ◆ Do some of the legwork yourself. For example, pick up and deliver papers yourself. Ask your attorney what you can do to assist him or her.
 ◆ Be prepared for appointments. Have all related papers with you, plan your visit to get to the point, and make an outline of what you want to discuss and what questions you want to ask.

No client gets prompt attention like a client who pays his or her lawyer on time. Many attorneys will have you sign an agreement that states how you will be charged.

Firing a Lawyer

If you find that you can no longer work with your lawyer or that you do not trust your lawyer, it is time to either go it alone or get a new attorney. You will need to send your lawyer a letter, stating that you no longer desire his or her services and are discharging him or her from representing you. Also, state that you will be coming by his or her office the following day to pick up your file. The attorney does not have to give you his or her own notes or other work that is in progress, but he or she must give you the essential contents of your file (such as copies of papers already prepared and billed for, and any documents you provided). If he or she refuses to give you your file for any reason, contact your state's bar association about filing a complaint or *grievance* against the lawyer. Of course, you will need to settle any remaining fees owed.

Chapter 4:
The Law of Prenuptial Agreements

This chapter will provide an overview of the law relating to prenuptial agreements. If you are going to enter into a prenuptial agreement, you should have some idea of the extent to which you can expect it to be enforced, what matters can be covered, and how the agreement relates to probate and divorce proceedings. All of this will be discussed in this chapter, as well as how to conduct additional legal research if you desire.

A Brief History

The law of prenuptial agreements has evolved over time. Originally, they were not recognized by some courts, because it was felt that prenuptial agreements somehow encouraged divorce. Eventually, they were enforced by courts, and the law regarding prenuptial agreements was slowly created in the opinions of the appellate courts.

Next, state legislatures became involved, and prenuptial agreements were officially made a part of probate laws. These laws did not specifically apply to divorce situations, but the divorce courts began unofficially using them anyway.

Finally, an independent *Uniform Premarital Agreement Act* was created, and that has been adopted in the District of Columbia and the following states: Arizona, Arkansas, California, Connecticut, Delaware, Hawaii, Idaho, Illinois, Indiana, Iowa, Kansas, Maine, Montana, Nebraska, Nevada, New Jersey, New Mexico, North Carolina, North Dakota, Oregon, Rhode Island, South Dakota, Texas, Utah, Virginia, and Wisconsin. In addition, the following states have a statute or case law that allows for prenuptial agreements in a form other than the Act: Alabama, Colorado, Florida, Georgia, Kentucky, Louisiana, Maryland, Massachusetts, Michigan, Minnesota, Mississippi, Missouri, New Hampshire, New York, Ohio, Oklahoma, Pennsylvania, Tennessee,

Washington, and West Virginia. The fact that the number of states that have adopted the *Uniform Premarital Agreement Act* has grown significantly in the past few years and the number of states otherwise allowing these types of agreements indicate that prenuptial agreements are becoming more popular and acceptable.

Uniform Probate Code Provision

A typical probate law provision is found in the Probate Code, which has been adopted in many states. The following is an example from Alaska.

> ***Sec. 13.11.085. Waiver of right to elect and of other rights.*** *The right of election of a surviving spouse and the rights of the surviving spouse to homestead allowance, exempt property and family allowance, or any of them, may be waived, wholly or partially, before or after marriage, by a written contract, agreement or waiver signed by the party waiving after full disclosure. Unless it provides to the contrary, a waiver of "all rights" (or equivalent language) in the property or estate of a present or prospective spouse or a complete property settlement entered into after or in antici-pation of separation or divorce is a waiver of all rights to elective share, homestead allowance, exempt property and family allowance by each spouse in the property of the other and a renunciation by each of all benefits which would otherwise pass to that spouse from the other by intestate succession or by virtue of the provisions of any will executed before the waiver or property settlement.*

The Courts and Prenuptial Agreements

Unfortunately, there is no absolute guarantee that a particular agreement will be enforced. Judges make the decisions, and there is no way to predict what a particular judge will do in a particular case. All you can do is look at various decisions made by various courts, and try to avoid the pit-falls that defeated similar agreements in the past. If the judge feels that both parties knew what they were doing and the agreement is fair, the agreement will be enforced. If the judge feels that one party took unfair advantage of the other, the agreement will be declared invalid.

Types of Prenuptial Agreements

How a court looks at a prenuptial agreement may depend upon the husband's and wife's situa-tions and the type of prenuptial agreement. Prenuptial agreements may be divided or broken down into three types of provisions:

1. those concerning the division of property upon the death of one party;
2. those that simply designate each party's separate property being brought into the marriage; and,
3. those that concern rights in property acquired during the marriage.

Any prenuptial agreement may contain one or more of these types of provisions.

Guidelines

To get an idea of how courts may look at a prenuptial agreement, it may be helpful to examine a particular case as an example. In *Del Vecchio v. Del Vecchio*, 143 So.2d 17 (Florida Supreme Court 1962), the prenuptial agreement gave a disproportionately small amount to the wife, especially considering the substantial property and income of the husband. The husband did not make full disclosure of his financial situation to the wife, although she did know that he had substantial business and property interests. The wife also did not have the advice of independent legal counsel before she signed the agreement.

The Florida Supreme Court did not address the particular agreement, but sent the case back to the trial court with instructions for the trial court to review the case again considering the following criteria.

1. Does the agreement make fair and reasonable provisions for the wife? (This could also be the husband if the wife is the person with the greater financial resources and the husband is giving up significant rights.) If it is fair and reasonable, then the agreement is valid. Whether the agreement is fair and reasonable should be determined by looking at the parties' relative situations, such as their ages, health, experience in financial matters, property held by each, and the needs of each spouse. After a divorce, each spouse must be able to live in a similar manner to what he or she enjoyed before the marriage. The person must be able to live "certainly no less comfortably than before the marriage" (from the *Del Vecchio* case). The question of whether the agreement is fair and reasonable is determined with reference to the time at which the agreement was signed.

2. If the agreement is not fair and reasonable, then the court should ask if there was full disclosure of each spouse's financial situation and if each spouse had an understanding of her or his rights. If there was full disclosure and an understanding of rights, the agreement is valid.

3. If the agreement was not fair and reasonable, and there was not full disclosure, then the court should ask if the wife (or husband) had actual knowledge of the husband's (or wife's) property, or if he or she should have had a general knowledge of it. If he or she had, or should have had, such knowledge, the agreement should probably be declared valid.

As courts now consider the above points in many prenuptial agreement matters, they will also look at whether each spouse had competent and independent legal advice, although such advice is not absolutely necessary to declare the agreement valid. Although the *Del Vecchio* case involved a probate situation, later cases followed it in divorce situations as well.

The *Del Vecchio* case is an example of how the Florida courts look at prenuptial agreements, but the same or similar factors are used in most states. For example, in the case of *In re Marriage of Kesler*, 4 Fam. L. Rptr. 2498 (Ohio Common Pleas 1978), the wife voluntarily chose not to have independent legal counsel advise her about the prenuptial agreement. The Ohio Court of Common Pleas decided that her choice was irrelevant, that she must have legal counsel even if she did not want it (due to the size and complexity of the husband's estate), and that the prenuptial agreement was therefore invalid. In this case, one party signs a prenuptial agreement after declining legal advice, then uses her own voluntary action to have the agreement set aside. This is a perfect example of how unpredictable courts can be.

The Parties

Where both parties have a similar value of property and are fairly equal in their knowledge of or experience with financial matters, the courts are likely to enforce the agreement. However, where one party has much more property or income than the other, or is much more financially sophisticated, the court will more closely consider the following questions.

♦ Did the party with the advantage fully disclose the extent of his or her property and income to the other party?

♦ Are the provisions of the agreement fair and reasonable to the other party?

♦ Did the other party freely and voluntarily sign the agreement?

♦ Did the other party have the advice of independent legal counsel before signing the agreement?

Division upon Death Provisions

Division upon death provisions relate to probate laws. Although the details of probate law vary from state to state, there are some general principles that apply in most, if not all, states. Upon the death of a spouse, the distribution of property depends upon whether there is a will. If there is not a will, the state laws will determine who gets the property. These laws assure that the surviving spouse receives a certain portion of the property. If there are no children, the spouse usually gets it all. If there are children, the property usually gets apportioned between the spouse and the children. The surviving spouse may get a set percentage of the estate or may have the right to live in the marital home until death. This right may only apply to the wife in some states.

If there is a will, it determines who gets the property. However, state laws still assure the surviving spouse (again, possibly only the wife) a minimal amount of the estate.

Example: *Suppose that Jack dies. His will leaves $1,000 to his wife Jill, and leaves the rest of his property (valued at $299,000) to The Wishing Well Foundation, Jack's favorite charity. Jill can take advantage of her state's law regarding a spouse's elective share, and get one-third of Jack's estate (or $100,000). The amount of the elective share varies from state to state, but the principle is the same.*

By signing a prenuptial agreement, a spouse can give up such rights to a minimum amount of his or her spouse's estate. In such cases, the judge will want to be sure that the surviving spouse will not be left destitute, and that he or she knew the extent of the other's estate when the agreement was signed and what rights were being given up.

Separate Property

Historically, courts would not enforce prenuptial agreements dealing with divorce. Such agreements were considered to encourage divorce, and the government wanted to encourage marriage. Now that divorce is much more common, the courts and the legislatures have come around to accepting prenuptial agreements.

Most, if not all, states recognize the concept of *separate property* in a marriage. You may also see separate property referred to as *nonmarital property* or *sole property*. Generally in a divorce, all property acquired during the marriage is considered *marital* property. In some states it is called *community* property. (There are legal technical differences between marital and community property, but for purposes of this discussion, these differences are not important.) Marital property is jointly owned by the parties, and will be fairly equally divided between them in a divorce. Typical examples of separate property include:

◆ property owned by one party before the marriage;
◆ property acquired during the marriage as a gift to one party individually;
◆ property acquired during the marriage as an inheritance by one party individually; or,
◆ any property acquired during the marriage by exchanging any of the types of property described above.

The listing for your state in Appendix A of this book gives you an idea of how your state laws view separate property.

Since the idea of separate property is so widely recognized and used, the courts will usually enforce a prenuptial agreement or provision that simply designates what property is separate. This is the type of provision that is the most likely to be enforced in court.

Property Acquired during Marriage

Prenuptial agreements dealing with how property acquired during the marriage will be distributed upon divorce or death will be more carefully reviewed by courts. Generally, property acquired during the marriage is considered joint property (or community property), regardless of how the title is held. The standard provision in a prenuptial agreement is to reverse this generality, and make how title is held the determining factor as to whether the property is joint or separate. This allows the couple to determine how each piece of property is held as they acquire it.

For example, if a couple wants a piece of property to be solely owned by the wife, only her name would appear on the title. Wherever title is unclear, the court will probably determine the property to be joint or community property.

Circumstances When Signed

The court may also look at the circumstances that existed at the time the prenuptial agreement was signed. If one person was threatened, pressured, coerced, or unduly influenced to sign the agreement, the court will declare the agreement invalid. Another point is whether the person had sufficient time to consider what he or she was about to sign. Each party should have a copy of the agreement for several days (a week or two would be even better) before signing it. This will allow enough time for each person to study it, think about it, and have it reviewed by independent legal and financial advisers before signing. It should also be signed well before the day of the wedding. (At least a week before would be advisable.)

Alimony, Child Support, and Child Custody

Provisions to eliminate or limit alimony will also be upheld where there was full disclosure. If both parties are in roughly equal financial situations, mutual waivers of alimony will be no problem. However, alimony provisions in prenuptial agreements are usually viewed in terms of the parties' situations at the time the agreement was signed. A later change in circumstances may cause problems with enforcing such provisions.

Example: *Suppose that Fred and Ginger are in fairly equal financial positions at the time they sign a prenuptial agreement mutually waiving alimony. Both have jobs earning about the same income, and they have property of approximately equal* *value. Five years later, Ginger is involved in a serious automobile accident that leaves her permanently disabled and unable to continue working. If either of them file for divorce, the court is unlikely to uphold the alimony waiver provision of the prenuptial agreement.*

Similarly, courts will not enforce an alimony waiver or limitation that would leave one spouse without sufficient support, especially if that spouse would need government assistance.

Child support and custody provisions that are reasonable and leave the child adequately cared for will probably be upheld. However, most state divorce laws have criteria for determining custody and a formula for determining child support. An agreement will not be upheld if it would not provide adequate child support (if it is substantially less than the state's child support formula) or has a custody arrangement that is clearly against the child's best interest (such as giving custody to a convicted child abuser).

Pension Plans

When it comes to divorce law, one of the most difficult assets to deal with is a pension or retirement plan. Generally, a pension plan is considered a marital asset to be divided between the parties. For some couples, this is one of the largest assets they have. If both parties are employed and have pension plans of fairly equal value, they will probably each keep their own plan. In this situation, a provision in a prenuptial agreement where both parties waive any stake in each other's plan will probably be upheld.

However, problems can arise when only one party has a pension plan, or when one party's plan is significantly more valuable than the other's. In these situations, one party's plan will need to be evaluated by an accountant or lawyer to determine how much of it belongs to the other. This can be a complex calculation, taking into consideration things such as the length of marriage, the length of time the parties will probably continue to work, the length of time the parties are likely to live beyond retirement, and so on. Still, if the party giving up these rights understands what is being given up, and does so voluntarily, the waiver will probably be upheld.

To further complicate things, the United States Circuit Court of Appeals for the Second Circuit has ruled that pension rights can only be waived by a spouse—not by a fiancé. This means that you may need a *postmarital* agreement (instead of a prenuptial agreement) in order to effectively waive pension rights. (See page 87 for examples of pension plan waivers.)

Legal Research

In order to be certain that you are doing things correctly, you may need to do a little research into the law in your state. Appendix A of this book provides some information regarding the law in each state, and will give you a starting point for looking further. To find out about the laws that apply to you, look for your state's listing in Appendix A of this book. This will give you some basic information about the law in your state. More information about how to use Appendix A is found in later chapters and at the beginning of Appendix A. It is also strongly suggested that you visit a law library to do more detailed research.

After this book, you may want to visit your local law library. One can usually be found in or near your county courthouse. If you live near a law school, you can also find a library there. Do not hesitate to ask the law librarian to help you find what you need. The librarian cannot give you legal advice, but can show you where to find your state's laws and other books on prenuptial agreements. Some typical sources are discussed in the following sections.

Statutes or Codes

The main source of information will be the set of volumes that contain the laws passed by your state legislature. Depending upon your state, these will be referred to as either the *statutes* or the *code* of your state; for example, Florida Statutes or Mississippi Code. The actual title of the books may also include words such as *revised* or *annotated*; for example, Annotated California Code, Illinois Statutes Annotated, Kentucky Revised Statutes, or Maine Revised Statutes Annotated. *Revised* simply means updated, and *annotated* means that the books contain summaries of court decisions and other information that explains and interprets the laws.

In some states, the titles will also include the name of the publisher, such as West's Colorado Revised Statutes Annotated, Vernon's Annotated Missouri Statutes, or Purdon's Pennsylvania Consolidated Statutes Annotated. The listing for your state in Appendix A gives the title of the set of laws for your state under the heading "The Law."

A few states have more than one set of laws by various publishers. (For example, Florida has both Florida Statutes and Florida Statutes Annotated, and Michigan has both Michigan Statutes Annotated and Michigan Compiled Laws Annotated.) Each state's listing in Appendix A will give the name of the set of books used by the author. Ask the law librarian for help if you have any problems in locating your state's laws.

Each year, the legislature meets and changes the law. Therefore, it is important to be sure you have the most current version. Once you locate the set of books at the library, you will find that they are updated in one of three ways. The most common way to update laws is with a softcover supplement, which will be found in the back of each volume. There will be a date on the cover of the supplement to tell you when it was published (such as "2007 Cumulative Supplement"). If it is more than one year old, ask the librarian if it is the most current supplement. Another way laws are updated is with a supplement volume, which will be found at the end of the regular set of volumes. This supplement will also have a date or year on it. A few states use a looseleaf binding, in which pages are removed and replaced, or a supplement section added as the law changes.

Practice Manuals

At the law library, you may also be able to find *practice manuals*, which are books containing detailed information about various aspects of the law. You may find practice manuals about prenuptial agreement law in your state, including sample forms for all different situations. Some of these books are written in connection with seminars for lawyers and can be very helpful in answering your questions about very specific situations. Again, ask the librarian to help you.

You probably will not need to do any more research than reviewing any laws your state may have regarding prenuptial agreements and looking at some of the forms in a practice manual. In addition to the laws passed by the legislature, law is also made by the decisions of the judges in various cases each year. You can find this *case law* at the law library. In addition to annotated codes or statutes, there are several types of books used to find the case law.

Digests

A *digest* is a set of volumes that gives short summaries of appeals court cases, and tells you where you can find the court's full written opinion. The information in the digest is arranged alphabetically by subject. First, try to find a digest for your state (such as New York Digest). There is a digest that covers the entire United States, but it will be easier to find your state's laws in a state digest. Look for the chapter on "Prenuptial Agreements," "Antenuptial Agreements," or "Marriage," then look for the headings for the subject you want. If you cannot find a chapter with one of these titles, look in the index under these words to find out what chapter title you should use.

Case Reporters

A case reporter is where the appeals courts publish their written opinions on the cases they hear. There may be a specific reporter for your state, or you may need to use a regional reporter that contains cases from several states in your area. Your librarian can help you locate the reporter for your state. There may be two *series* of the regional reporter, the second series being newer than the first. For example, if the digest gives a reference to "*Del Vecchio v. Del Vecchio*, 143 So.2d 17 (1962)," this tells you that you can find the case titled *Del Vecchio v. Del Vecchio* by going to Volume 143 of the Southern Reporter 2d Series, and turning to page 17. The number in parentheses (1962) is the year the court issued its opinion. In its opinion, the court will discuss what the case was about, what questions of law were presented for consideration, and what the court decided and why.

pedia

       is similar to a regular encyclopedia. You simply look up the subject you want
prenuptial agreements, marriage, divorce, etc.) in alphabetical order, and it gives you a
summary of the law on that subject. It will also refer to specific court cases, which can then be
found in the Reporter. On a national level, the two main sets are *American Jurisprudence* (abbreviated "Am. Jur.") and *Corpus Juris Secundum* (C.J.S.). You may also find a set for your state, such
as Florida Jurisprudence.

Internet Research

Much of the type of research discussed above is available on the Internet. The statutes or codes
for all fifty states and the District of Columbia can be found at **www.findlaw.com**. Once you get
to the Findlaw site, click on the tab titled "For Legal Professionals," then click on "US Laws: Cases
& Codes." Then, scroll down to the heading "US Statutes and Cases" and click on the desired
state. Next, click on the state's code or statutes. From this point, navigating the state's website will
vary depending upon how the site operates. Generally, you will either be able to enter a specific
statute section number, go to a list of the various titles or chapters of the statutes, or do a search
by statute number or keyword.

Chapter 5:
Talking to Your Partner

There is no clear-cut way to talk to your partner about a prenuptial agreement. Each person has a different experience, background, and attitude about the subject, so the same approach will not work with everyone. All that can be done is to offer several suggestions and ideas, so that you can choose or design an approach that you think will be the best for your situation.

It is important for you to realize that discussion of a prenuptial agreement will probably contain both logical and emotional aspects. The emotional aspect will be more difficult to anticipate and deal with.

Many people do not like the idea of a prenuptial agreement. The main reason for this discomfort is that prenuptial agreements appear to be looking toward a divorce even before the couple is married. Similarly, many people do not make a will because it means they have to think about death. The world would probably be a much more pleasant place if no one had to deal with death, divorce, and taxes. Unfortunately, people do not have this luxury.

Many people also think that a prenuptial agreement diminishes the romance of marriage. Therefore, it can be important to bring up the subject in the right way. This may depend upon the relative financial positions of you and your intended spouse. If you are both of roughly equal wealth, you would approach the subject differently than if you are a wealthy person about to marry someone of lesser means.

First of all, think about the central question—why would someone want to sign a prenuptial agreement? Because the agreement is fair and to get some kind of protection or advantage from it. You cannot expect your partner to sign (or even be receptive to the idea of) a one-sided agreement.

Financial Future

To deal with the potential emotional reaction, you may want to begin with a general discussion of planning your financial future together. This is important for any individual or couple, even if they do not want a prenuptial agreement. Several years ago, Harvard University conducted a study of its graduates. It found that 3% had specific written goals, 10% had goals in mind but not written, and 87% had not set goals. The 3% with specific written goals accomplished fifty to one hundred times more in their lifetimes than the 10% with goals in their mind only. Comparatively, very little was accomplished by the 87% with no *written* goals.

Therefore, it is important for the two of you to plan for your future. Such planning will involve talking about your dreams and desires for your careers, for having children and for their future, and for what kind of a lifestyle you want to seek. Part of financial planning includes examining your life insurance needs, and this consideration may lead to a discussion of having wills prepared. As was discussed earlier, there are many situations in which a will may be insufficient to accomplish what is intended, and a prenuptial agreement can cure this problem.

Plan and Write Together

The ideal way to prepare a prenuptial agreement is for the two of you to prepare it together. This way, it is not perceived that one of you is asking the other to sign one. In fact, Dale Carnegie, in his book *How To Win Friends and Influence People*, says the best way to win someone to your point of view is to make that person think it was his or her idea. This tactic might be accomplished by describing a possible problem to your partner, and asking him or her how to resolve it. A little prompting might be necessary, of course: "Do you think some kind of prenuptial agreement might take care of this?"

Verbal Approaches

Other approaches to this discussion that you might want to consider include the following.

- ◆ "I read somewhere that a prenuptial agreement is a good idea. I'm not sure what I think of the idea. Do you think we should consider it?"
- ◆ "My lawyer (or accountant, financial planner, estate planner, mother, business partner, etc.) suggested we should get wills and a prenuptial agreement prepared. What do you think?"
- ◆ "Someone at work gave me this book to look at. I looked through it briefly, and it looks like a prenuptial agreement might be a good idea in addition to wills."

An alternative approach is for you to prepare a prenuptial agreement, then present it to your partner for his or her consideration and comment. If you take this route, however, you should approach it with how it will protect or benefit your intended spouse. You might also begin by explaining a problem you had with a previous marriage.

Fairness

In any event, you will both need to believe the agreement is fair. If the agreement is not fair to your partner, do not expect him or her to sign it. If you truly feel it is fair and your partner will not sign it, then maybe you should reconsider the marriage. Of course, be sure to listen to his or her objections, because you will want to be sure your proposal is fair. If you and your partner cannot discuss this, then maybe one or both of you are not ready (mature, honest, practical, or communicative enough) for marriage.

Chapter 6:
Preparing Your Prenuptial Agreement

This chapter guides you in preparing a very basic prenuptial agreement, using form 1 from Appendix C of this book. Form 1 is designed for when both persons are in fairly simple and equal financial situations.

When to Use a Basic Prenuptial Agreement

The basic PRENUPTIAL AGREEMENT (see form 1, p.171) is designed for a couple who are of fairly equal financial and career situations, and want to keep most or all of their finances separate. With this form, each person gives up all interests in the other's property and earnings, unless they indicate otherwise in writing (such as by purchasing property together and having it titled in both names). If your situation is more complex, and especially if either you or your partner has any children from a prior marriage, you will need to use the more complex PRENUPTIAL AGREEMENT. (see form 2, p.175.) If you need to use form 2, read Chapter 7 instead of this chapter.

Completing the Basic Prenuptial Agreement

As you will see, there are not many blank spaces that need to be filled in on the basic PRENUPTIAL AGREEMENT. (see form 1, p.171.) On pages 31–36 is a sample of form 1 completed for a fictional couple. There are two boxes at the bottom right-hand corner of each page. These are for you and your partner to initial to indicate that you have read and approved each page.

NOTE: *Paragraph 30 allows for you to use the* ADDENDUM TO MARITAL AGREEMENT *(form 9) for any additional provisions needed for your particular circumstances. See Chapter 9 for more information about form 9.*

After you have completed your agreement, you will need to get two witnesses and go to a notary public for the signing. You, your partner, and your two witnesses will sign the agreement before the notary. The notary will complete rest of the form.

NOTE: *Your witnesses should not be anyone who would inherit from either of you, either by law or in your wills.*

PRENUPTIAL AGREEMENT

This Agreement is entered into on **August 23**   , **2007** , by and
between **Stanley I. Kowalski**   (hereafter referred to as the Husband), and
Blanche E. Dubois   (hereafter referred to as the Wife), who agree that:

1.   **MARRIAGE.** The parties plan to marry each other, and intend to provide in this agreement for their property and other rights that may arise because of their contemplated marriage.

2.   **PURPOSE OF AGREEMENT.** Both parties currently own assets, and anticipate acquiring additional assets, which they wish to continue to control and they are executing this Agreement to fix and determine their respective rights and duties during the marriage, in the event of a divorce or dissolution of the marriage, or on the death of one of the parties.

3.   **FINANCIAL DISCLOSURE.** The parties have fully revealed to each other full financial information regarding their net worth, assets, holdings, income, and liabilities; not only by their discussions with each other, but also through copies of their current financial statements, copies of which are attached hereto as Exhibit A and Exhibit B. Both parties acknowledge that they have had sufficient time to review the other's financial statement, are familiar with and understand the other's financial statement, have had any questions satisfactorily answered, and are satisfied that full and complete financial disclosure has been made by the other.

4.   **ADVICE OF COUNSEL.** Each party has had legal and financial advice, or has the opportunity to consult independent legal and financial counsel, prior to executing this agreement. Either party's failure to so consult legal and financial counsel constitutes a waiver of such right. By signing this agreement, each party acknowledges that he or she understands the facts of this agreement, and is aware of his or her legal rights and obligations under this agreement or arising because of their contemplated marriage.

5.   **CONSIDERATION.** The parties acknowledge that each of them would not enter into the contemplated marriage except for the execution of this agreement in its present form.

6.   **EFFECTIVE DATE.** This Agreement shall become effective and binding upon the marriage of the parties. In the event the marriage does not take place, this agreement shall be null and void.

SIK   *BED*

7.   **DEFINITIONS.** As used in this agreement, the following terms shall have the following meanings:

(a)   "Joint Property" means property held and owned by the parties together. Such ownership shall be as tenants by the entirety in jurisdictions where such a tenancy is permitted. If such jurisdiction does not recognize or permit a tenancy by the entirety, then ownership shall be as joint tenants with rights of survivorship. The intention of the parties is to hold joint property as tenants by the entirety whenever possible.

(b)   "Joint Tenancy" means tenancy by the entirety in jurisdictions where such a tenancy is permitted, and joint tenancy with rights of survivorship if tenancy by the entirety is not recognized or permitted. The intention of the parties is to hold joint property as tenants by the entirety whenever possible.

8.   **HUSBAND'S SEPARATE PROPERTY.** The Husband is the owner of certain property, which is set forth and described in Exhibit C attached hereto and made a part hereof, which he intends to keep as his nonmarital, separate, sole, and individual property. All income, rents, profits, interest, dividends, stock splits, gains, and appreciation in value relating to any such separate property shall also be deemed separate property.

9.   **WIFE'S SEPARATE PROPERTY.** The Wife is the owner of certain property, which is set forth and described in Exhibit D attached hereto and made a part hereof, which she intends to keep as her nonmarital, separate, sole, and individual property. All income, rents, profits, interest, dividends, stock splits, gains, and appreciation in value relating to any such separate property shall also be deemed separate property.

10.   **JOINT OR COMMUNITY PROPERTY.** The parties intend that certain property shall, from the beginning of the marriage, be marital, joint, or community property, which is set forth and described in Exhibit E attached hereto and made a part hereof.

11.   **PROPERTY ACQUIRED DURING MARRIAGE.** The parties recognize that either or both of them may acquire property during the marriage. The parties agree that the manner in which such property is titled during the marriage shall control such property's ownership and distribution in the event of any divorce, dissolution of marriage, separation, or death of either party. Such property shall be held as provided in the instrument conveying or evidencing title to such property. If the instrument does not specify or if there is no instrument, the property shall be held as a tenancy by the entirety, or as a joint tenancy with rights of survivorship in the event tenancy by the entirety is not recognized by the court having jurisdiction over the distribution of such property. Any property acquired that does not normally have a title or ownership certificate shall be considered as joint property unless otherwise specified by the parties in writing. All wedding gifts shall be deemed joint property, unless specified as separate property in either Exhibit C or D.

STK   BED

12. **BANK ACCOUNTS.** Any funds deposited in either party's separate bank accounts shall be deemed that party's separate property. Any funds deposited in a bank account held by the parties jointly shall be deemed joint property.

13. **PAYMENT OF EXPENSES.** The parties agree that their expenses shall be paid as set forth in Exhibit F attached hereto and made a part hereof.

14. **DISPOSITION OF PROPERTY.** Each party retains the management and control of the property belonging to that party and may encumber, sell, or dispose of the property without the consent of the other party. Each party shall execute any instrument necessary to effectuate this paragraph on the request of the other party. If a party does not join in or execute an instrument required by this paragraph, the other party may sue for specific performance or for damages, regardless of the doctrine of spousal immunity, and the defaulting party shall be responsible for the other party's costs, expenses, and attorney's fees. This paragraph shall not require a party to execute a promissory note or other evidence of debt for the other party. If a party executes a promissory note or other evidence of debt for the other party, that other party shall indemnify the party executing the note or other evidence of debt from any claims or demands arising from the execution of the instrument. Execution of an instrument shall not give the executing party any right or interest in the property or the party requesting execution.

15. **PROPERTY DIVISION UPON DIVORCE, DISSOLUTION OF MARRIAGE, OR SEPARATION.** In the event of divorce, dissolution of marriage, or separation proceedings being filed and pursued by either party, the parties agree that the terms and provisions of this agreement shall govern all of their rights as to property, alimony including permanent periodic, rehabilitative, and lump sum, property settlement, rights of community property, and equitable distribution against the other. Each party releases and waives any claims for special equity in the other party's separate property or in jointly owned property. If either party files for divorce, dissolution, alimony, or spousal support unconnected with divorce, separation, or separate maintenance, the parties agree that either shall, in the filing of said proceedings, ask the court to follow the provisions and terms of this premarital agreement and be bound by the terms of this agreement.

16. **ALIMONY.** In the event of divorce or dissolution of marriage proceedings being filed by either party in any state or country, each party forever waives any right to claim or seek any form of alimony or spousal support, attorney's fees and costs from the other. Any rights concerning distribution of property are otherwise covered by this agreement, and any rights to community property or claims of special equity are waived and released. In the event that a final judgment or decree of divorce or dissolution of marriage is entered for whatever reason, the parties agree that the provisions of this agreement are in complete settlement of all rights to claim or seek any form of financial support, except child support for any living minor children of the parties, from the other.

|SIK| |BED|

17.   DISPOSITION UPON DEATH. Each party consents that his or her estate, or the estate of the other, may be disposed of by will, codicil, or trust, or in the absence of any such instrument, according to the laws of descent and distribution and intestate succession as if the marriage of the parties had not taken place. In either event, the estate shall be free of any claim or demand of inheritance, dower, curtesy, elective share, family allowance, homestead election, right to serve as executor, administrator, or personal representative, or any spousal or other claim given by law, irrespective of the marriage and any law to the contrary. Neither party intends by this agreement to limit or restrict the right to give to, or receive from, the other an inter vivos or testamentary gift. Neither party intends by this agreement to release, waive, or relinquish any devise or bequest left to either by specific provision in the will or codicil of the other, any property voluntarily transferred by the other, any joint tenancy created by the other, or any right to serve as executor or personal representative of the other's estate if specifically nominated in the other's will or codicil.

18.   DEBTS. Neither party shall assume or become responsible for the payment of any pre-existing debts or obligations of the other party because of the marriage. Neither party shall do anything that would cause the debt or obligation of one of them to be a claim, demand, lien, or encumbrance against the property of the other party without the other party's written consent. If a debt or obligation of one party is asserted as a claim or demand against the property of the other without such written consent, the party who is responsible for the debt or obligation shall indemnify the other from the claim or demand, including the indemnified party's costs, expenses, and attorney's fees.

19.   HOMESTEAD. Each party releases any claim, demand, right, or interest that the party may acquire because of the marriage in any real property of the other because of the homestead property provisions of the laws of any state concerning the descent of the property as homestead.

20.   FREE AND VOLUNTARY ACT. The parties acknowledge that executing this agreement is a free and voluntary act, and has not been entered into for any reason other than the desire for the furtherance of their relationship in marriage. Each party acknowledges that he or she has had adequate time to fully consider the consequences of signing this agreement, and has not been pressured, threatened, coerced, or unduly influenced to sign this agreement.

21.   GOVERNING LAW. This agreement shall be governed by the laws of _____.

22.   SEVERABILITY. If any part of this agreement is adjudged invalid, illegal, or unenforceable, the remaining parts shall not be affected.

$\boxed{SIK}$ $\boxed{BED}$

23.   FURTHER ASSURANCE. Each party shall execute any instruments or documents at any time requested by the other party that are necessary or proper to effectuate this agreement.

24.   NO OTHER BENEFICIARY. No person shall have a right or cause of action arising or resulting from this agreement except those who are parties to it and their successors in interest.

25.   RELEASE. Except as otherwise provided in this agreement, each party releases all claims or demands to the property or estate of the other, however and whenever acquired, including acquisitions in the future.

26.   ENTIRE AGREEMENT. This instrument, including any attached exhibits, constitutes the entire agreement of the parties. No representations or promises have been made except those that are set out in this agreement. This agreement may not be modified or terminated except in writing signed by the parties.

27.   PARAGRAPH HEADINGS. The headings of the paragraphs contained in this agreement are for convenience only, and are not to be considered a part of this agreement or used in determining its content or context.

28.   ATTORNEYS' FEES IN ENFORCEMENT. A party who fails to comply with any provision or obligation contained in this agreement shall pay the other party's attorney's fees, costs, and other expenses reasonably incurred in enforcing this agreement and resulting from the noncompliance.

29.   SIGNATURES AND INITIALS OF PARTIES. The signatures of the parties on this document, and their initials on each page, indicate that each party has read, and agrees with, this entire Prenuptial Agreement, including any and all exhibits attached hereto. Any provisions containing a box, ❏, that does not contain an "X" does not apply and is not a part of the agreement of the parties.

30.   ❏ OTHER PROVISIONS. Additional provisions are contained in the Addendum to Prenuptial Agreement attached hereto and made a part hereof.

Stanley I. Kowalski
Husband

Blanche E. Dubois
Wife

SIK   BED

Executed in the presence of:

Ralph Kramden   _Alice Kramden_

Name: Ralph Kramden   Name: Alice Kramden

Address: 142 Tennessee Ave.   Address: 142 Tennessee Ave.

Williams, VA 10234   Williams, VA 10234

STATE OF   Virginia)

COUNTY OF   Wise   )

The foregoing instrument was acknowledged before me this 23rd day of August, 2007, by Stanley I. Kowalski, Blanche E. Dubois, Ralph Kramden, and Alice Kramden the above-named Husband, Wife, and Witnesses respectively, who are personally known to me or who have produced VAdr.lic.K-492-729, D603-997, K559-382, K193-449 as identification.

Trixie Norton

Signature

Trixie Norton

(Typed Name of Acknowledger)

NOTARY PUBLIC

Commission Number: 97-299384

My Commission Expires: Nov. 23, 2008

SIK   BED

Additional Forms

In addition to the basic **Prenuptial Agreement** (form 1), there are some forms you will need to complete and other forms you may need to use. All of these forms are discussed in more detail in Chapter 9, but they will be summarized here.

In addition to the basic **Prenuptial Agreement**, you will also need to use the following forms.

- ◆ **Husband's Financial Statement** (form 3)—This satisfies the husband's duty for full financial disclosure.
- ◆ **Wife's Financial Statement** (form 4)—This satisfies the wife's duty for full financial disclosure.
- ◆ **Husband's Schedule of Separate Property** (form 5)—This lists all of the property the husband currently owns that will remain his separate property after the marriage.
- ◆ **Wife's Schedule of Separate Property** (form 6)—This lists all of the property the wife currently owns that will remain her separate property after the marriage.

Depending upon your situation, you may also use some or all of the following forms.

- ◆ **Schedule of Joint Property** (form 7)—If either or both of you have property that you wish to consider as your joint property, you need to list it on this form.
- ◆ **Expense Payment Schedule** (form 8)—This describes how you and your partner will handle your monthly living expenses.
- ◆ **Addendum to Marital Agreement** (form 9)—This is used if there are any special matters that are not covered by the **Prenuptial Agreement** form.

Chapter 7:
Customizing Your Prenuptial Agreement

If you determine that the basic **Prenuptial Agreement** (form 1) does not meet your needs, you will need to create your own agreement using the more complex, or *customized*, **Prenuptial Agreement** (see form 2, p.175) as a guide.

How to Use the Customized Prenuptial Agreement

Form 2 from Appendix C may be used as is, by checking the boxes that are appropriate to your situation. Alternatively, you may instead want to write a new agreement using only the provisions you have selected or agreed upon. There are advantages and disadvantages to each method.

If you are trying to get your partner to agree to the provisions you want, you may not want him or her to see the alternatives. In this case, it would be better to prepare an agreement containing only those provisions you want. On the other hand, if the other alternatives are in your agreement, it will show that the agreement was voluntarily signed and agreed to with knowledge of alternatives. This will help your position later, should your partner try to say that you talked him or her into signing, or that he or she did not understand the options.

Creating Your Prenuptial Agreement

In this section, you will be guided in making your customized agreement. You may also find it helpful to review the sample **Prenuptial Agreement** on pages 48 through 56, where a fictional couple have created their own agreement by selecting various optional provisions from form 2, as found in Appendix C. The following instructions and information relate to each of the paragraphs in form 2. (Of course, if you decide not to use one or more of these paragraphs you will need to renumber them.)

Introductory Paragraph

In the first (unnumbered) paragraph, type in the date, the husband's name, and the wife's name where indicated. The date should be the same date as you will sign the agreement before the witnesses and notary public.

Paragraph 1

The paragraph designated "1. Marriage" is a general, introductory statement that should be part of your agreement.

Paragraph 2

The paragraph designated "2. Purpose of Agreement" states the basic reasons you are entering into a prenuptial agreement. Either subparagraph (A) or both subparagraphs (A) and (B) should be included in your agreement. In all cases, you should check subparagraph (A). If you or your partner have children from a prior marriage, you should also check subparagraph (B); then, check the appropriate box or boxes to indicate whose children they are, and type in the names of the children on the line.

Paragraph 3

The paragraph designated "3. Financial Disclosure" is used to describe the manner in which you and your partner informed each other about your respective financial situations. As mentioned earlier, a court may invalidate a prenuptial agreement if one of the parties was not fully aware of the other's financial situation. It is preferable to check subparagraph (A), as this indicates full financial disclosure. Subparagraph (B) should only be used if one or both parties is not provided with the other's financial statement. Keep in mind that using (B) is more likely to prompt a court challenge to the agreement. If (B) is checked, the box for either "Husband" or "Wife" should also be checked.

Paragraph 4

The paragraph designated "4. Advice of Counsel" is used to indicate whether each of you consulted an attorney before signing the agreement. As mentioned earlier, a person who consulted an attorney prior to signing a prenuptial agreement is less likely to be able to successfully challenge the validity of the agreement. Only check one box. Be sure to read each subparagraph to determine which fits your situation. Check (A) if both of you have consulted an attorney. Check (B) if one of you consulted an attorney and the other did not. Check (C) if neither you nor your partner consulted an attorney. Keep in mind that if you check (B) or (C), it is more likely to prompt a court challenge to the agreement. For (A) or (B), the name of the attorney should be typed in on the appropriate lines. For (B), either the box for "Husband" or "Wife" should be checked.

Paragraph 5

The paragraph designated "5. Consideration" is standard language designed to satisfy a basic legal requirement for a valid contract. The legal concept of *consideration* is fairly complex, and it is not necessary that you understand it to enter into a prenuptial agreement. Basically, it is something of value that one party to a contract gives or promises in exchange for the performance or promise of the other party. This can be as simple as both parties promising to do something they are not otherwise legally required to do (such as enter into a marriage). It is consideration that distinguishes a contract from a gift.

Paragraph 6

The paragraph designated "6. Effective Date" simply states that the agreement will not become binding upon you and your partner until you are married. If you end up not getting married, the agreement means nothing.

Paragraph 7

The paragraph designated "7. Definitions" gives the legal definitions of various types of property ownership. Because various states use different terms for types of property ownership, this will make the terms used in the agreement clear in all states. This may also become important if you and your spouse move to or purchase property in another state.

Paragraph 8

The paragraph designated "8. Husband's Separate Property" describes what will be considered the husband's separate property. (This relates to property owned at the time you get married. Property acquired after marriage is covered in paragraph 11 of the agreement.) This paragraph does not list the property, but merely refers to "Exhibit C," which is the HUSBAND'S SCHEDULE OF SEPARATE PROPERTY. (see form 5, p.191.) This is discussed in more detail in Chapter 9.

Paragraph 9

The paragraph designated "9. Wife's Separate Property" describes what will be considered the wife's separate property. (This relates to property owned at the time you get married. Property acquired after marriage is covered in paragraph 11 of the agreement.) This paragraph does not list the property, but merely refers to "Exhibit D," which is the WIFE'S SCHEDULE OF SEPARATE PROPERTY. (see form 6, p.193.) This is discussed in more detail in Chapter 9.

Paragraph 10

The paragraph designated "10. Joint or Community Property" describes what will be considered joint (or community) property. *Community property* is property considered owned by a husband or wife together in Arizona, California, Idaho, Louisiana, Nevada, New Mexico, Texas, Washington, and Wisconsin. In all other states, joint ownership between a husband and wife will be called *joint tenancy* or *tenancy by the entireties*. (This relates to property owned at the time you get married. Property acquired after marriage is covered in paragraph 11 of the agreement.) This paragraph does not list the property, but merely refers to "Exhibit E," which is the **Schedule of Joint Property**. (see form 7, p.195.) This is discussed in more detail in Chapter 9.

Paragraph 11

The paragraph designated "11. Property Acquired During Marriage" states that ownership of any property acquired during your marriage will be determined by how title is designated on the ownership documents. For example, if you and your spouse agree that you alone are buying a piece of real estate, you would need to have the deed convey the property to you alone. If you were buying it together, you would need to have the deed convey the property to both of you.

This paragraph also provides that property will be considered jointly owned if ownership is not specified in the documents or if there is no document designating ownership. For example, suppose you buy a new camera. There will not be any title document to show ownership. It would therefore be considered joint property, unless you and your spouse sign a piece of paper stating that the camera belongs only to you. You can use the **Property Ownership Agreement** (see form 13, p.213) to designate separate property. Form 13 is discussed in more detail in Chapter 9.

Paragraph 12

The paragraph designated "12. Bank Accounts" provides that the ownership of funds in bank accounts will be determined by ownership of the account. A bank account in your name alone will contain your separate funds, a bank account in your spouse's name alone will contain your spouse's separate funds, and a bank account in both your and your spouse's names will be joint funds. This would also cover accounts owned by you and someone other than your spouse. For example, you and your brother could own a joint account, or you and your child could own a joint account.

Nothing prevents you or your spouse from designating the other as a beneficiary of the funds upon the death of the owner of the account. However, doing so will defeat any contrary provisions in a will.

Example: *While Mary and John are married, Mary executed a will stating that all of her separate property goes to her son from a previous marriage. Mary later opens a bank account in her name alone, and designates the funds that are payable upon her death to John. Upon Mary's death, the funds in that account will go to John, not to her son.*

Paragraph 13

The paragraph designated "13. Payment of Expenses" allows you to specify how expenses will be divided between you and your spouse. This paragraph does not list the expenses, but merely refers to "Exhibit F," which is the **Expense Payment Schedule**. (see form 8, p.197.) This is discussed in more detail in Chapter 9. Although it is strongly recommended that you include this paragraph (and Exhibit F) in your agreement, it may be deleted if you desire. In addition to making your relative contributions to expenses clear, using this paragraph will help you to plan a budget, which should be done by every household, even if there is no prenuptial agreement.

Paragraph 14

The paragraph designated "14. Income From and Reinvestment of Separate Property" gives two options for how to treat income from, reinvestment of, or appreciation of separate property. Each of these matters will be discussed separately.

Income

Some separate property may generate income. For example, a home you rent out will (hopefully) produce rental income. Funds in a separate bank account will generate interest income. Stocks or bonds will generate dividends or interest. Although the property itself is clearly separate property, a question may arise as to the nature of the income from the property. Just as income from employment is often legally considered joint property, so is income from separately held property. By checking either subparagraph (A) or subparagraph (B) in paragraph 14, all of the income from separate property will be separate property.

Reinvestment

An ownership issue can also arise if you sell separate property and reinvest the proceeds in other property. Although the original property is clearly separate under your prenuptial agreement, after it is sold, new property is property acquired during the marriage. By checking either subparagraph (A) or subparagraph (B) in paragraph 14, any proceeds or other property obtained by the sale or transfer of separate property will remain separate property.

Appreciation

Especially in the case of real estate, separate property can increase in value over time. Legally, this appreciation in value can be considered joint property, as it was technically acquired during the marriage. This can be further complicated if the spouse of the owner contributes funds to the property (such as helping with capital improvements, paying a portion of the taxes, etc.). By checking subparagraph (A) of paragraph 14, the full current value of the property will all be separate property, regardless of any other circumstances. Subparagraph (A) keeps it entirely separate property. By checking subparagraph (B), the appreciated portion of the property's value will be joint property in proportion to the other party's financial contribution.

Paragraph 15

The paragraph designated "15. Residence of the Parties" sets forth the ownership of the property you and your spouse will occupy as your residence. Check subparagraph (A) if you intend for the residence to be jointly owned. If the residence is to be separate property, you will need to choose between subparagraphs (B) and (C). Check (B) if the residence is to be one party's separate property, regardless of the circumstances. This means that even if the nonowner spouse contributes money for mortgage payments, utilities, repairs, maintenance, or capital improvements, the nonowner will have no interest in the property. Check (C) if you want the nonowner spouse to be entitled to a lien against the property for contributing funds to capital improvements. He or she will still not have any interest for contributions for mortgage payments, utilities, repairs, and maintenance.

Paragraph 16

The paragraph designated "16. Disposition of Property" describes how separate property may be sold, encumbered, or otherwise transferred. It also requires the nonowner to execute documents necessary to enable the property to be sold, encumbered, or transferred; however, it does not require the nonowner to become personally indebted.

Paragraph 17

The paragraph designated "17. Property Division Upon Divorce, Dissolution of Marriage, or Separation" states what happens to property in the event of divorce or separation.

Paragraph 18

The paragraph designated "18. Alimony" sets forth the agreement of the parties regarding alimony. This paragraph gives four options, and only one should be checked. The options are for no alimony, lump sum alimony, temporary alimony, or permanent alimony. You should review your state's guidelines for determining alimony to see what rights you may be giving up. A summary of these guidelines may be found in Appendix A of this book.

Subparagraph (A) will completely waive alimony for both parties.

Subparagraph (B) provides for one party to get a lump sum of alimony, with the exact amount based upon the length of the marriage. You will need to check the appropriate box to indicate whether the husband or wife will pay alimony, and fill in the amount agreed upon for each year of marriage.

Subparagraph (C) provides for one party to get temporary alimony, which will be in periodic payments and for a limited amount of time. You will need to check the appropriate box to indicate whether the husband or wife will pay alimony, and fill in the amount, the periodic payment time (e.g., "$500 per month"), and the duration (e.g., "for a period of five years"). Where alimony is deemed appropriate, most courts prefer temporary alimony to allow the spouse time to get sufficient education, training, and time to find employment.

Subparagraph (D) provides for one party to get permanent alimony, which will be in periodic payments until death or remarriage. You will need to check the appropriate box to indicate whether the husband or wife will pay alimony, and fill in the amount and periodic payment time (e.g., "$500 per month"). Where alimony is deemed appropriate, the trend is not to require permanent alimony, unless the spouse is likely to be unable to obtain employment and become self-sufficient (such as due to age, illness, or disability).

Paragraph 19

The paragraph designated "19. Child Support" outlines how the parties would like child support to be determined in the event the parties divorce or separate when they have a minor child. It is important to understand that this paragraph is not binding on a court. In all states and the District of Columbia, the law requires that minor children be adequately supported by their parents. The amount of child support and which portion is the responsibility of each parent is calculated according to state law. Although an agreement of the parties can be one factor considered by the court, it will not be followed if the agreement does not appear to provide sufficient support for the child. Also, any child support order is subject to change in the event circumstances change. A change in circumstances can be a change in the child's needs or a change in the income of either parent. Paragraph 19 can be deleted from your agreement if you desire.

Check subparagraph (A) if you want to indicate what portion of the needed support will be paid by each party. This basically follows the law in many states, which requires each party to be responsible for a percentage of the needed support, in proportion to each party's percentage of total combined income. If you check (A), you will need to fill in a percentage for the husband and wife. Make sure the two percentages total 100%.

Check subparagraph (B) if you want to try to agree on a support amount later or want to leave the matter up to the court.

Regardless of whether you check (A) or (B), complete the paragraph beginning "Such support shall continue..." by checking one of the three options. The last paragraph acknowledges that you understand that the ultimate decision about child support will be with the court.

Paragraph 20

The paragraph designated "20. Disposition Upon Death" provides choices about how property will be disposed of upon death. You will need to select either subparagraph (A) or subparagraph (B), but not both. Either option in this paragraph serves to waive certain rights a spouse typically has in the estate of the other. You should check your state's laws regarding inheritance rights of a spouse to understand what rights you may be waiving. A summary of each state's inheritance laws may be found in Appendix A of this book.

Checking subparagraph (A) will completely waive each party's rights to any portion of the other's estate. This paragraph will more often be used when the parties are fairly equal in their financial situations. This paragraph will not prohibit either party from making a gift to the other, holding property jointly, designating the other as a beneficiary, or leaving property to each other by way of a will or trust.

Checking subparagraph (B) allows one party to give the other a fixed amount, in lieu of all other rights of inheritance. This paragraph will more often be used when one party is in a substantially better financial situation than the other.

Example: *At the time Bob and Carol married, Bob was in business with his son from a prior marriage, and had a net worth of six million dollars. Carol was a teacher with a net worth of $250,000. Bob wanted to preserve most of his estate for his son, but the law in his state would allow his wife to claim one-half of his estate, regardless of what was in his will. Bob and Carol used subparagraph (B) to provide that Carol would get one million dollars in the event of Bob's death, and the balance of Bob's estate would go to his son.*

To complete (B), you will need to check either "Husband" or "Wife" in two places (whichever will be receiving the fixed amount), and fill in the amount.

Paragraph 21

The paragraph designated "21. Life Insurance" requires the parties to maintain life insurance for the benefit of each other. This is an optional provision. You should both evaluate your need for life insurance, and if you decide this is a good idea, evaluate the amount of insurance necessary to meet your desired goals.

Paragraph 22

The paragraph designated "22. Debts" limits your liability for each other's debts. It is self-explanatory and should be included in your prenuptial agreement.

Paragraph 23

The paragraph designated "23. Homestead" waives any homestead rights one party may have in the real property of the other. This paragraph should be included in your prenuptial agreement.

Paragraph 24

The paragraph designated "24. Commingling of Income and Assets" provides that the terms of your agreement will not be negated if your income or assets become commingled. This paragraph should be included in your prenuptial agreement.

Paragraph 25

The paragraph designated "25. Tax Returns/Gifts/Legal Proceedings" states that your agreement will not be negated because of the manner in which you file tax returns, make gifts to each other, or become involved in a divorce or other legal proceeding against each other. This paragraph should be included in your prenuptial agreement.

Paragraphs 26–35

Paragraphs 26 through 35 are standard provisions commonly included in most prenuptial agreements and other contracts. They are designed to prevent common arguments for having a contract declared invalid or unenforceable by a court, and should be included in your prenuptial agreement. Paragraph 27 requires you to fill in the name of the state whose law will govern your agreement. This will be the state in which you have your primary residence (or where you intend to have your primary residence if you plan to move shortly after your marriage).

Paragraph 36

The paragraph designated "36. Other Provisions" should be checked if you will be using the ADDENDUM TO MARITAL AGREEMENT (see form 9, p.199) to add matters not covered elsewhere. See Chapter 9 for more information on using form 9.

PRENUPTIAL AGREEMENT

This Agreement is entered into on __March 23__, __2007__, by and between __George Washington__ (hereafter referred to as the Husband), and __Martha Dandridge Curtis__ (hereafter referred to as the Wife), who agree that:

1.   **MARRIAGE.** The parties plan to marry each other, and intend to provide in this agreement for their property and other rights that may arise because of their contemplated marriage.

2.   **PURPOSE OF AGREEMENT.**
   ❏ (A) Both parties currently own assets, and anticipate acquiring additional assets, which they wish to continue to control, and are executing this Agreement to establish and determine their respective rights and responsibilities during the marriage, in the event of a divorce or dissolution of the marriage, or the death of one of the parties.

   ❏ (B) The parties desire that each party having any child(ren) of a prior marriage be able to identify and maintain a separate estate so as to provide for such child(ren), and each party has the following children of a prior marriage:

   ❏ Husband: _____.

   ☒ Wife:_____John Parke Curtis_____.

3.   **FINANCIAL DISCLOSURE.** The parties have fully revealed to each other complete financial information regarding their net worth, assets, holdings, income, and liabilities; both by their discussions with each other, and through their current financial statements, copies of which are attached hereto as Exhibit A and Exhibit B. Both parties acknowledge that they have had sufficient time to review the other's financial statement, are familiar with and understand the other's financial statement, have had any questions satisfactorily answered, and are satisfied that full and complete financial disclosure has been made by the other.

GW   *MDC*

4. **ADVICE OF COUNSEL.** Each party has had advice of independent counsel prior to executing this agreement.

The Husband received such counsel from ___John Jay, attorney at law___ .

The Wife received such counsel from ___Daniel Webster, attorney at law___ .

As a result of such independent counsel, both parties acknowledge that they have been informed of their legal rights in the property currently owned by each of them, rights in any property which may be acquired by either or both of them during their marriage, rights to claim interests in such property, rights to seek alimony upon divorce or dissolution of marriage, rights of inheritance and support as a surviving spouse, rights to take a certain share of the other's estate in the event the other's will makes unacceptable provisions for him or her, and has been informed of the consequences of any waivers, releases, and surrenders of such rights pursuant this agreement.

5. **CONSIDERATION.** The parties acknowledge that each of them would not enter into the contemplated marriage except for the execution of this agreement.

6. **EFFECTIVE DATE.** This Agreement shall become effective and binding upon the marriage of the parties. In the event the marriage does not take place, this agreement shall be null and void.

7. **DEFINITIONS.** As used in this agreement, the following terms shall have the following meanings:

(a) "Joint Property" means property held and owned by the parties together. Such ownership shall be as tenants by the entirety in jurisdictions where such a tenancy is permitted. If such jurisdiction does not recognize or permit a tenancy by the entirety, then ownership shall be as joint tenants with rights of survivorship. The intention of the parties is to hold joint property as tenants by the entirety whenever possible. "Joint property" also means community property as to any property which may be subject to community property laws.

(b) "Joint Tenancy" means tenancy by the entirety in jurisdictions where such a tenancy is permitted, and joint tenancy with rights of survivorship if tenancy by the entirety is not recognized or permitted. The intention of the parties is to hold joint property as tenants by the entirety whenever possible. "Joint tenancy" also refers to community property as to any property which may be subject to community property laws.

GW *MDC*

(c) "Separate Property" means property owned by either party which is and will remain, or may be acquired, as that party's individual property, free from any claims of the other party. "Separate property" is not part of the community property estate in any state recognizing community property.

8. **HUSBAND'S SEPARATE PROPERTY.** The Husband is the owner of certain property, which is set forth and described in Exhibit C attached hereto and made a part hereof, which he intends to keep as his nonmarital, separate, sole, and individual property. All income, rents, profits, interest, dividends, stock splits, gains, and appreciation in value relating to any such separate property shall also be deemed separate property. All inheritances or gifts received by the Husband individually during the marriage shall also be deemed separate property.

9. **WIFE'S SEPARATE PROPERTY.** The Wife is the owner of certain property, which is set forth and described in Exhibit D attached hereto and made a part hereof, which she intends to keep as her nonmarital, separate, sole, and individual property. All income, rents, profits, interest, dividends, stock splits, gains, and appreciation in value relating to any such separate property shall also be deemed separate property. All inheritances or gifts received by the Wife individually during the marriage shall also be deemed separate property.

10. **JOINT OR COMMUNITY PROPERTY.** The parties intend that certain property shall, from the beginning of the marriage, be joint property, as set forth and described in Exhibit E attached hereto and made a part hereof.

11. **PROPERTY ACQUIRED DURING MARRIAGE.** The parties recognize that either or both of them may acquire property during the marriage. The parties agree that the manner in which such property is titled during the marriage shall control such property's ownership and distribution in the event of divorce, dissolution of marriage, separation, or death of either party. Such property shall be held as stated in the instrument conveying or evidencing title. If the instrument does not specify or if there is no instrument, the property shall be held as a tenancy by the entirety, or as a joint tenancy with rights of survivorship in the event tenancy by the entirety is not recognized by the state having jurisdiction over the distribution of such property. Any property acquired that does not normally have a title or ownership certificate shall be considered as joint property unless otherwise specified by the parties in writing. All wedding gifts shall be deemed joint property, unless specified as separate property in either Exhibit C or D.

12.   **BANK ACCOUNTS.** Any funds deposited in either party's separate bank accounts shall be deemed that party's separate property. Any funds deposited in a bank account held by the parties jointly shall be deemed joint property.

13.   **PAYMENT OF EXPENSES.** The parties agree that their expenses shall be paid as set forth in Exhibit F attached hereto and made a part hereof.

14.   **INCOME FROM AND REINVESTMENT OF SEPARATE PROPERTY.** Any property obtained by either party due to the use, investment, reinvestment, or any transfer of any portion of his or her separate property, and any income from any such property shall remain that party's separate property. Any appreciation or other increase in the value of either party's separate property, shall remain that party's separate property, unless the other party has made a direct financial contribution to the increase in value, but only to the proportion of the increase attributable to his or her contribution.

15.   **RESIDENCE OF THE PARTIES.** It is expressly recognized that the ❑ Husband ☒ Wife is the sole owner of the residence to be occupied by the parties at   123 Mount Vernon Avenue , and that the use of any joint funds, or separate funds of the other party, for the mortgage payments, utilities, and repair or maintenance of the residence and grounds for the joint benefit of the parties shall not create any interest in the property in the other party. However, if joint funds or the other party's separate funds are used to make capital improvements on the property, the other party shall have a lien against the property to the extent of one-half of the total joint funds, or the full amount of the separate funds contributed, which lien shall be paid upon the sale of the property, the termination of the marriage, or the death of the Husband or Wife, whichever occurs first.

16.   **DISPOSITION OF PROPERTY.** Each party retains the ownership, management, and control of his or her separate property, and may encumber, sell, or dispose of the property without the other party's consent. Each party shall, on the request of the other, execute any instrument necessary to effectuate this paragraph. The failure or refusal of a party to join in or execute an instrument required by this paragraph shall entitle the other party to sue for specific performance or for damages, regardless of the doctrine of spousal immunity, and the defaulting party shall pay the other party's costs, expenses, and attorney's fees. This paragraph shall not require a party to execute a promissory note or other evidence of debt for the other party; but if a party executes a promissory note or other evidence of debt for the other party, that other party shall indemnify the party executing the note or other evidence of debt from any claims or demands arising from the execution of the instrument. Execution of an instrument shall not give the executing party any right or interest in the property of the party requesting execution.

17.   PROPERTY DIVISION UPON DIVORCE, DISSOLUTION OF MARRIAGE, OR SEPARATION. In the event of divorce, dissolution of marriage, or separation proceedings being filed and pursued by either party, the parties agree that the terms and provisions of this agreement shall govern all of their rights as to property; alimony including permanent periodic, rehabilitative, and lump sum; property settlement; rights of community property; and, equitable distribution against the other. Each party releases and waives any claims for special equity in the other party's separate property or in jointly owned property. If either party files for alimony, or spousal support unconnected with divorce, dissolution of marriage, separation, or separate maintenance, the parties agree that the party filing said proceedings shall ask the court to follow the provisions and terms of this prenuptial agreement.

18.   ALIMONY. In the event divorce, dissolution of marriage, separation, or similar proceedings are filed by either party in any state or country, the parties agree that neither party will request or receive alimony or support, whether temporary, rehabilitative, permanent, or lump sum. In consideration for not requesting alimony, the ☒ Husband ❏ Wife shall pay to the other party a sum equal to $___5,000___ for each full year of marriage up to the date a divorce, dissolution of marriage, separation, or similar action is filed. Said sum shall be paid regardless of which party files, and shall terminate on either the death or remarriage of the payee, or on the death of the payor, whichever occurs first.

19.   CHILD SUPPORT. In the event of divorce, dissolution of marriage, or separation, and if there are any minor children of the parties, the parties agree that each shall contribute to the support of any such children in the following proportions:

___75___% from the Husband.

___25___% from the Wife.

Such support shall continue until: age 18, or graduation from high school, whichever occurs last, provided any such child is enrolled as a full-time student and is making a good faith effort to graduate. The amount of support shall be determined by agreement of the parties. If the parties cannot agree, the amount of support shall be determined by the court. Both parties acknowledge that they are aware that the court has the ultimate authority to determine child support, taking into consideration the needs of the children and any other factors required by law to be considered.

GW   MDC

20.   DISPOSITION UPON DEATH. Subject to the conditions set forth in this paragraph, the ❏ Husband   ☒ Wife shall receive from the other party after his/her death, the sum of $____35,000____, free of any and all inheritance and estate taxes, in place of, and in full and final settlement and satisfaction of, any and all rights and claims which he/she might otherwise have in the other party's estate and property under any law now or hereafter in force in this or any other jurisdiction, whether as a right of election to take against the other party's will, as an intestate share of the estate, or otherwise. The ❏ Husband   ☒ Wife shall only be entitled to receive said amount if all of the following conditions are met: (1) the parties were married at the time of death, (2) he/she survives the decedent, (3) the parties were not separated at the time of death, and (4) no divorce, dissolution of marriage, or separation proceedings were in progress at the time of death. If any of the above conditions are not met, then he/she shall not be entitled to any sums from the other party's estate. Neither party intends by this agreement to release, waive, or relinquish any devise or bequest left to either by specific provision in the will or codicil of the other, any property voluntarily transferred by the other, any joint tenancy created by the other, or any right to serve as executor or personal representative of the other's estate if specifically nominated in the other's will or codicil.

21.   LIFE INSURANCE. The parties shall maintain the following life insurance policies payable to the other party on death in the face amounts of at least:

Life insurance on the life of the Husband payable to the Wife or a person she designates of at least $____100,000____.

Life insurance on the life of the Wife payable to the Husband or a person he designates of at least $____25,000____.

22.   DEBTS. Neither party shall assume or become responsible for the payment of any preexisting debts or obligations of the other party because of the marriage. Neither party shall do anything that would cause the debt or obligation of one of them to become a claim, demand, lien, or encumbrance on the other's property without the other party's written consent. If a debt or obligation of one party is asserted as a claim or demand against the other's separate property without such written consent, the party who is responsible for the debt or obligation shall indemnify the other from the claim or demand, including the payment of the other party's costs, expenses, and attorney's fees.

GW   *MDC*

23.   HOMESTEAD. Each party releases any claim, demand, right, or interest that the party may acquire because of the marriage in any real property of the other because of the homestead property provisions of the laws of any state concerning the descent of the property as homestead.

24.   COMMINGLING OF INCOME AND ASSETS. The parties recognize that it is possible for their income or assets to become, or appear to become, commingled. It is the parties' intention that any commingling of income or assets shall not be interpreted to imply any abandonment of the terms and provisions of this agreement, that the provisions contained herein regarding the parties' interests in jointly held property be applied, and that in other instances each party's interest be determined by each party's proportionate contribution toward the total funds or value of assets in question.

25.   TAX RETURNS/GIFTS/LEGAL PROCEEDINGS. The fact that the parties may file joint local, state, or federal income tax returns, or any other joint tax papers or documents, or make gifts of property or cash to each other, or not account to each other with regard to the expenditure of income, shall not be interpreted to imply any abandonment of the terms and provisions of this agreement. The filing of a divorce, dissolution of marriage, separation, or other legal action or proceeding shall not be deemed as any abandonment of the terms and provisions of this agreement.

26.   FREE AND VOLUNTARY ACT. The parties acknowledge that executing this agreement is a free and voluntary act, and has not been entered into for any reason other than the desire for the furtherance of their relationship in marriage. Each party acknowledges that he or she has had adequate time to fully consider the consequences of signing this agreement, and has not been pressured, threatened, coerced, or unduly influenced to sign this agreement.

27.   GOVERNING LAW. This agreement shall be governed by the laws of _____Virginia_____.

28.   SEVERABILITY. If any part of this agreement is adjudged invalid, illegal, or unenforceable, the remaining parts shall not be affected.

29.   FURTHER ASSURANCE. Each party shall execute any instruments or documents at any time requested by the other party that are necessary or proper to effectuate this agreement.

GW   *MDC*

30. BINDING AGREEMENT / NO OTHER BENEFICIARY. This agreement shall be binding upon the parties, and upon their heirs, executors, personal representatives, administrators, and assigns. No person shall have a right or cause of action arising or resulting from this agreement except those who are parties to it and their successors in interest.

31. RELEASE. Except as otherwise provided in this agreement, each party releases all claims or demands to the property or estate of the other, however and whenever acquired, including acquisitions in the future.

32. ENTIRE AGREEMENT. This instrument, including any attached exhibits, constitutes the entire agreement of the parties. No representations or promises have been made except those that are set out in this agreement. This agreement may not be modified or terminated except in writing signed by the parties.

33. PARAGRAPH HEADINGS. The headings of the paragraphs contained in this agreement are for convenience only, and are not to be considered a part of this agreement or used in determining its content or context.

34. ATTORNEYS' FEES IN ENFORCEMENT. A party who fails to comply with any provision or obligation contained in this agreement shall pay the other party's attorney's fees, costs, and other expenses reasonably incurred in enforcing this agreement and resulting from the noncompliance.

35. SIGNATURES AND INITIALS OF PARTIES/UNMARKED BOXES. The signatures of the parties on this document, and their initials on each page, indicate that each party has read, and agrees with, this entire Prenuptial Agreement, including any and all exhibits attached hereto. Any provision containing a box, ❏ , that does not contain an "X" does not apply and is not a part of the agreement of the parties.

36. ❏ OTHER PROVISIONS. Additional provisions are contained in the Addendum to Prenuptial Agreement attached hereto and made a part hereof.

George Washington
Husband

Martha Dandridge Curtis
Wife

GW *MDC*

Executed in the presence of:

Alexander Hamilton

Name: __Alexander Hamilton__

Address: __286 Duelist Avenue__

__Washington, DC 20064__

Dolley Madison

Name: __Dolley Madison__

Address: __1642 Cupcake Lane__

__Fairfax, VA 20599__

STATE OF   Virginia)

COUNTY OF   Wise   )

The foregoing instrument was acknowledged before me this __23rd__ day of __March__, __2007__, by __George Washington, Martha Dandridge Curtis, Dolley__, __Madison, and Alexander Hamilton__ the above-named Husband, Wife, and Witnesses respectively, who are personally known to me or who have produced __VAdr.lic.K-492-729,__ __D603-997, K559-382, K193-449__ as identification.

Trixie Norton

Signature

__Trixie Norton__

(Typed Name of Acknowledger)

NOTARY PUBLIC

Commission Number: __97-299384__

My Commission Expires: Nov. 23, 2008

GW   *MDC*

Additional Forms

In addition to the PRENUPTIAL AGREEMENT (form 2), there are some forms you will need to complete and other forms you may need to use. All of these forms are discussed in more detail in Chapter 9, but they will be summarized here.

In addition to the PRENUPTIAL AGREEMENT, you will also need to use the following forms.

- ◆ HUSBAND'S FINANCIAL STATEMENT (form 3)—This satisfies the husband's duty for full financial disclosure.
- ◆ WIFE'S FINANCIAL STATEMENT (form 4)—This satisfies the wife's duty for full financial disclosure.
- ◆ HUSBAND'S SCHEDULE OF SEPARATE PROPERTY (form 5)—This lists all of the property the husband currently owns that will remain his separate property after the marriage.
- ◆ WIFE'S SCHEDULE OF SEPARATE PROPERTY (form 6)—This lists all of the property the wife currently owns that will remain her separate property after the marriage.

Depending upon your situation, you may also use some or all of the following forms.

- ◆ SCHEDULE OF JOINT PROPERTY (form 7)—If either or both of you have property that you wish to consider as your joint property, you need to list it on this form.
- ◆ EXPENSE PAYMENT SCHEDULE (form 8)—This describes how you and your partner will handle your monthly living expenses.
- ◆ ADDENDUM TO MARITAL AGREEMENT (form 9)—This is used if there are any special matters that are not covered by the PRENUPTIAL AGREEMENT form.

Chapter 8:
Postnuptial Agreements

Even if you are already married, you and your spouse can still create an agreement to accomplish the things discussed throughout this book. Such agreements between already married couples are called *postnuptial agreements*, *postmarital agreements*, or *marital agreements*. All they typically require are some slight changes to reflect that you are already married.

From a legal standpoint, there is one difference between a *pre*nuptial and a *post*nuptial agreement. This relates to the duty owed by one spouse to another. Generally, married people owe each other a higher degree of duty than unmarried people.

How to Use the Customized Postnuptial Agreement

This POSTNUPTIAL AGREEMENT from Appendix C may be used as is by checking the boxes that are appropriate to your situation, or you may want to write a new agreement only using the provisions you have selected or agreed upon. Using it as is may be easier and quicker. Creating a new document using only the provisions you want will make a cleaner, and possibly less confusing, document.

Creating Your Postnuptial Agreement

In this section, you will be guided in making your customized agreement. You may also find it helpful to review the sample POSTNUPTIAL AGREEMENT on pages 68 through 78, where a fictional couple have created their own agreement by selecting various optional provisions from form 12, as found in Appendix C. The following instructions and information relates to each of the paragraphs in form 12. (Of course, if you decide not to use one or more of these paragraphs, you will need to renumber them.)

Introductory Paragraph

In the first (unnumbered) paragraph, type in the date, the husband's name, and the wife's name where indicated. The date should be the same date as you will sign the agreement before the witnesses and notary public.

Paragraph 1

The paragraph designated "1. Purpose of Agreement" states the basic reasons you are entering into a postnuptial agreement. Either subparagraph (A) or both subparagraphs (A) and (B) should be included in your agreement. In all cases, you should check subparagraph (A). If you or your partner have children from a prior marriage, you should also check subparagraph (B); then, check the appropriate box or boxes to indicate whose children they are, and type in the names of the children on the line.

Paragraph 2

The paragraph designated "2. Financial Disclosure" describes how you and your partner informed each other about your financial situations. A court may invalidate a postnuptial agreement if one of the parties was not fully aware of the other's financial situation. It is preferable to check subparagraph (A), which indicates full financial disclosure. Subparagraph (B) should only be used if one or both or the parties has not provided a financial statement. A court challenge is more likely if (B) is used. If (B) is checked, the box for either "Husband" or "Wife" should also be checked.

Paragraph 3

The paragraph designated "3. Advice of Counsel" is used to indicate whether each of you consulted an attorney before signing the agreement. As mentioned earlier, a person who consulted an attorney prior to signing a postnuptial agreement is less likely to be able to successfully challenge the validity of the agreement. Only check one box. Be sure to read each subparagraph to determine which fits your situation. Check (A) if both of you have consulted an attorney. Check (B) if one of you consulted an attorney and the other did not. Check (C) if neither you nor your partner consulted an attorney. Keep in mind that if you check (B) or (C), it is more likely to prompt a court challenge to the agreement. For (A) or (B), the name of the attorney should be typed in on the appropriate lines. For (B), either the box for "Husband" or "Wife" should be checked.

Paragraph 4

The paragraph designated "4. Effective Date" simply states that the agreement becomes effective immediately.

Paragraph 5

The paragraph designated "5. Definitions" gives the legal definitions of various types of property ownership. Because various states use different terms for types of property ownership, this will make the terms used in the agreement clear in all states. This may also become important if you and your spouse move to or purchase property in another state.

Paragraph 6

The paragraph designated "6. Husband's Separate Property" describes what will be considered the husband's separate property. (This relates to property owned at the time you sign the postnuptial agreement. Property acquired later is covered in paragraph 9 of the agreement.) This paragraph does not list the property, but merely refers to "Exhibit C," which is the **HUSBAND'S SCHEDULE OF SEPARATE PROPERTY**. (see form 5, p.191.) This form is discussed in more detail in Chapter 9.

Paragraph 7

The paragraph designated "7. Wife's Separate Property" describes what will be considered the wife's separate property. (This relates to property owned at the time you sign the agreement. Property acquired later is covered in paragraph 9 of the agreement.) This paragraph does not list the property, but merely refers to "Exhibit D," which is the **WIFE'S SCHEDULE OF SEPARATE PROPERTY**. (see form 6, p.193.) This form is discussed in more detail in Chapter 9.

Paragraph 8

The paragraph designated "8. Joint or Community Property" describes what will be considered joint (or community) property. *Community property* is property considered owned by a husband or wife together in Arizona, California, Idaho, Louisiana, Nevada, New Mexico, Texas, Washington, and Wisconsin. In all other states, joint ownership between a husband and wife will be called *joint tenancy* or *tenancy by the entireties*. (This relates to property owned at the time you sign the agreement. Property acquired later is covered in paragraph 9 of the agreement.) This paragraph does not list the property, but merely refers to "Exhibit E," which is the **SCHEDULE OF JOINT PROPERTY**. (see form 7, p.195.) This form is discussed in more detail in Chapter 9.

Paragraph 9

The paragraph designated "9. Property Acquired During Marriage" states that ownership of any property acquired in the future will be determined by how title is designated on the ownership documents. For example, if you and your spouse agree that you alone are buying a piece of real estate, you would need to have the deed convey the property to you alone. If you were buying it together, you would need to have the deed convey the property to both of you.

This paragraph also provides that property will be considered jointly owned if ownership is not specified in the documents, or if there is no document designating ownership. For example, suppose you buy a new camera. There will not be any title document to show ownership. It would therefore be considered joint property, unless you and your spouse sign a piece of paper stating that the camera belongs only to you. You can use the **Property Ownership Agreement** (form 13, p.213) to designate separate property. Form 13 is discussed in more detail in Chapter 9.

Paragraph 10

The paragraph designated "10. Bank Accounts" provides that the ownership of funds in bank accounts will be determined by ownership of the account. A bank account in your name alone will contain your separate funds, a bank account in your spouse's name alone will contain your spouse's separate funds, and a bank account in both your and your spouse's names will be joint funds. This would also cover accounts owned by you and someone other than your spouse. For example, you and your brother could own a joint account, or you and your child could own a joint account.

Nothing prevents you or your spouse from designating the other as a beneficiary of the funds upon the death of the owner of the account. However, doing so will defeat any contrary provisions in a will.

Example: *Mary and John are married, and Mary executes a will stating that all of her separate property goes to her son from a previous marriage. Mary later opens a bank account in her name alone, and designates the funds that are payable upon her death to John. Upon Mary's death, the funds in that account will go to John, not to her son.*

Paragraph 11

The paragraph designated "11. Payment of Expenses" allows you to specify how expenses will be divided between you and your spouse. This paragraph does not list the expenses, but merely refers to "Exhibit F," which is the **Expense Payment Schedule**. (see form 8, p.197.) This form is discussed in more detail in Chapter 9. Although it is strongly recommended that you include this paragraph (and Exhibit F) in your agreement, it may be deleted if you desire. In addition to making your relative contributions to expenses clear, using this paragraph will help you to plan a budget, which should be done by every household, even if there is no prenuptial or postnuptial agreement.

Paragraph 12

The paragraph designated "12. Income From and Reinvestment of Separate Property" gives two options for how to treat income from, reinvestment of, or appreciation of separate property. Each of these matters will be discussed separately.

Income

Some separate property may generate income. For example, a home you rent out will (hopefully) produce rental income. Funds in a separate bank account will generate interest income. Stocks or bonds will generate dividends or interest. Although the property itself is clearly separate property, a question may arise as to the nature of the income from the property. Just as income from employment is often legally considered joint property, so is income from separately held property. By checking either subparagraph (A) or subparagraph (B) in paragraph 14, all of the income from separate property will be separate property.

Reinvestment

An ownership issue can also arise if you sell separate property and reinvest the proceeds in other property. Although the original property is clearly separate under your prenuptial agreement, after it is sold, new property is property acquired during the marriage. By checking either subparagraph (A) or subparagraph (B) in paragraph 14, any proceeds or other property obtained by the sale or transfer of separate property will remain separate property.

Appreciation

Especially in the case of real estate, separate property can increase in value over time. Legally, this appreciation in value can be considered joint property, as it was technically acquired during the marriage. This can be further complicated if the spouse of the owner contributes funds to the property (such as helping with capital improvements, paying a portion of the taxes, etc.). By checking subparagraph (A) of paragraph 14, the full current value of the property will all be separate property, regardless of any other circumstances. Subparagraph (A) keeps it entirely separate property. By checking subparagraph (B), the appreciated portion of the property's value will be joint property in proportion to the other party's financial contribution.

Paragraph 13

The paragraph designated "13. Residence of the Parties" sets forth the ownership of the property you and your spouse occupy as your residence. Check subparagraph (A) if you intend for the residence to be jointly owned. If the residence is to be separate property, you will need to choose between subparagraphs (B) and (C). Check (B) if the residence is to be one party's separate property, regardless of the circumstances. This means that even if the nonowner spouse contributes money for mortgage payments, utilities, repairs, maintenance, or capital improvements, the nonowner will have no interest in the property. Check (C) if you want the nonowner spouse to be entitled to a lien against the property for contributing funds to capital improvements. He or she will still not have any interest for contributions for mortgage payments, utilities, repairs, and maintenance.

Paragraph 14

The paragraph designated "14. Disposition of Property" describes how separate property may be sold, encumbered, or otherwise transferred. It also requires the nonowner to execute documents necessary to enable the property to be sold, encumbered, or transferred, except that it does not require the nonowner to become personally indebted.

Paragraph 15

The paragraph designated "15. Property Division Upon Divorce, Dissolution of Marriage, or Separation" states what happens to property in the event of divorce or separation.

Paragraph 16

The paragraph designated "16. Alimony" sets forth the agreement of the parties regarding alimony. This paragraph gives four options, and only one should be checked. The options are for no alimony, lump sum alimony, temporary alimony, or permanent alimony. You should review your state's guidelines for determining alimony to see what rights you may be giving up. A summary of these guidelines may be found in Appendix A of this book.

Subparagraph (A) will completely waive alimony for both parties.

Subparagraph (B) provides for one party to get a lump sum of alimony, with the exact amount based upon the length of the marriage. You will need to check the appropriate box to indicate whether the husband or wife will pay alimony, and fill in the amount agreed upon for each year of marriage.

Subparagraph (C) provides for one party to get temporary alimony, which will be in periodic payments for a limited amount of time. You will need to check the appropriate box to indicate whether the husband or wife will pay alimony, and fill in the amount, periodic payment time (e.g., "$500 per month"), and the duration (e.g., "for a period of five years"). Where alimony is deemed appropriate, most courts prefer temporary alimony to allow the spouse time to get sufficient education, training, and time to find employment.

Subparagraph (D) provides for one party to get permanent alimony, which will be in periodic payments, until death or remarriage. You will need to check the appropriate box to indicate whether the husband or wife will pay alimony, and fill in the amount and periodic payment time (e.g., "$500 per month"). Where alimony is deemed appropriate, the trend is not to require permanent alimony, unless the spouse is likely to be unable to obtain employment and become self-sufficient (such as due to age, illness, or disability).

Paragraph 17

The paragraph designated "17. Child Support" outlines how the parties would like child support to be determined in the event the parties divorce or separate when they have a minor child. It is important to understand that this paragraph is not binding on a court. In all states and the District of Columbia, the law requires that minor children be adequately supported by their parents. The amount of child support and which portion is the responsibility of each parent is calculated according to state law. Although an agreement of the parties can be one factor considered by the court, it will not be followed if the agreement does not appear to provide sufficient support for the child. Also, any child support order is subject to change in the event circumstances change. A change in circumstances can be a change in the child's needs or a change in the income of either parent. Paragraph 17 can be deleted from your agreement if you desire.

Check subparagraph (A) if you want to indicate what portion of the needed support will be paid by each party. This basically follows the law in many states, which requires each party to be responsible for a percentage of the needed support in proportion to each party's percentage of total combined income. If you check (A), you will need to fill in a percentage for the husband and wife. Make sure the two percentages total 100%.

Check subparagraph (B) if you want to try to agree on a support amount later or leave the matter up to the court.

Regardless of whether you check (A) or (B), complete the paragraph beginning "Such support shall continue..." by checking one of the three options. The last paragraph acknowledges that you understand that the ultimate decision about child support will be with the court.

Paragraph 18

The paragraph designated "18. Disposition Upon Death" provides for how property will be disposed of upon death. You need to select either subparagraph (A) or (B), but not both. Either option waives certain rights a spouse has in the estate of the other. Check your state's laws on inheritance rights of a spouse to understand what you may be waiving. A summary of state inheritance laws may be found in Appendix A of this book.

Checking subparagraph (A) will completely waive each party's rights to any portion of the other's estate. This paragraph will more often be used when the parties are fairly equal in their financial situations. This paragraph will not prohibit either party from making a gift to the other, holding property jointly, designating the other as a beneficiary, or leaving property to each other by way of a will or trust.

Checking subparagraph (B) allows one party to give the other a fixed amount, in lieu of all other rights of inheritance. This paragraph will more often be used when one party is in a substantially better financial situation than the other.

Example: *At the time Bob and Carol married, Bob was in business with his son from a prior marriage, and had a net worth of six million dollars. Carol was a teacher with a net worth of $250,000. Bob wanted to preserve most of his estate for his son, but the law in his state would allow his wife to claim one-half of his estate, regardless of what was in his will. Bob and Carol used subparagraph (B) to provide that Carol would get one million dollars in the event of Bob's death, and the balance of Bob's estate would go to his son.*

To complete (B), you will need to check either "Husband" or "Wife" in two places (whichever will be receiving the fixed amount); and fill in the amount.

Paragraph 19

The paragraph designated "19. Life Insurance" requires the parties to maintain life insurance for the benefit of each other. This is an optional provision. You should both evaluate your need for life insurance, and if you decide this is a good idea, evaluate the amount of insurance necessary to meet your desired goals.

Paragraph 20

The paragraph designated "20. Debts" limits your liability for each other's debts. It is self-explanatory, and should be included in your postnuptial agreement.

Paragraph 21

The paragraph designated "21. Homestead" waives any homestead rights one party may have in the real property of the other. This paragraph should be included in your postnuptial agreement.

Paragraph 22

The paragraph designated "22. Commingling of Income and Assets" provides that the terms of your agreement will not be negated if your income or assets become commingled. This paragraph should be included in your postnuptial agreement.

Paragraph 23

The paragraph designated "23. Tax Returns/Gifts/Legal Proceedings" states that your agreement will not be negated because of the manner in which you file tax returns, make gifts to each other, or become involved in a divorce or other legal proceeding against each other. This paragraph should be included in your postnuptial agreement.

Paragraphs 24–33

Paragraphs 24 through 33 are standard provisions commonly included in most postnuptial agreements and other contracts. They are designed to prevent common arguments for having a contract declared invalid or unenforceable by a court, and should be included in your prenuptial agreement. Paragraph 25 requires you to fill in the name of the state whose law will govern your agreement. This will be the state in which you have your primary residence (or where you intend to have your primary residence if you plan to move in the near future).

Paragraph 34

The paragraph designated "34. Other Provisions" should be checked if you will be using the **ADDENDUM TO MARITAL AGREEMENT** (form 9, p.199) to add matters not covered elsewhere. See Chapter 9 for more information on using form 9.

POSTNUPTIAL AGREEMENT

This Agreement is entered into on ___March 23___, __2007__, by and between __George Washington__ (hereafter referred to as the Husband), and __Martha Curtis Washington__ (hereafter referred to as the Wife), who agree that:

1.   **PURPOSE OF AGREEMENT.**

❑ (A) Both parties currently own assets, and anticipate acquiring additional assets, which they wish to continue to control, and are executing this agreement to establish and determine their respective rights and responsibilities during the marriage, in the event of a divorce or dissolution of the marriage, or the death of one of the parties.

❑ (B) The parties desire that each party having any child(ren) of a prior marriage be able to identify and maintain a separate estate so as to provide for such child(ren), and each party has the following children of a prior marriage:

Husband: __Thomas Gunter Washington__.
Wife: ___Kittie and Samantha Curtis___.

2.   **FINANCIAL DISCLOSURE.**

❑ (A) The parties have fully disclosed to each other complete financial information regarding their net worth, assets, holdings, income, and liabilities; both by their discussions with each other, and through their current financial statements, copies of which are attached hereto as Exhibit A and Exhibit B. Both parties acknowledge that they have had sufficient time to review the other's financial statement, are familiar with and understand the other's financial statement, have had any questions satisfactorily answered, and are satisfied that full and complete financial disclosure has been made by the other.

❑ (B) The ☒ Husband ❑ Wife acknowledges that he/she is fully acquainted with the business and resources of the other party; that the other party is a person of substantial wealth; that the other party has answered all questions asked about his/her income and assets; that he/she understands that by entering into this agreement he/she may receive less than he/she would otherwise be entitled to under law in the event of divorce, dissolution of marriage, separation, or death of the other party; that he/she has carefully weighed all facts and circumstances; and that he/she desires to enter into this agreement regardless of any financial arrangements made for his/her benefit.

3.   **ADVICE OF COUNSEL.**

❑ (A) Each party has had advice of independent counsel prior to executing this agreement.

The Husband received such counsel from _____.

The Wife received such counsel from_____.

As a result of such independent counsel, both parties acknowledge that they have been informed of their legal rights in the property currently owned by each of them, rights in any property which may be acquired by either or both of them during their marriage, rights to claim interests in such property, rights to seek alimony upon divorce or dissolution of marriage, rights of inheritance and support as a surviving spouse, rights to take a certain share of the other's estate in the event the other's will makes unacceptable provisions for him or her, and has been informed of the consequences of any waivers, releases, and surrenders of such rights pursuant this agreement.

☒ (B) Each party has had sufficient opportunity to seek advice of independent counsel prior to executing this agreement.

The ❑ Husband ☒ Wife has received the advice of independent counsel from ___Christopher Christopherson, attorney at law___, prior to executing this agreement.

The ☒ Husband ❑ Wife has not sought the advice of independent counsel, despite urging by the other party to do so, and despite being given sufficient time in which to seek such advice. Such party's failure to consult independent counsel constitutes a waiver of such right. By signing this agreement, each party acknowledges that he or she understands the terms of this agreement, is aware of his or her legal rights and obligations under this agreement or arising because of their marriage, and understands the consequences of his or her waivers, releases, and surrenders of such rights pursuant to this agreement.

❑ (C) Each party has had legal and financial advice, or has had the opportunity to consult independent legal and financial counsel, prior to executing this agreement. Either party's failure to consult legal and financial counsel constitutes a waiver of such right. By signing this agreement, each party acknowledges that he or she understands the terms of this agreement, is aware of his or her legal rights and obligations under this agreement or arising because of their marriage, and understands the consequences of his or her waivers, releases, and surrenders of such rights under this agreement.

4.   EFFECTIVE DATE. This agreement shall become effective and binding upon the execution of this agreement by both of the parties.

5.   DEFINITIONS. As used in this agreement, the following terms shall have the following meanings:

(a) "Joint Property" means property held and owned by the parties together. Such ownership shall be as tenants by the entirety in jurisdictions where such a tenancy is permitted. If such jurisdiction does not recognize or permit a tenancy by the entirety, then ownership shall be as joint tenants with rights of survivorship. The intention of the parties is to hold joint property as tenants by the entirety whenever possible. "Joint property" also means community property as to any property which may be subject to community property laws.

(b) "Joint Tenancy" means tenancy by the entirety in jurisdictions where such a tenancy is permitted, and joint tenancy with rights of survivorship if tenancy by the entirety is not recognized or permitted. The intention of the parties is to hold joint property as tenants by the entirety whenever possible. "Joint property" also refers to community property as to any property which may be subject to community property laws.

(c) "Separate Property" means property owned by either party which is and will remain, or may be acquired, as that party's individual property, free from any claims of the other party. "Separate property" is not part of the community property estate in any state recognizing community property.

6.   HUSBAND'S SEPARATE PROPERTY. The Husband is the owner of certain property, which is set forth and described in Exhibit C attached hereto and made a part hereof, which he intends to keep as his nonmarital, separate, sole, and individual property. All income, rents, profits, interest, dividends, stock splits, gains, and appreciation in value relating to any such separate property shall also be deemed separate property. All inheritances or gifts received by the Husband individually during the marriage shall also be deemed separate property.

7.   WIFE'S SEPARATE PROPERTY. The Wife is the owner of certain property, which is set forth and described in Exhibit D attached hereto and made a part hereof, which she intends to keep as her nonmarital, separate, sole, and individual property. All income, rents, profits, interest, dividends, stock splits, gains, and appreciation in value relating to any such separate property shall also be deemed separate property. All inheritances or gifts received by the Wife individually during the marriage shall also be deemed separate property.

8.   JOINT OR COMMUNITY PROPERTY. The parties intend that certain property shall, from the beginning of the marriage, be joint, as set forth and described in Exhibit E attached hereto and made a part hereof.

9.   PROPERTY ACQUIRED DURING MARRIAGE. The parties recognize that either or both of them may acquire property during the marriage. The parties agree that the manner in which such property is titled during the marriage shall control such property's ownership and distribution in the event of divorce, dissolution of marriage, separation, or death of either party. Such property shall be held as stated in the instrument conveying or evidencing title. If the instrument does not specify or if there is no instrument, the property shall be held as a tenancy by the entirety, or as a joint tenancy with rights of survivorship in the event tenancy by the entirety is not recognized by the state having jurisdiction over the distribution of such property. Any property acquired that does not normally have a title or ownership certificate shall be considered as joint property unless otherwise specified by the parties in writing. All wedding gifts shall be deemed joint property, unless specified as separate property in either Exhibit C or D, or otherwise so specified in writing by the parties.

10.   BANK ACCOUNTS. Any funds deposited in either party's separate bank accounts shall be deemed that party's separate property. Any funds deposited in a bank account held by the parties jointly shall be deemed joint property.

11.   PAYMENT OF EXPENSES. The parties agree that their expenses shall be paid as set forth in Exhibit F attached hereto and made a part hereof.

12.   INCOME FROM AND REINVESTMENT OF SEPARATE PROPERTY.

☒ (A) Any property obtained by either party due to the use, investment, reinvestment, or any transfer of any portion of his or her separate property, and any income from any such property, and any appreciation in the value of such property, shall remain that party's separate property.

❑ (B) Any property obtained by either party due to the use, investment, reinvestment or any transfer of any portion of his or her separate property, and any income from any such property, shall remain that party's separate property. Any appreciation or other increase in the value of either party's separate property, shall remain that party's separate property, unless the other party has made a direct financial contribution to the increase in value, such as by investing his or her own funds, and then only to the proportion of the increase attributable to his or her investment.

13.   RESIDENCE OF THE PARTIES.

☒ (A) It is expressly recognized that the Husband and Wife are joint owners of the residence occupied by the parties at _____1642 Cupcake Lane_____
_____Fairfax, VA 20599_____.

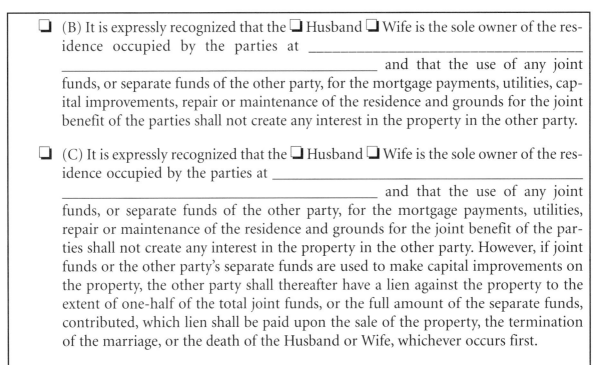

❏ (B) It is expressly recognized that the ❏ Husband ❏ Wife is the sole owner of the residence occupied by the parties at _____ _____ and that the use of any joint funds, or separate funds of the other party, for the mortgage payments, utilities, capital improvements, repair or maintenance of the residence and grounds for the joint benefit of the parties shall not create any interest in the property in the other party.

❏ (C) It is expressly recognized that the ❏ Husband ❏ Wife is the sole owner of the residence occupied by the parties at _____ _____ and that the use of any joint funds, or separate funds of the other party, for the mortgage payments, utilities, repair or maintenance of the residence and grounds for the joint benefit of the parties shall not create any interest in the property in the other party. However, if joint funds or the other party's separate funds are used to make capital improvements on the property, the other party shall thereafter have a lien against the property to the extent of one-half of the total joint funds, or the full amount of the separate funds, contributed, which lien shall be paid upon the sale of the property, the termination of the marriage, or the death of the Husband or Wife, whichever occurs first.

14.   DISPOSITION OF PROPERTY. Each party retains the ownership, management, and control of his or her separate property, and may encumber, sell, or dispose of the property without the other party's consent. Each party shall, on the request of the other, execute any instrument necessary to effectuate this paragraph. The failure ore refusal of a party to join in or execute an instrument required by this paragraph shall entitle the other party to sue for specific performance or for damages, regardless of the doctrine of spousal immunity, and the defaulting party shall pay the other party's costs, expenses, and attorney's fees. This paragraph shall not require a party to execute a promissory note or other evidence of debt for the other party; but if a party executes a promissory note or other evidence of debt for the other party, that other party shall indemnify the party executing the note or other evidence of debt from any claims or demands arising from the execution of the instrument. Execution of an instrument shall not give the executing party any right or interest in the property of the party requesting execution.

15.   PROPERTY DIVISION UPON DIVORCE, DISSOLUTION OF MARRIAGE, OR SEPARATION. In the event of divorce, dissolution of marriage, or separation proceedings being filed and pursued by either party, the parties agree that the terms and provisions of this agreement shall govern all of their rights as to property; alimony including permanent, periodic, rehabilitative, and lump sum; property settlement; rights of community property; and, equitable distribution against the other. Each party releases and waives any claims for special equity in the other party's separate property or in jointly owned property. If either party files for alimony, or spousal support unconnected with divorce, dissolution of marriage, separation, or separate maintenance, the parties agree that the party filing said proceedings shall ask the court to follow the provisions and terms of this postmarital agreement.

16. **ALIMONY.**

   ❏ (A) In the event of divorce or dissolution of marriage proceedings being filed by either party in any state or country, each party forever waives any right to claim or seek any form of alimony or spousal support, and attorneys' fees and costs from the other. Any rights regarding distribution of property are otherwise covered by this agreement, and any rights to community property or claims of special equity are waived and released. In the event that a final judgment or decree of divorce or dissolution of marriage is entered, the parties agree that the provisions of this agreement are in complete settlement of all rights to claim or seek any form of financial support, except child support for any living minor children of the parties, from the other.

   ❏ (B) In the event divorce, dissolution of marriage, separation, or similar proceedings are filed by either party in any state or country, the parties agree that neither party will request or receive alimony or support, whether temporary, rehabilitative, permanent, or lump sum. In consideration for not requesting alimony, the ❏ Husband ❏ Wife shall pay to the other party a sum equal to $_____ for each full year of marriage up to the date a divorce, dissolution of marriage, separation, or similar action is filed. Said sum shall be paid regardless of which party files, and shall terminate on either the death or remarriage of the payee, or on the death of the payor, whichever occurs first.

   ☒ (C) In the event of divorce or dissolution of marriage proceedings being filed by either party in any state or country, the ❏ Husband ☒ Wife agrees to pay to the other party temporary and rehabilitative alimony in the sum of $__5,000__ per ___year___, for a period of __eight__ years after the date a divorce, dissolution of marriage, or separation action is filed. Said sum shall be paid regardless of which party files, and shall terminate at the end of the period stated above, or on either the death or remarriage of the payee, or on the death of the payor, whichever occurs first.

   ❏ (D) In the event of divorce or dissolution of marriage proceedings being filed by either party in any state or country, the ❏ Husband ❏ Wife agrees to pay to the other party temporary and permanent periodic alimony in the sum of $_____ per _____. Said sum shall be paid regardless of which party files, and shall terminate on either the death or remarriage of the payee, or on the death of the payor, whichever occurs first.

17. **CHILD SUPPORT.**

   ☒ (A) In the event of divorce, dissolution of marriage, or separation, and there are any minor children of the parties' marriage, the parties agree that each shall contribute to the support of any such children in the following proportions:

_____25_____% from the Husband.

_____75_____% from the Wife.

❏ (B) The amount of support shall be determined by agreement of the parties. If the parties cannot agree, the amount of support shall be determined by the court.

Such child support shall continue until:
- ❏ Age 18.
- ☒ Age 18, or graduation from high school, whichever occurs last, provided any such child is enrolled as a full-time student and is making a good faith effort to graduate.
- ❏ Graduation from college or trade school, provided any such child is enrolled as a full-time student and is making a good faith effort to graduate.

Both parties acknowledge that they are aware that the court has the ultimate authority to determine child support, taking into consideration the needs of the children and any other factors required by law to be considered.

18. DISPOSITION UPON DEATH.

☒ (A) Each party consents that his or her estate, or the estate of the other, may be disposed of by will, codicil, or trust, or in the absence of any such instrument, according to the laws of descent and distribution and intestate succession as if the marriage of the parties had not taken place. In either event, the estate shall be free of any claim or demand of inheritance, dower, curtesy, elective share, family allowance, homestead election, right to serve as executor, administrator, or personal representative, or any spousal or other claim given by law, irrespective of the marriage and any law to the contrary. Neither party intends by this agreement to limit or restrict the right to give to, or receive from, the other an inter vivos or testamentary gift. Neither party intends by this agreement to release, waive, or relinquish any devise or bequest left to either by specific provision in the will or codicil of the other, any property voluntarily transferred by the other, any joint tenancy created by the other, or any right to serve as executor or personal representative of the other's estate if specifically nominated in the other's will or codicil.

❏ (B) Subject to the conditions set forth in this paragraph, the ❏ Husband ❏ Wife shall receive and accept from the other party after his/her death, the sum of $_____, free of any and all inheritance and estate taxes, in place of, and in full and final settlement and satisfaction of, any and all rights and claims which he/she might otherwise have in the other party's estate and property under any law now or hereafter in force in this or any other jurisdiction, whether by way of a right of election to take against the other party's will, as a share of the estate in intestacy, or otherwise. The ❑ Husband ❑ Wife shall only be entitled to receive said amount if all of the following conditions are met: (1) the parties were married at the time of death, (2) he/she survives the decedent, (3) the parties were not separated at the time of death, and (4) no divorce, dissolution of marriage, or separation proceedings were in progress at the time of death. If any of the above conditions are not met, then he/she shall not be entitled to any sums from the other party's estate.

19.   LIFE INSURANCE. The parties shall maintain the following life insurance policies payable to the other party on death in the face amounts of at least:

Life insurance on the life of the Husband payable to the Wife or a person she designates of at least $_____185,000_____.

Life insurance on the life of the Wife payable to the Husband or a person he designates of at least $_____200,000_____.

20.   DEBTS. The parties may incur debts either individually or jointly. Neither party shall assume or become responsible for the payment of any debts or obligations of the other party because of their marriage. Neither party shall do anything that would cause any debt or obligation of one of them to become a claim, demand, lien, or encumbrance on the other's property without the other party's written consent. If a debt or obligation of one party is asserted as a claim or demand against the other's separate property without such written consent, the party who is responsible for the debt or obligation shall indemnify the other from the claim or demand, including the payment of the other party's costs, expenses, and attorney's fees.

21.   HOMESTEAD. Each party releases any claim, demand, right, or interest that the party may have acquired because of their marriage in any real property of the other because of the homestead property provisions of the laws of any state concerning the descent of the property as homestead.

22.   COMMINGLING OF INCOME AND ASSETS. The parties recognize that it is possible for their income or assets to become, or appear to become, commingled. It is the parties' intention that any commingling of income or assets shall not be interpreted to imply any abandonment of the terms and provisions of this agreement, that the provisions contained herein regarding the parties' interests in jointly held property be applied, and that in other instances each party's interest be determined by each party's proportionate contribution toward the total funds or value of assets in question.

23.   TAX RETURNS/GIFTS/LEGAL PROCEEDINGS. The fact that the parties may file joint local, state, or federal income tax returns, or any other joint tax papers or documents, or make gifts of property or cash to each other or not account to each other with regard to the expenditure of income shall not be interpreted to imply any abandonment of the terms and provisions of this agreement. The filing of a divorce, dissolution of marriage, separation, or other legal action or proceeding shall not be deemed as any abandonment of the terms and provisions of this agreement.

24.   FREE AND VOLUNTARY ACT. The parties acknowledge that executing this agreement is a free and voluntary act, and has not been entered into for any reason other than the desire for the furtherance of their relationship in marriage. Each party acknowledges that he or she has had adequate time to fully consider the consequences of signing this agreement, and has not been pressured, threatened, coerced, or unduly influenced to sign this agreement.

25.   GOVERNING LAW. This agreement shall be governed by the laws of _____Virginia_____.

26.   SEVERABILITY. If any part of this agreement is adjudged invalid, illegal, or unenforceable, the remaining parts shall not be affected.

27.   FURTHER ASSURANCE. Each party shall execute any instruments or documents at any time requested by the other party that are necessary or proper to effectuate this agreement.

28.   BINDING AGREEMENT/NO OTHER BENEFICIARY. This agreement shall be binding upon the parties, and upon their heirs, executors, personal representatives, administrators, and assigns. No person shall have a right or cause of action arising or resulting from this agreement except those who are parties to it and their successors in interest.

29.   RELEASE. Except as otherwise provided in this agreement, each party releases all claims or demands to the property or estate of the other, however and whenever acquired, including acquisitions in the future.

30.   ENTIRE AGREEMENT. This instrument, including any attached exhibits, constitutes the entire agreement of the parties. No representations or promises have been made except those that are set out in this agreement. This agreement may not be modified or terminated except in writing signed by the parties.

31.   PARAGRAPH HEADINGS. The headings of the paragraphs contained in this agreement are for convenience only, and are not to be considered a part of this agreement or used in determining its content or context.

32.   ATTORNEYS' FEES IN ENFORCEMENT. A party who fails to comply with any provision or obligation contained in this agreement shall pay the other party's attorney's fees, costs, and other expenses reasonably incurred in enforcing this agreement and resulting from the noncompliance.

33.   SIGNATURES AND INITIALS OF PARTIES. The signatures of the parties on this document, and their initials on each page, indicate that each party has read, and agrees with, this entire Postmarital Agreement, including any and all exhibits attached hereto. Any provision containing a box, ❏, that does not contain an "X" does not apply and is not a part of the agreement of the parties.

34.   ❏   OTHER PROVISIONS. Additional provisions are contained in the Addendum to Postmarital Agreement attached hereto and made a part hereof.

George Washington
Husband

Martha Curtis Washington
Wife

Executed in the presence of:

Alexander Hamilton
Name: Alexander Hamilton
Address: 286 Duelist Avenue
    Washington, DC 20064

Gertrude Hamilton
Name: Gertrude Hamilton
Address: 286 Duelist Avenue
    Washington, DC 20064

STATE OF   Virginia   )
COUNTY OF   Wise   )

      The foregoing Postmarital Agreement, consisting of __eight__ pages and Exhibits __one__ through __five__, was acknowledged before me this __twenty-third__ day of __March__, __2007__, by _George Washington,_ _Martha Curtis Washington, and Gertrude and Alexander Hamilton_, the above-named Husband, Wife, and Witnesses respectively, who are personally known to me or who have produced __VAdr.lic.K-492-729, D603-997,__ __97-299384, and B-234-956-2285634-L__ as identification.

Trixie Norton
Signature

Trixie Norton
(Typed Name of Acknowledger)

NOTARY PUBLIC
Commission Number: __97-299384__
My Commission Expires: November 23, 2008

Additional Forms

In addition to the **Postnuptial Agreement** (form 12), there are some forms you will need to complete and other forms you may need to use. All of these forms are discussed in more detail in Chapter 9, but they will be summarized here.

In addition to the Postnuptial Agreement, you will also need to use the following forms.

- ◆ **Husband's Financial Statement** (form 3)—This satisfies the husband's duty for full financial disclosure.
- ◆ **Wife's Financial Statement** (form 4)—This satisfies the wife's duty for full financial disclosure.
- ◆ **Husband's Schedule of Separate Property** (form 5)—This lists all of the currently owned property that will be owned solely by the husband.
- ◆ **Wife's Schedule of Separate Property** (form 6)—This lists all of the currently owned property that will be owned solely by the wife.

Depending upon your situation, you may also use some or all of the following forms.

- ◆ **Schedule of Joint Property** (form 7)—If there is property that you wish to consider as your joint property, you need to list it on this form.
- ◆ **Expense Payment Schedule** (form 8)—This describes how you and your spouse will handle your monthly living expenses.
- ◆ **Addendum to Marital Agreement** (form 9)—This is used if there are any special matters that are not covered by the Postnuptial Agreement form.

Chapter 9:
Additional Forms

Regardless of which **PRENUPTIAL AGREEMENT** (or **POSTNUPTIAL AGREEMENT**) form you use, you will need to complete some additional forms. This chapter helps you decide which forms you need and how to complete them.

Listing Assets and Debts

Regardless of whether you are preparing a prenuptial or postnuptial agreement, you and your partner will need to list assets and debts on the **HUSBAND'S FINANCIAL STATEMENT** (form 3) or the **WIFE'S FINANCIAL STATEMENT** (form 4), in each party's **SCHEDULE OF SEPARATE PROPERTY** (forms 5 and 6), and in the **SCHEDULE OF JOINT PROPERTY** (form 7). It is important to list everything and to list it accurately and precisely. The following information is provided to help you determine what and how to list things.

Cash and Bank Accounts

For the **FINANCIAL STATEMENT**, it is sufficient to just give the total from all accounts. However, for the schedules of property, list each account separately, giving the name of the bank, credit union, etc., and the account number. This includes savings and checking accounts, and certificates of deposit (CDs).

Stocks, Bonds, Notes, Annuities, Pensions, and Other Investments

All stocks, bonds, or other *paper investments* should be listed. Write down the number of shares, the certificate numbers (if any), and the name of the company or other organization that issued them. Also copy any notation such as *common* or *preferred* stock or shares. This information can be obtained from the certificate itself, or from a statement from your stock broker, financial planner, issuing company or organization, etc. Such a statement should also give you a current value for your **FINANCIAL STATEMENT.** If you do not have an exact value as of the date you sign your **FINANCIAL STATEMENT**, note that it is an "approximate value," "estimated value," or "value as of _____ " (fill in the most recent date you were able to determine a value). Also list retirement or pension plans (see page 21 on pension plans).

Real Estate

List each piece of property separately. The description might include a legal description (these can be quite long, and are not necessary if there is another way to clearly and unmistakably identify the property), street address for the property, a subdivision name and lot number, or anything that indicates the piece of property you are referring to. In assigning a value to the property, consider the market value, which is how much you could probably sell the property for. This might be what similar properties in the area have sold for recently. You might also consider how much you paid for the property, or how much the property is insured for.

NOTE: *Do not use the tax assessment value, as this is usually considerably lower than the market value. Make a note on your Financial Statement to indicate how the value was determined, such as "purchase price on _____ " (fill in the date of purchase), "estimated value based on recent sales of similar property," "appraised value as of _____ " (fill in the date of the appraisal), and so on.*

Automobiles, Boats, and Other Vehicles

All cars, trucks, motor homes, recreational vehicles (RVs), motorcycles, boats, trailers, airplanes, and any other means of transportation for which the state requires a title and registration should be listed. You should include the make, model, year and serial number of each. Regarding a value, you can go the the public library and ask to look at the *blue book* for cars, trucks, or whatever it is you are looking for. A blue book (which may actually be any color) gives the average values for used vehicles. Your librarian can help you find what you need. Another source is to look in the classified advertising section of a newspaper to see what similar vehicles are selling for. You might also try calling a dealer to see if he or she can give you a rough idea of the value. Be sure you consider the condition of the vehicle.

Other Personal Property

This general category is further broken down on the **FINANCIAL STATEMENT.** For each type of property listed on the form, type in an estimate of the value. Some of the items that fit in this category are discussed in more detail below.

Appliances, Electronic Equipment, Yard Machines, Etc.

Include such things as televisions, VCRs, refrigerators, lawn mowers, and power tools on the **FINANCIAL STATEMENT**. Include the make, model, serial number, size, or whatever identifying information is available. You will probably only be able to estimate the value.

Furniture

Furniture will be included in the "Contents of home" line of the **FINANCIAL STATEMENT**. On the **SCHEDULE OF SEPARATE PROPERTY** and **SCHEDULE OF JOINT PROPERTY**, list furniture as specifically as possible. You should include the type of piece (such as sofa, coffee table, etc.), the color, and if you know it, the manufacturer, line name, or the style. Furniture usually will not have a serial number, although if you find one, be sure to write it on the list. Once again, estimate the value.

Jewelry and Collections

You do not need to list individual items of inexpensive or costume jewelry. However, if you own an expensive piece, you should list it separately, along with an appraised, insured, or estimated value. Be sure to include silverware, furs, original art, gold, coin collections, etc. Again, be as detailed and specific as possible.

Recreation/Sports Equipment

Examples of recreation or sports equipment include golf clubs, guns, skis, cameras, pool tables, and camping or fishing equipment. Just give a total on the **FINANCIAL STATEMENT**. On the schedules of property, be as specific as possible, and give an appraised, insured, or estimated value.

Trade Tools/Equipment

If you have tools, equipment, or other things that you use in your business or job, give a total estimated value on your **FINANCIAL STATEMENT**. On the schedules of property, describe these items as specifically as possible.

Life Insurance

Fill in the total of your life insurance policy on the **FINANCIAL STATEMENT**. On the schedules of property, type in the name of the company issuing the policy, the policy number, the face amount, cash surrender value (if any), and any other information that may specifically identify the policy.

Business Ownerships and Interests

If you own a business or any interest in a business, list the name of the company or business, and describe your interest in the business (such as "sole owner," "50% active partner," "5% silent partner," "10% shareholder"). Estimate the value as best as you can for your **FINANCIAL STATEMENT.**

Other Assets

The category for Other Assets is simply a general reference to anything of value that does not fit in one of the above categories, or that is of such a value that you feel it should be listed separately. Examples might be a pet, portable spa, above-ground swimming pool, and farm animals or machinery.

Debts

In "ITEM 3: LIABILITIES" on the **FINANCIAL STATEMENT**, you will list all debts. For each debt, fill in the name of the creditor, what property (if any) serves as security for the debt, and the balance owed. If you have a mortgage on real estate, the property will usually be the security for the debt.

If you have a car or boat loan, the car or boat will probably be the security. If you purchased household furniture or appliances using the store's in-house credit, the furniture or appliance may serve as security.

If you bought anything using a credit card, it is unlikely that the debt is secured by any property. Be sure to include any loans by family members or friends (significant amounts—not if you owe your friend five dollars you borrowed for lunch last week).

Financial Statement

You and your spouse each need to complete a **FINANCIAL STATEMENT**. These forms must be completed accurately, and must list all of your income, assets, and debts. If there is ever a challenge to the prenuptial agreement, your **FINANCIAL STATEMENT** will be your evidence that you fully disclosed your financial situation to your spouse.

The **HUSBAND'S FINANCIAL STATEMENT** and the **WIFE'S FINANCIAL STATEMENT** in Appendix C are designed for information on a monthly basis. If you are paid weekly or every two weeks, you will need to convert your income to a monthly figure. To convert weekly amounts to monthly amounts, just take the weekly figure and multiply it by 4.3. (There are roughly 4.3 weeks to a month.) To convert from every two weeks, divide by 2, and then multiply by 4.3.

Most of the blanks in either **FINANCIAL STATEMENT** clearly indicate what information is to be filled in there. (see form 3, p.183 and form 4, p.187.) However, the following may answer some questions.

- ❖ Type your name (or your spouse's name) in the blank in the first paragraph.
- ❖ Complete the information called for in ITEM 1 for your occupation, employer's name and address, Social Security number, pay period, and rate of pay. "PAY PERIOD" refers to how often you receive your paycheck, such as "weekly," "every two weeks," or "twice a month." "RATE OF PAY" refers to your hourly rate, or weekly, monthly, or yearly salary, whichever applies to your situation.
- ❖ "AVERAGE GROSS MONTHLY INCOME" refers to your total income before any deductions for taxes or other items. The other items listed on the form are some of the more common types of income other than wages or salary. Add these items (if any) to

your average gross monthly income and type in the total on the line for "TOTAL MONTHLY GROSS INCOME."

⟡ "DEDUCTIONS" refers to deductions from gross income. The items listed on the form are some of the more common deductions.

⟡ "TOTAL NET INCOME" is calculated by subtracting the "TOTAL DEDUCTIONS" from the "TOTAL GROSS MONTHLY INCOME."

⟡ "ITEM 2" on "ASSETS" is where you list everything you own. Refer to pages 82–83 for more information on how to list assets.

⟡ "ITEM 3" on "LIABILITIES" is where you list everything you owe. Refer to page 85 for more information on how to list debts. In the column marked "Creditor," type in the name of the company or person you owe the debt to. This will include such creditors as Visa, Mastercard, Sears, and other credit cards with an outstanding balance, as well as mortgages, car and boat loans, student loans, and so on. In the column marked "Security," type in what property secures the debt. Be as specific as possible, such as giving the VIN number of a car. Some of your debts may not be secured, such as most credit cards. In these cases, simply type in the word "Unsecured." In the column marked "Balance," type in the total amount still owed. Finally, add the amounts in the "Balance" column, and type in the total on the last line.

⟡ This form should be dated and signed by you (or your spouse if it is his or her **FINANCIAL STATEMENT**) where indicated. Next, two copies should be made of each **FINANCIAL STATEMENT**. The original will be attached to the **PRENUPTIAL AGREEMENT**. You should keep a copy, and your spouse should keep a copy.

⟡ The "ACKNOWLEDGMENT OF RECEIPT" is where each of you verify that you have received a copy of the other's **FINANCIAL STATEMENT**. The wife will complete this section on the **HUSBAND'S FINANCIAL STATEMENT**, and the husband will complete this section on the **WIFE'S FINANCIAL STATEMENT**. Type in the spouse's name in the first blank. In the second blank, write in the date the spouse received a copy. The spouse would then fill in the date after the word "DATED" and sign where indicated.

Schedules of Separate Property

The **HUSBAND'S SCHEDULE OF SEPARATE PROPERTY** and the **WIFE'S SCHEDULE OF SEPARATE PROPERTY** forms will be used for you and your partner to list property that will remain separate. (see form 5, p.191 and form 6, p.193.) In the introductory paragraph, fill in the title of your agreement (either "Prenuptial Agreement" or "Postnuptial Agreement") and the date of that agreement. Below that paragraph, describe the items in the same manner as you described the property on the **FINANCIAL STATEMENT**. Refer back to the subsection of Chapter 4 on "Separate Property" for more information about how to list items here. Be sure that each of you initial one of the boxes at the bottom of each form.

Schedule of Joint Property

The SCHEDULE OF JOINT PROPERTY is completed in the same manner as forms 5 and 6, except it is for property that you and your partner want to be considered as joint property. (see form 7, p.195.) If there is no such property, simply type in the word "None." Describe each item in the same manner as you described the property in the FINANCIAL STATEMENT. Be sure that each of you initials one of the boxes at the bottom of each form.

If any real property listed here is currently titled in one name, you will need to prepare a deed to add the other person's name to the title. As each state has its own requirements for deeds (e.g., the format, the number of witnesses required, notary requirements, and recording procedures), you will need to either find out what is required or have a deed professionally prepared. If any separately owned mobile homes, motor vehicles, or other items with title papers are to become joint property, you may need to contact the appropriate governmental agency to arrange to have the other person's name added to the title documents.

Expense Payment Schedule

The EXPENSE PAYMENT SCHEDULE is for you and your partner to describe how you intend to pay for your living expenses. (form 8, p.197.) This is to be sure you are in agreement about who is to be responsible for what bills, or for what portion of each bill. This will also assist you in making a budget, which can help to avoid financial difficulties in the future. In the introductory paragraph, fill in the title of your agreement (either "Prenuptial Agreement" or "Postnuptial Agreement") and the date of that agreement.

Addendum to Marital Agreement

The ADDENDUM TO MARITAL AGREEMENT will only be used if there are provisions that are not included in your PRENUPTIAL AGREEMENT or your POSTNUPTIAL AGREEMENT. (see form 9, p.199.) In the introductory paragraph, fill in the title of your agreement (i.e., either "Prenuptial Agreement" or "Postnuptial Agreement") and the date of that agreement. Below the first paragraph, type in the additional provisions. Be sure that each of you initials one of the boxes at the bottom of each form.

The ADDENDUM TO MARITAL AGREEMENT is to be used to write any provisions that are not included in the main part of the agreement or to further explain provisions of the main part of the agreement. (see form 9, p.199.) Type in the date of your main prenuptial agreement in the first paragraph. Next, type in the additional provisions. At the bottom of the form, be sure that each of you initial where indicated.

If you are modifying or explaining a provision in the main part of your **PRENUPTIAL AGREEMENT**, refer to the paragraph number (for example, "Paragraph 17 is modified to provide that _____").

Two of the more common provisions you may want to include in your agreement, or in an addendum, relate to pension plans and businesses.

As stated earlier, one federal court has decided that only a spouse, not a fiancé, may waive pension plan rights. The spouse can only waive such rights if the agreement states that all federal pension rights are being waived, and it names a beneficiary. If you or your partner intend to give up pension plan rights, you may want to consult a lawyer, or use one of the following two provisions.

With the following provision, both parties waive their rights in each other's pension plan. This should be used when each party has his or her own plan.

> **WAIVER OF PENSION RIGHTS.** Each party waives any and all state and federal rights he or she may otherwise have in any pension, retirement, or profit-sharing plan of the other party. In the event of the death of either party, _____ is named as the beneficiary of the deceased Husband's plan, and _____ is named as the beneficiary of the deceased Wife's plan. Each party further agrees to execute an agreement within ____ days after the parties' marriage, whereby such rights are waived in accordance with this paragraph. Failure of one party to execute such an agreement after the parties' marriage shall entitle the other party to declare this Prenuptial Agreement null and void upon written notice of such declaration to the other party.

With the following provision, one party gives up rights in the other's pension. In three places you will need to cross out either the word "HUSBAND" or "WIFE," whichever does not apply.

> **WAIVER OF PENSION RIGHTS.** The HUSBAND/WIFE waives any and all state and federal rights in any pension, retirement, or profit-sharing plan of the other party. In the event of the plan holder's death, _____ is named as the beneficiary of the plan. The HUSBAND/WIFE further agrees to execute an agreement within _____ days after the parties' marriage, whereby such rights are waived in accordance with this paragraph. Failure of the HUSBAND/WIFE to execute such an agreement after the parties' marriage shall entitle the other party to declare this Prenuptial Agreement null and void upon written notice of such declaration to the other party.

A postnuptial agreement could also use either of the provisions on page 87, except you would delete the last sentence that begins "Failure of...." You cannot force your spouse to sign a post-nuptial agreement, so the only protection you would have is to put some kind of penalty in the prenuptial agreement if he or she refuses to sign the required pension agreement. In the paragraphs above, the penalty is that you would be able to cancel the prenuptial agreement. However, this may actually harm you further, depending upon what is in your prenuptial agreement. An alternative would be to have your spouse give up something he or she would otherwise receive under the prenuptial agreement, as a penalty for refusing to sign the postnuptial agreement.

The **ADDENDUM TO MARITAL AGREEMENT** is to be used to add any provisions that are not included in the **PRENUPTIAL AGREEMENT** or **POSTNUPTIAL AGREEMENT**. (see form 9, p.199.)

Career and Business Interests

If either or both of you have a business to keep separate, you can simply list that business on the appropriate **SCHEDULE OF SEPARATE PROPERTY** (form 5 or form 6). If one or both or you are professionals and want to avoid the problem of having the other claim an interest in your earnings, or if you prefer to state your business interest more specifically, you may use one of the following provisions.

With the following provision, one party waives his/her claims on the other's business. You will need to delete the word "HUSBAND" or "WIFE," and "he" or "she," whichever does not apply.

> **WAIVER OF INTERESTS IN BUSINESS.** The HUSBAND/WIFE acknowledges that he/she has no interest in, and will claim no interest in, the business of the HUS-BAND/WIFE known as _____, in the event of divorce, dissolution of marriage, legal separation, or death; regardless of whether there is any appreciation in said business or whether he/she provides any personal labor, services, or other contribution to said business. Nothing in this paragraph shall prevent an *inter vivos* or testamentary transfer of an interest in said business.

With the following provision, one party waives interest in the other party's career. You will need to delete the word "HUSBAND" or "WIFE" and "he" or "she," whichever does not apply. The name or description or the person's career goes on the blank line (e.g., "dentist," "attorney," "CPA").

> **WAIVER OF INTERESTS IN BUSINESS.** The HUSBAND/WIFE acknowledges that he/she has no interest in, and will claim no interest in, the earnings and profits of the career of the HUSBAND/WIFE as _____, in the event of divorce, dissolution of marriage, or legal separation.

You may need to make variations to these provision or even combine them to fit your needs. You may also wish to consult an attorney.

Chapter 10:
Changing or Canceling Your Agreement

A prenuptial agreement is not necessarily carved in stone for all time. Sometimes circumstances change that lead the parties to want to change, or even cancel, the agreement. A prenuptial agreement can be changed or cancelled, provided this is the agreement of both parties. This chapter will explain how to go about modifying or cancelling a prenuptial agreement.

Amendment to Marital Agreement

As long as you and your spouse agree, you prenuptial or postnuptial agreement can be changed. As your financial situation changes, you may need to modify your agreement. You may also want to modify your agreement if you and your spouse have children together. **AMENDMENT TO MARITAL AGREEMENT** is to be used anytime you and your spouse want to change any of the provisions of your prenuptial or postnuptial agreement. (see form 10, p.201.) To complete form 10 you need to do the following.

⟐ Type in the current date in the first blank of the first (unnumbered) paragraph. In the second and third blanks, type in your name and your spouse's, with the husband's name first. In the fourth blank, fill in the title of your agreement (either "Prenuptial Agreement" or "Postnuptial Agreement"), and in the fifth blank fill in the date of that agreement.

⟐ In paragraph 1, type in whatever changes you want to make.

⟐ Below paragraph 3, both parties need to sign (in the presence of the witnesses and notary) where indicated. Type in the name and address of the two witnesses. The notary will then complete the notary section at the bottom.

Release of Marital Agreement

If, for whatever reason, you and your spouse decide to cancel your prenuptial agreement, you can use the **RELEASE OF MARITAL AGREEMENT**. (see form 11, p.203.) To complete form 11, you need to do the following.

⬦ Type in the current date in the first blank of the first (unnumbered) paragraph. In the second and third blanks, type in your name and your spouse's, with the husband's name first.

⬦ In paragraph 1, type in the title and date of your original premarital agreement.

⬦ If any agreement was made in connection with canceling the agreement (such as the payment of any money or the transfer of any item of property), type in an explanation of the agreement after paragraph 3. If no agreement was made, type in the word "None."

⬦ Below paragraph 5, both parties need to sign (in the presence of the witnesses and notary) where indicated. Type in the name and address of the two witnesses. The notary will then complete the notary section at the bottom.

Glossary

A

addendum. Provisions of a contract that are on a separate sheet of paper from the basic contract form.

administrator (or **administratrix**). A person appointed by the court to oversee distribution of the property of someone who died without leaving a will. Administrator applies to a male, and administratrix applies to a female.

alimony. In a divorce, a payment to be made by one spouse for the support of the other.

antenuptial agreement. Another name for a prenuptial agreement.

augmented estate. A term defined by the law of a particular state that describes exactly what property is included in the estate for particular purposes, such as in determining the spouse's intestate or elective share. This may include property that is in addition to property in the probate estate, may not include some property that is in the probate estate, or may simply be different from property in the probate estate. For example, a typical definition is: "the value of the probate assets reduced by funeral expenses, homestead, family allowances and exemptions, liens, mortgages, and enforceable claims."

B

beneficiary. A person who receives property from a person who has died, or who benefits from an agreement between two other persons.

C

code. (1) The collection of a state's laws, such as "Code of Alabama." Many states use the term statutes instead. (2) The collection of a state's laws on a particular subject, such as "Probate Code."

codicil. A change or amendment to a will.

commingling. The mixing of two types of property. In the context of premarital agreements, divorce, and probate, it typically refers to mixing marital and nonmarital property. For example, prior to marriage the wife has a bank account, which would be nonmarital property under the laws of her state. After marriage she adds money from her paychecks, which would be marital property under the laws of her state. She now has a bank account with marital and nonmarital property commingled.

community property. Property owned by a husband and wife together in any of the following nine states: Arizona, California, Idaho, Louisiana, Nevada, New Mexico, Texas, Washington, and Wisconsin.

D

decedent. In probate law, the person who has died.

devise. Real property left to someone in a will.

devisee. A person who is left real property in another person's will.

E

elective share. The minimal portion of property that a state allows a surviving spouse to receive when the decedent leaves a will. The surviving spouse must choose or elect to take what he or she was left in the will, or to take the elective share. This generally comes into play when the decedent has left little in the will to the surviving spouse, so that he or she would receive more by taking the elective share.

equitable distribution. A legal term for how property is divided in a divorce in most states. Equitable distribution is *not* used in those states with community property laws.

executor (or **executrix**). A person appointed by the court, or by a will, to oversee distribution of the property of someone who has died with a will. Executor applies to a male, and executrix applies to a female.

exempt property. Property set aside by a state's laws that is exempt from attachment by creditors, to which a surviving spouse is entitled in addition to any other rights such as the intestate or elective share, homestead, and family allowance.

F

family allowance. Money or other property that a surviving spouse or children may keep in addition to other rights such as the intestate or elective share, homestead, and exempt property. It is designed to provide living expenses for a certain period of time, usually up to one year from the date of death.

forced share. Another term for the spouse's elective share.

H

heir. A person who receives property owned by a person who has died without a will.

homestead. Real property where an individual or married couple had their primary residence. This is used in some states that give special rights and protection to such property against the claims of creditors or for property tax purposes. In probate law, many states allow the surviving spouse certain rights in homestead property that cannot be given away to others by a will.

I

intestate. Dying without leaving a will.

intestate share. The portion of property a family member receives when a person dies without leaving a will. (As used in Appendix A of this book, the intestate share refers to the share the surviving spouse would receive if there is no will.)

J

joint property. Property owned by a husband and wife together.

joint tenancy. A type of property ownership by two or more persons. If one owner dies, his or her interest in the property goes to the surviving owner or owners. Some states may require the ownership document to include the phrase "as joint tenants with rights of survivorship."

L

legacy. Personal property left to someone in a will.

legatee. A person who is left personal property in another person's will.

M

maintenance. The term used in some states for alimony.

marital property. Property considered by some state laws as owned by husband and wife together.

N

nonmarital property. Property owned by one spouse individually, and free from claims of the other spouse.

P

personal property. Property that is not real property.

personal representative. A person appointed by the court or a will to oversee distribution of the property of someone who has died. This is a more modern trend and generally replaces the terms administrator, administratrix, executor, and executrix.

postnuptial agreement (or **postmarital agreement**). An agreement between a husband and wife, executed after they are married, providing for the division of their property in the event of death or divorce.

premarital agreement. Another name for a prenuptial agreement.

prenuptial agreement. An agreement between a man and woman, executed before they are married, providing for the division of their property in the event of death or divorce.

probate estate. Generally, those assets of a decedent that are subject to probate; typically it does not include property passing automatically to a joint owner, pay-on-death accounts, or life insurance proceeds. This is matter of definition in a particular state's laws, and therefore varies from state to state.

property division (or **property distribution**). The allocation of property between the husband and wife in a divorce case.

R

real property. Land and things permanently attached to the land, such as a house.

S

separate maintenance. Another name for alimony, used in some states.

separate property. Another name for sole property or nonmarital property, used in some states.

severability clause. A provision in a contract that says that if a court declares one provision of the contract invalid, it does not invalidate the entire contract.

sole property. Another name for separate property or nonmarital property, used in some states.

spousal support. Another name for alimony, used in some states.

statutes. The collection of a state's laws, such as "Oregon Revised Statutes." Many states use the term code instead.

supplemental amount. The minimal amount of a spouse's elective share when married less than one year in a state where the spouse's elective share is a based on the duration of the marriage. It is typically a somewhat complicated calculation, starting with a minimal amount and subtracting what was received through certain other legal provisions (such as the homestead and family allowance). Where referred to in Appendix A, you will need to read the law of that particular state to figure out exactly what this would be in a given situation.

T

taking against the will. When a surviving spouse chooses to take the elective share of the estate, instead of taking what was left to him or her in the will.

tenancy by the entirety (or **tenancy by the entireties**). A type of property ownership by a married couple. This is generally the same as joint tenancy, except that it is specifically and only between spouses.

tenancy in common. A type of property ownership by two or more persons. If one owner dies, his or her interest in the property goes to his or her heirs or devisees, not to the other owners.

testate. Someone who dies leaving a will.

Appendix A:
State Laws

This appendix contains information about the laws of each state that have some impact on prenuptial agreements. It is strongly suggested that you read the law as it is actually written. To find the law, see the section on "Legal Research" in Chapter 4 of this book. The fifty states and the District of Columbia are listed in alphabetical order. Under each state's listing you will find the following headings.

The Law

"The Law" tells about how your state's law books are organized, and where to find the basic law regarding prenuptial agreements. The following subheadings may also be found.

In General. The "In General" section will give the title of the volume of books containing your state's law, and the title, chapter, article, or section number of a sample provision. It will also show you how your state's laws are abbreviated. There may also be additional information to help you find the law for your state. For example, look at the listing in this appendix for Alabama. The laws of Alabama are found in the set of books called the Code of Alabama. For the example given, you would look for the volume of the Code of Alabama, which contains Title 43, then look for Chapter 8, then Section 43-8-72. This would be abbreviated "C.A., Sec. 43-8-72." "C.A." stands for Code of Alabama. "Sec. 43-8-72" stands for "Section 43-8-72," which is also "Title 43, Chapter 8, Section 72."

UPAA. The "UPAA" section will tell you if your state uses the *Uniform Premarital Agreement Act* (UPAA). If so, the reference for this law in your state will be given. The basic UPAA is reproduced in Appendix B, although the section numbers will be different in each state. Also, be sure to check your state's UPAA, because some states have made small changes in the wording.

Misc. A few states have their own laws relating to premarital agreements, which are not the UPAA, nor are they in sections of the law relating to probate or divorce. If your state has such a law, it will be listed here. There is not a "Misc" subheading for most states.

Probate. The "Probate" section is where you will find the reference for any premarital agreement laws in your state's probate laws.

Divorce. The "Divorce" section is where you will find the reference for any premarital agreement laws in your state's divorce laws.

Probate Laws

"Probate Law" tells you where to find your state's probate laws, and gives you some basic information about probate laws relating to premarital agreements, and what kind of rights you may have in your spouse's property. This is to give you a rough idea of what you may be giving up by signing a premarital agreement, and where you can look to get the details of the law in your state. You will find the following subheadings.

In General. The "In General" section gives a reference to where your state's probate laws can be found. If your state has adopted the Uniform Probate Code, the letters "UPC" will appear. For example, Alabama has adopted the Uniform Probate Code, and it begins in the Code of Alabama at Section 43-8-1.

Elective Share. The "Elective Share" section gives the reference to where you can find your state's law regarding a surviving spouse's elective share. It will also give basic information about what the elective share is for your state. For example, the elective share in Alabama is the lesser of $1/3$ of the deceased spouse's estate, or all of the estate minus the surviving spouse's separate property. Of course, you would need to read the specific law to get all of the details, and to find out what is considered separate property, etc. The elective share statute is found in the Alabama Code at Section 43-8-70.

Intestate Share. The "Intestate Share" section will tell you what portion of your spouse's estate you would receive if he or she died without leaving a will (providing there is no premarital agreement). For example, the surviving spouse's intestate share in Alabama is $1/2$ to all of the estate. This is typical of most states, with the range depending upon how many children or other heirs there are. The law relating to the intestate share is found in the Alabama Code at Section 43-8-41.

Divorce Laws

"Divorce Law" tells you where to find your state's divorce laws, and gives you some basic information about divorce laws relating to premarital agreements, and what kind of rights you may have in your spouse's property in the event of divorce. This is to give you a rough idea of what you may be giving up by signing a premarital agreement, and where you can look to get the details of the law in your state. You will find the following subheadings.

Title. The "Title" section tells you what a divorce action is called in your particular state. It will either be "Divorce" or "Dissolution of Marriage," depending on how it is referred to in your state. You may want to use the proper term for your state in your premarital agreement, or keep the more all-inclusive language found in the forms in Appendix C. For example, Alabama uses the term *divorce*, whereas Alaska uses the term *dissolution of marriage*.

Property. The "Property" section gives you a summary of the law in your state regarding the factors used to divide property in a divorce case. It will also give a reference to where you can find this in your state's laws.

Alimony. The "Alimony" section gives you a summary of the law in your state regarding the factors used in a divorce case to determine whether alimony should be awarded, and if so, how much alimony. It will also give a reference to where you can find this in your state's laws.

You may find most state statutes on the Internet, although they can vary dramatically in user-friendliness. Some of these sites are maintained by the state government, and others are maintained by private companies or law firms. For a few states, the laws are only available by paying for a subscription service. A single site, **www.findlaw.com**, provides access to all of the state websites, except Colorado and the District of Columbia, which may only be accessed by paying for a subscription service. Findlaw will take you to the website specific to your site. Additional help in navigating a particular state's website may be included in the state's listing in this appendix.

ALABAMA

THE LAW

In General:
Code of Alabama, Title 43, Chapter 8 (C.A., Sec. 43-8-72).

UPAA:
No.

Probate:
C.A., Sec. 43-8-72. Standard UPC waiver provision. Allows spouse to waive elective share, homestead (C.A., Sec. 43-8-110), exempt property (C.A., Sec. 43-8-111), and family allowance (Sec. 43-8-112). Any other interest may also be waived, C.A., Secs. 43-8-290 through 43-8-298.

Divorce:
C.A., Sec. 30-4-9, which provides that: "The husband and wife may contract with each other, but all contracts into which they enter are subject to the rules of law as to contracts by and between persons standing in confidential relations." Case law indicates that if the agreement is not "fair, just and equitable" as to one party, that party must have "competent, independent advice." *Tibbs v. Anderson*, 580 So.2d 1337 (Ala. 1991). Marriage itself is sufficient consideration for a premarital agreement.

PROBATE LAWS

In General:
UPC: C.A., Sec. 43-8-1.

Elective share:
The lesser of $1/3$, or all minus the survivor's separate estate. (C.A., Sec. 43-8-70.)

Intestate share:
$1/2$ to all. (C.A., Sec. 43-8-41.)

DIVORCE LAWS

Title:
Divorce.

Property:
Equitable distribution under case law. Fault may be considered. No statutory factors. Courts recognize separate property as property acquired (1) before marriage; or (2) by gift or inheritance (unless used for the benefit of both parties). See C.A., Secs. 30-4-1 through 30-4-4 on separate property of wife.

Alimony:
Alimony may be awarded if the party seeking alimony has insufficient property or income for support. Factors: (1) value of each party's estate; and (2) financial condition of recipient spouse's family. However, property acquired before marriage is not considered unless it was regularly used for the common benefit during the marriage. (C.A., Sec. 30-2-51.) Fault may limit or bar alimony altogether. (C.A., Sec. 30-2-52.) Alimony must terminate upon remarriage or cohabitation with a member of the opposite sex. (C.A., Sec. 30-2-55.)

ALASKA

THE LAW

In General:
Alaska Statutes, Title 13, Section 13.12.213 (A.S., Sec. 13.12.213).

UPAA:
No.

Probate:
A.S., Sec. 13.12.213. Standard UPC waiver provision.

Divorce:
None.

PROBATE LAW

In General:
UPC: A.S., Sec. 13.06.005.

Elective share:
$1/3$. (A.S., Sec. 13.12.202.)

Intestate share:
$1/2$ to all. (A.S., Sec. 13.12.102.)

DIVORCE LAW

Title:
Divorce (standard procedure), or Dissolution of Marriage (simplified procedure).

Property:
Equitable distribution. Fault is not a factor. All property acquired during marriage is marital property. Factors for dividing marital property: (1) length of marriage and parties' station in life during marriage; (2) age and health of parties; (3) each party's earning capacity, including educational background, training, employment skills, work experience, length of absence from job market, and child custodial responsibilities during the marriage; (4) each party's financial condition, including availability and cost of health insurance; (5) con-duct of the parties, including whether there has been unreasonable depletion of marital assets; (6) desirability of the child custodian remaining in the marital home; (7) circumstances and necessities of the parties; (8) time and manner of acquisition of the assets; and (9) the income producing capacity of the property and the value of the property. (A.S., Secs. 25.24.160(a)(4) and 25.24.230.)

Alimony:
Called *maintenance*. Fault not considered. Factors: (1) length of marriage and parties' station in life during marriage; (2) age and health of parties; (3) each party's earning capacity, including educational background, training, employment skills, work experience, length of absence from job market, and child custodial responsibilities during the marriage; (4) each party's financial condition, including availability and cost of health insurance; (5) conduct of the parties, including whether there has been unreasonable depletion of marital assets; (6) property division; and (7) any other relevant factor. (A.S., Sec. 25.24.160(a)(2).)

ARIZONA

THE LAW

In General:
Arizona Revised Statutes, Title 25, Section 25-201 (A.R.S., Sec. 25-201).

UPAA:
A.R.S., Sec. 25-201.

Probate:
A.R.S., Sec. 14-2207. Standard UPC waiver provision.

Divorce:
None.

PROBATE LAW

In General:
UPC: A.R.S., Sec. 14-1102.

Elective share:
$1/2$ to all of community property and decedent's separate property. (A.R.S., Sec. 14-3101.)

Intestate share:
Same as elective share. (A.R.S., Sec. 14-2102.)

DIVORCE LAW

Title:
Dissolution of Marriage.

Property:
Community property. Fault not considered. Each party retains their "sole and separate property." In dividing property the court may consider "excessive or abnormal expenditures, destruction, concealment or fraudulent disposition of community, joint tenancy and other property held in common." No other statutory factors. (A.R.S., Sec. 25-318.)

Alimony:
Called *maintenance.* Alimony may be awarded if the party: (1) lacks sufficient property to provide for his or her reasonable needs; and (2) is unable to support self through employment, or is custodian of young child so is not required to seek employment, or lacks earning ability; or (3) contributed to spouse's education; or (4) is of an age which may preclude adequate employment and the marriage was of long duration. Amount and duration factors: (1) standard of living established during the marriage; (2) duration of marriage; (3) age, employment history, earning ability, and physical and emotional condition of the party seeking alimony; (4) ability of the other party to meet his or her own needs while paying alimony; (5) comparative financial resources and earning abilities; (6) contribution of the party seeking alimony to the other's earning ability; (7) extent to which the party seeking alimony has reduced income or career opportunity for the other's benefit; (8) ability of both to contribute to the child's future educational costs; (9) financial resources of the party seeking alimony, and the ability to meet own needs; (10) time needed to acquire education and training to find appropriate employment; (11) "excessive or abnormal expenditures, destruction, concealment or fraudulent disposition of community, joint tenancy and other property held in common"; (12) cost for spouse seeking maintenance to obtain health insurance and the reduction in cost of insurance for other spouse if able to convert family health insurance to employee insurance; and, (13) actual damages and judgments from conduct resulting in criminal conviction of either spouse in which the other spouse or child was the victim. (A.R.S., Sec. 25-319.)

ARKANSAS

THE LAW

In General:

Arkansas Code of 1987 Annotated, Title 9, Chapter 11, Section 9-11-401 (A.C.A., Sec. 9-11-401).

UPAA:

A.C.A., Sec. 9-11-401.

Probate:

None.

Divorce:

None.

PROBATE LAW

In General:

A.C.A., Sec. 28-1-101 ("Probate Code").

Elective share:

Same as intestate share; must have been married at least one year to claim. (A.C.A., Sec. 28-39-401.)

Intestate share:

$^1/_3$ to $^1/_2$; but only a life estate as to real property that constitutes the decedent's "ancestral estate." (A.C.A., Secs. 28-11-301, 28-11-305, and 28-11-307.)

DIVORCE LAW

Title:

Divorce.

Property:

Equitable distribution. Nonmarital property is property: (1) acquired prior to marriage; (2) acquired by gift or inheritance; (3) acquired in exchange for nonmarital property; (4) designated nonmarital by a valid agreement; (5) from an increase in value of, or income from, nonmarital property; and (6) claims for workers' compensation, personal injuries, or Social Security that is for permanent disability or future medical expenses. Marital property is divided equally, unless judge includes his reasons for an unequal distribution considering: (1) length of marriage; (2) age, health, and station in life of the parties; (3) occupation; (4) amount and sources or income; (5) vocational skills; (6) employability; (7) each party's estate, liabilities, and needs, and opportunity for further acquisition of capital assets and income; (8) each party's contribution to the acquisition, preservation, or appreciation of marital property; and (9) federal income tax consequences. (A.C.A., Sec. 9-12-315.)

Alimony:

No statutory factors, other than that it is to be awarded as "reasonable from the circumstances of the parties and the nature of the case." (A.C.A., Sec. 9-12-312.)

CALIFORNIA

THE LAW

In General:

West's Annotated California Codes, Family Code Sec. 1600 (A.C.C., Family Code Sec. 1600). Ignore the "Title" numbers. California has several Annotated California Codes, arranged by subject, so be sure you have the properly titled set.

UPAA:

A.C.C., Family Code Sec. 1600.

Probate:

A.C.C., Probate Code Sec. 140.

Divorce:

None.

PROBATE LAW

In General:

A.C.C., Probate volumes.

Elective share:

Same as intestate share, except no more than $1/2$ of decedent's separate property. (A.C.C., Probate Code Sec. 21610.) However, spouse gets nothing if decedent's will shows a clear intent not to provide anything for spouse, or if decedent clearly provided for spouse outside of probate, or if there is a valid waiver by the spouse. (A.C.C., Probate Code Sec. 21611.)

Intestate share:

$1/2$ community and quasi-community property of deceased plus $1/3$ of separate property. (A.C.C., Probate Sec. 6401.)

DIVORCE LAWS

Title:

Dissolution of Marriage.

Property:

Community property. Separate property is property: (1) owned before the marriage; (2) acquired by gift or inheritance; and (3) income and profits from separate property. (A.C.C., Family Code Sec. 770.) Basically, each party keeps their separate property, and gets $1/2$ of community property. However, there are numerous qualifications and exceptions. (A.C.C., Family Code Secs. 2500 through 2660.)

Alimony:

Marital misconduct is not considered. Factors: The standard of living established during the marriage, considering: (1) the extent of each party's earning capacity to maintain the standard of living, considering marketable skills, the job market, the time and expense required for the party requesting alimony to acquire education and training, the need for retraining to acquire other more marketable skills, and the extent earning capacity was impaired by periods of unemployment during the marriage due to domestic responsibilities; (2) the extent the party seeking alimony contributed to the education, training, and employment of the other; (3) the spouse's ability to pay; (4) the needs of each party, based on the standard of living; (5) the assets and debts of each party; (6) the duration of the marriage; (7) the ability of the custodial parent to earn without interfering with the best interest of the children; (8) the age and health of the parties; (9) the tax consequences; (10) the balance of hardships to each party; and any other relevant factor. (A.C.C., Family Code Sec. 4320.)

COLORADO

THE LAW

In General:

West's Colorado Revised Statutes Annotated, Title 14, Article 2, Section 14-2-301 (C.R.S.A., Sec. 14-2-301).

UPAA:

C.R.S.A., Sec. 14-2-301. "Colorado Marital Agreement Act."

Probate:

C.R.S.A., Sec. 15-11-204. Standard UPC waiver provision.

Divorce:

None.

PROBATE LAWS

In General:

UPC: C.R.S.A., Sec. 15-10-101 ("Colorado Probate Code").

Elective share:

5% to 50%, based on length of marriage. Supplemental amount for less than one year. (C.R.S.A., Sec. 15-11-201.)

Intestate share:

$^1/_2$ to all. (C.R.S.A., Sec. 15-11-102.)

DIVORCE LAWS

Title:

Dissolution of Marriage.

Property:

Equitable distribution. Fault is not considered. Separate property includes property: (1) acquired before marriage; (2) acquired by gift or inheritance; (3) acquired in exchange for nonmarital property; (4) acquired after a legal separation decree; or (5) designated separate by an written agreement of the parties. Factors in dividing marital property: (1) each party's contribution to acquisition of marital property; (2) value of separate property; (3) economic circumstances of the parties, including whether custodial party should remain in marital home; and (4) any increase or decrease in value of separate property during the marriage, and any depletion of separate property for marital purposes. (C.R.S.A., Sec. 14-10-113.)

Alimony:

Called *maintenance*. Fault is not considered. A party may be awarded alimony if he or she: (1) lacks sufficient property to meet own needs; and (2) is unable to support self by employment, or has child custody responsibilities such that employment outside the home is inappropriate. Factors in determining amount and duration of alimony: (1) financial resources and ability of spouse seeking alimony to meet his or her own needs; (2) time needed to obtain education or training to find appropriate employment, and future earning capacity; (3) standard of living established during the marriage; (4) duration of the marriage; (5) age and physical and emotional condition of the party seeking alimony; and (6) ability of other party to meet own needs while paying alimony. (C.R.S.A., Sec. 14-10-114.)

CONNECTICUT

THE LAW

In General:
Connecticut General Statutes Annotated, Title 46b, Section 46b-36a (C.G.S.A., Sec. 46b-36a). If using the statutes in books, ignore "Chapter" numbers. If using statutes from website, the UPAA will be found in Title 46b, Chapter 815e; divorce laws will be found in Title 45, Chapter 815j; and probate laws will be found in Title 45a, Chapter 802b.

UPAA:
C.G.S.A., Sec. 46b-36a. "Connecticut Premarital Agreement Act."

Probate:
C.G.S.A., Sec. 45a-436(f). This law states: "The provisions of this section with regard to the statutory share of the surviving spouse in the property of the deceased spouse shall not apply to any case in which, by written contract made before or after marriage, either party has received from the other what was intended as a provision in lieu of the statutory share."

Divorce:
None.

PROBATE LAWS

In General:
C.G.S.A., Sec. 45a-273.

Elective Share:
Life estate in $1/3$ of the property. (C.G.S.A., Sec. 45a-436.)

Intestate Share:
$1/2$ to all. (C.G.S.A., Sec. 45a-437.)

DIVORCE LAWS

Title:
Dissolution of Marriage.

Property:
Equitable distribution. Factors: (1) length of the marriage; (2) causes of the divorce; (3) each party's age, health, station, occupation, amount and sources of income, vocational skills, employability, estate, liabilities, needs, and opportunity for future acquisition of capital assets and income; and (4) contribution of each spouse to the acquisition, preservation or appreciation of assets. (C.G.S.A., Sec. 46b-81.)

Alimony:
Factors: (1) length of marriage; (2) cause of divorce; (3) age, health, station, occupation, amount and sources of income, vocational skills, employability, estate, and needs of each party; and (4) property division; and (5) desirability of child custodian obtaining employment. (C.G.S.A., Sec. 46b-82.)

DELAWARE

THE LAW

In General:
Delaware Code Annotated, Title 12, Section 905 (D.C.A., 12 Sec. 905). Ignore "chapter" numbers.

UPAA:
D.C.A., 13 Sec. 321.

Probate:
D.C.A., 12 Sec. 905. Standard UPC-type waiver provision.

Divorce:
None.

PROBATE LAWS

In General:
D.C.A., 12 Sec. 101.

Elective share:
$^1/_3$. (D.C.A., 12 Secs. 901 to 908.)

Intestate share:
$^1/_2$ personal property and life estate in real property, to all. (D.C.A., 12 Sec. 502.)

DIVORCE LAWS

Title:
Divorce.

Property:
Equitable distribution. Nonmarital property includes property: (1) acquired before marriage, including any increase in value; (2) acquired after marriage if acquired by inheritance, or in exchange for other nonmarital property; and (3) by written agreement. Fault not considered. Factors: (1) length of the marriage; (2) any prior marriages; (3) each party's age, health, station, amount and sources of income, vocational skills, employability, estate, liabilities, and needs; and (4) whether property award is in lieu of, or in addition to, alimony; (5) each party's opportunity for future acquisition of assets and income; (6) contribution or dissipation of assets, including as homemaker or husband; (7) value of separate property; (8) economic circumstances of each party, including whether the custodial parent should remain in the marital home; (9) whether property was acquired as a gift; (10) each party's debts; and (11) tax consequences. (D.C.A., 13 Sec. 1513.)

Alimony:
Marriage for less than 20 years: alimony limited to a time period of 50% of the length of marriage. Marriage of 20 years or more: no limit. Fault is not a factor. Spouse seeking alimony must be (1) dependent upon spouse; (2) lack sufficient property for his or her needs; and (3) unable to support self through employment, or is not required to seek employment because he or she has child custody which makes employment inappropriate. The amount is determined by the following factors: (1) financial resources and ability to meet needs of the party seeking alimony; (2) time and expense required to acquire education and training for employment; (3) standard of living established during the marriage; (4) duration of the marriage; (5) age and physical and emotional condition of each party; (6) contribution of the party seeking alimony to the other's career; (7) ability of the other party to pay and meet his or her own needs; (8) tax consequences; (9) whether either party has forgone or postponed education and career opportunities during the marriage; and (10) any other relevant factor. (D.C.A., 13 Sec. 1512.)

DISTRICT OF COLUMBIA

THE LAW

In General:

District of Columbia Code, Title 30, Section 141 (D.C.C., Sec. 30-141).

UPAA:

D.C.C., Sec. 30-141

Probate:

D.C.C., Sec. 19-113(f). This law states: "A valid antenuptial or postnuptial agreement entered into by the spouses determines the rights of the surviving spouse in the real and personal estate of the deceased spouse and the administration thereof, but a spouse may accept the benefits of a devise or bequest made to him by the deceased spouse."

Divorce:

D.C.C., Sec. 16-910. This law provides for how property is to be divided "…in the absence of a valid ante-nuptial or post-nuptial agreement…"

PROBATE LAWS

In General:

D.C.C., Sec. 18-101.

Elective Share:

Basically ¹/₂, although the statute is more complex. (D.C.C., Sec. 19-113(e).)

Intestate Share:

¹/₂ to all. (D.C.C., Secs. 19-302 through 19-305.)

DIVORCE LAWS

Title:

Divorce.

Property:

Equitable distribution. Fault is not a factor. "Sole property" is property (1) acquired before marriage; (2) acquired by gift or inheritance; (3) acquired in exchange for such property; and (4) increased value of sole property. Marital property divided according to following factors: (1) duration of the marriage; (2) any prior marriages; (3) each party's age, health, occupation, amount and sources of income, vocational skills, and employability; (4) each party's assets, debts, and needs; (5) child custody provisions; (6) whether property division is in lieu of or in addition to alimony; (7) each party's opportunity for future acquisition of assets and income; (8) each party's contribution to the acquisition, preservation, appreciation, dissipation, or depreciation of marital assets; (9) each party's contribution as a homemaker or to the family unit; and (10) any other relevant factor. (D.C.C., Sec. 16-910.)

Alimony:

Fault may be considered. Statute merely states that alimony may be awarded "if it seems just and proper." (D.C.C., Secs. 16-912 and 16-913.) No other statutory factors or guidelines.

FLORIDA

THE LAW

In General:

Florida Statutes, Chapter 732, Section 732.702 (F.S., Sec. 732.702). If using Florida Statutes books, ignore "Title" and "Part" numbers. If using statutes from website, you will need to use title and part number indicated below.

UPAA:

No.

Probate:

F.S., Sec. 732.702. Similar to standard UPC-type waiver provision.

Divorce:

None.

PROBATE LAWS

In General:

F.S., Secs. 731.005 to 735.302.

Elective Share:

30% of the "elective estate." F.S., Sec. 732.2065 [on website, Title XLII, Part II]. See F.S., Secs. 732.2035 – 732.2055 for what constitutes the "elective estate." Also, see spouse's rights to homestead (F.S., Secs. 732.401 and 732.4015); exempt property (F.S., Sec. 732.402); and family allowance (F.S., Sec. 732.403).

Intestate Share:

$1/2$ to all. F.S., Sec. 732.102 [on website, Title XLII, Part I].

DIVORCE LAWS

Title:

Dissolution of Marriage.

Property:

Equitable distribution. Fault is not considered. A "special equity" claim for nonmarital property must be included in the petition. Nonmarital property is property: (1) acquired before marriage; (2) acquired by gift or inheritance; (3) designated nonmarital in an agreement between the parties; (4) acquired in exchange for property in (1), (2), or (3) above; and (5) income from nonmarital property, unless the parties treated or used it as marital income. (F.S., Sec. 61.075(5).) Marital property includes all retirement, profit-sharing, and deferred compensation plans. F.S., Sec. 61.076. Marital property divided considering: (1) each party's contribution to the marriage; (2) each party's economic circumstances; (3) duration of the marriage; (4) either party's interruption of personal career or educational opportunities; (5) either party's contribution to the personal career or educational opportunities of the other; (6) desirability of retaining any asset intact and free of any claim of or interference from the other; (7) each party's contribution to the acquisition, enhancement, and production on income or the improvement of both marital and nonmarital property; (8) desirability for the custodial parent to remain in the marital home; (9) any intentional dissipation, waste, depletion, or destruction of marital assets after filing petition or within two years prior to filing; and (10) any other relevant factor. (F.S., Sec. 61.075.)

Alimony:

Factors: (1) adultery; (2) standard of living established during marriage; (3) duration of marriage; (4) each party's age and physical and emotional condition; (5) each party's financial resources, and the marital and nonmarital property distribution; (6) time needed to acquire sufficient education and training to find appropriate employment; (7) each party's contribution to the marriage; (8) all sources of income available; and (9) any other relevant factor. (F.S., Sec. 61.08.)

GEORGIA

THE LAW

In General:

Official Code of Georgia Annotated, Title 19, Chapter 3, Section 19-3-62. (C.G.A., Sec. 19-3-62). This is not the "Georgia Code," which is a separate, outdated set of books with a completely different numbering system. If all you can find is the Georgia Code, look for a cross-reference table to the Official Code of Georgia.

UPAA:

No.

Probate:

Spouse may renounce rights, C.G.A., Sec. 53-2-115. These include those rights under C.G.A., Secs. 53-2-10 (limit on gifts to charity), 53-5-1 (elective share of 1 year's support), and 53-4-2 (share of intestate estate).

Divorce:

C.G.A., Secs. 19-3-62 to 19-3-68. Requires two witnesses. (C.G.A., Sec. 19-3-63.)

PROBATE LAWS

In General:

C.G.A., Sec. 53-1-1.

Elective Share:

One year's support. (C.G.A., Secs. 53-3-1(c) and 53-3-3.)

Intestate Share:

$1/3$ to all. (C.G.A., Sec. 53-2-1(b).)

DIVORCE LAWS

Title:

Divorce.

Property:

Equitable distribution. No factors in statute.

Alimony:

To qualify for alimony, proof of the cause of the divorce must be presented. Desertion or adultery is a bar to alimony. See C.G.A., Sec. 19-6-1. The amount is based upon the need of the party seeking alimony and the other party's ability to pay, considering: (1) standard of living established during the marriage; (2) duration of the marriage; (3) age and physical and emotional condition of the parties; (4) financial resources of each party; (5) time needed to acquire education and training to obtain employment; (6) contribution of each party to the marriage; (7) condition of the parties, including the separate estate, earning capacity and fixed liabilities; and (8) any other relevant factor. (C.G.A., Sec. 19-6-5.)

HAWAII

THE LAW

In General:
Hawaii Revised Statutes, Title 572D, Section 572D-1 (H.R.S., Sec. 572D-1). For Internet search, scroll down to "2000 Hawaii Revised Statutes" (or "2001 Hawaii Revised Statutes," when that is finally listed), then either type in a word or phrase for a search, or click on "Browse" which will then allow you to select a volume number, followed by a section number. Ignore "Title" numbers.

UPAA:
H.R.S., Sec. 572D-1.

Probate:
H.R.S., Sec. 560:2-213. Standard UPC waiver provision.

Divorce:
None.

PROBATE LAWS

In General:
UPC: H.R.S., Sec. 560:1-101.

Elective Share:
3% to 50%, based on length of marriage. (H.R.S., Sec. 560:2-202.)

Intestate Share:
The first $100,000 plus $1/2$ of the balance, to all. (H.R.S., Sec. 560:2-102.)

DIVORCE LAWS

Title:
Divorce.

Property:
Equitable distribution. Factors: (1) respective merits of the parties; (2) relative abilities of the parties; (3) condition each party will be in after divorce; (4) burdens imposed on either spouse for the benefit of the children; and (5) any other relevant circumstances. (H.R.S., Sec. 580-47.)

Alimony:
Called *spousal support and maintenance.* Marital misconduct is not considered. Factors: (1) each party's financial resources; (2) ability of party seeking alimony to meet own needs; (3) duration of marriage; (4) standard of living established during marriage; (5) ages of parties; (6) each party's physical and emotional condition; (7) each party's usual occupation during the marriage; (8) vocational skills and employability of party seeking alimony; (9) needs of the parties; (10) either party's child custodial and support responsibilities; (11) ability of party to pay alimony and meet own needs; (12) condition each party will be in after divorce; (13) probable duration of the need for alimony; and (14) any other relevant factor. (H.R.S., Sec. 580-47.)

IDAHO

THE LAW

In General:
Idaho Code, Title 32, Section 32-921 (I.C., Sec. 32-921). If using statutes from website, you will need to use title, chapter, and part numbers; for example, to find Section 15-2-201 you would need to click on "Title 15," then "Chapter 2," then "Part 2," then the section number (e.g., 15-2-201).

UPAA:
I.C., Sec. 32-921.

Probate:
I.C., Sec. 15-2-208. Standard UPC waiver provision.

Divorce:
I.C., Sec. 32-916. This law states: "The property rights of husband and wife are governed by this chapter, unless there is a marriage settlement agreement entered into prior to or during marriage containing stipulations contrary thereto."

PROBATE LAWS

In General:
UPC: I.C., Sec. 15-1-101.

Elective Share:
$^1/_2$. (I.C., Sec. 15-2-203.)

Intestate Share:
Separate property: $^1/_2$ to all. Community property: $^1/_2$ of decedent's community property. Also have rights to homestead (I.C., Sec. 15-2-401), exempt property (I.C., Sec. 15-2-402), and family allowance (I.C., Sec. 15-2-403).

DIVORCE LAWS

Title:
Divorce.

Property:
Community property. Separate property is property acquired: (1) before marriage; (2) by gift or inheritance; and (3) as proceeds of separate property and acquired with proceeds of separate property. I.C., Sec. 32-903. Marital property is to be divided equally, unless judge gives reasons based upon: (1) duration of marriage; (2) any premarital agreement; (3) each party's age, health, occupation, amount and sources of income, vocational skills, employability, and liabilities; (4) each party's needs; (5) whether property division is in lieu of or in addition to alimony; (6) each party's present and potential earning capacity; and (7) each party's retirement benefits, including Social Security, civil service, military and railroad pensions. (I.C., Secs. 32-712.)

Alimony:
Called *maintenance*. Either party may be awarded alimony if he or she: (1) lacks sufficient property to be self-supporting; and (2) is unable to be self-supporting through employment. Factors for determining amount and duration: (1) financial resources of the party seeking alimony, including property awarded and ability to meet own needs; (2) time needed to acquire education and training to become employed; (3) duration of marriage; (4) age, and physical and emotional condition of party seeking alimony; (5) ability of party paying alimony to meet own needs while paying; (6) tax consequences; (7) fault of either party; and (8) any other relevant factor. (I.C., Sec. 32-705.)

ILLINOIS

THE LAW

In General:

There are two sets of books containing the laws of Illinois; references are given to both. West's Smith-Hurd Illinois Compiled Statutes Annotated, Chapter 750, Act 10, Article 1 (750 ILCS 10/1); Smith-Hurd Illinois Annotated Statutes, Chapter 40, Paragraph 2601 (I.A.S., 40 Para. 2601). The website uses the ILCS numbers. If using statutes from website, you will need to click on the "part" or "article" numbers indicated below.

UPAA:

750 ILCS 10/1 (click on "Part V, Property, Support and Attorney Fees"); I.A.S., 40 Para. 2601. Known as the "Illinois Uniform Premarital Agreement Act."

Probate:

None.

Divorce:

None.

PROBATE LAWS

In General:

755 ILCS 5/1-1; I.A.S., 110 ^{1}/$_2$ Para. 1-1. Known as the "Probate Act of 1975."

Elective Share:

^{1}/$_2$ if no children; ^{1}/$_3$ if children. 755 ILCS 5/2-8 (click on "Article XV, Spouse and Child Awards"); I.A.S., 110 Para. 2-8. Also 9 months of support; which shall be not less than $10,000 plus $5,000 for each child. 755 ILCS 5/15-1 (click on "Article XV, Spouse and Child Awards"); I.A.S., 110 Para. 15-1.

Intestate Share:

^{1}/$_2$ to all. 755 ILCS 5/2-1 (click on "Article II, Descent and Distribution"); I.A.S., 110 Para. 2-1.

DIVORCE LAWS

Title:

Dissolution of Marriage.

Property:

Equitable distribution. Fault is not considered. Nonmarital property is property: (1) acquired before marriage; (2) acquired after marriage by gift, inheritance, in exchange for other nonmarital property, or after a legal separation; (3) designated nonmarital by written agreement of the parties; (4) designated nonmarital by a judgment from the spouse; or (5) increased value or income from property in (1) through (4). Division of marital property based on following factors: (1) contribution or dissipation of each party; (2) value of separate property; (3) duration of the marriage; (4) economic circumstances of the parties, including whether custodial parent should remain in marital home; (5) prior marriage obligations; (6) any premarital agreements; (7) age, health, station, occupation, income, skills, employability, estate, liabilities, and needs of each party; (8) child custody provisions; (9) whether property is in lieu of, or in addition to, alimony; (10) each party's opportunity for future acquisition of assets and income; and (11) tax consequences. 750 ILCS 5/503 (click on "Part V, Property, Support and Attorney Fees"); I.A.S., 40 Para. 503.

Alimony:

Called *maintenance.* Fault is not considered. Factors: (1) each party's income and property, (2) each party's needs; (3) each party's present and future earning capacity; (4) any impairment of present or future earning capacity of the party seeking maintenance due to "devoting time to domestic duties or having forgone or delayed education, training, employment, or career opportunities due to the marriage," (5) time necessary for party seeking maintenance to acquire education or training, or whether being a child's custodian makes it inappropriate to seek employment; (6) standard of living established during the marriage; (7) duration of marriage; (8) age, and physical and emotional condition of each party; (9) tax consequences of the property division; (10) the contribution by party seeking maintenance to the education or career of the other; (11) any valid agreement of the parties; and (12) any other relevant factor. 750 ILCS 5/504 (click on "Part V, Property, Support and Attorney Fees"); I.A.S., 40 Para. 504.

INDIANA

THE LAW

In General:

West's Annotated Indiana Code, Title 31, Article 11, Chapter 3, Section 1 (A.I.C., Sec. 31-11-3-1). If using statutes from website, you can either type in the section number or use the "Table of Contents to the Code."

UPAA:

A.I.C., Sec. 31-11-3-1.

Probate:

A.I.C., Secs. 29-1-2-13 and 29-1-3-6. Similar to standard UPC-type waiver provision. A.I.C., Secs. 29-1-2-13 and 29-1-3-6.

Divorce:

A.I.C., Sec. 31-15-2-17. Specifically authorizes and encourages agreements as to alimony, property, and custody and support of children.

PROBATE LAWS

In General:

A.I.C., Sec. 29-1-1-1. Known as the "Probate Code," which somewhat follows UPC.

Elective Share:

$^1/_3$ personal property plus life estate in $^1/_3$ real property, to $^1/_2$ of personal and real property. (A.I.C., Sec. 29-1-3-1.)

Intestate Share:

$^1/_2$ of personal property plus life estate in $^1/_3$ real property, to all. (A.I.C., Sec. 29-1-2-1.)

DIVORCE LAWS

Title:

Dissolution of Marriage.

Property:

Equitable distribution. Fault is not a factor. Property acquired before marriage is a part of the marital estate, although time of acquisi- tion is a factor to be considered in dividing the property. Equal division is presumed. Factors considered in unequal distribution claim are: (1) contribution of each party to acquisition; (2) extent of property acquired prior to marriage, or by gift or inheritance; (3) economic circumstances at the time of distribution, including whether custodial parent should remain in marital home; (4) conduct of the parties as related to disposition or dissipation of assets; (5) the earnings, or earning capacity, of each party; and (6) any other relevant evidence. (A.I.C., Sec. 31-15-7-5.) Also must consider tax consequences. (A.I.C., Sec. 31-15-7-7.) If insufficient marital property, court may award money to a party for contribution to the other's education. (A.I.C., Sec. 31-15-7-6.)

Alimony:

Fault is not a factor. Alimony may be awarded for a necessary period of time if (1) the party seeking alimony is physically or mentally incapacitated; or (2) lacks financial ability and is custodian of a physically or mentally incapacitated child which requires that party to forego employment. Rehabilitative alimony for up to three years may be awarded after considering: (1) each party's educational level at the time of the marriage and at the time the petition was filed; (2) whether the party seeking alimony had his or her education, training or employment interrupted due to homemaking or child care responsibilities; (3) earning capacity of each party; and (4) time and expense required to acquire education and training to obtain employment. (A.I.C., Sec. 31-15-7-2.)

IOWA

THE LAW

In General:

Iowa Code Annotated, Section 596.1 (I.C.A., Sec. 596.1). If using statutes from website, you may either click on "Browse"; or enter either the chapter or section number.

UPAA:

I.C.A., Sec. 596.1.

Probate:

None.

Divorce:

None.

PROBATE LAWS

In General:

I.C.A., Sec. 633.1. Known as the "Iowa Probate Code."

Elective Share:

$^1/_3$ of real property, all personal property of decedent as head of a family and exempt from execution, and $^1/_3$ of all other personal property not necessary for payment of debts; to all. I.C.A., Sec. 633.238.

Intestate Share:

$^1/_2$ of real property, all personal property of decedent as head of a family and exempt from execution, and $^1/_2$ of all other personal property not necessary for payment of debts (but at least the first $50,000); to all. I.C.A., Secs. 633.211 and 633.212.

DIVORCE LAWS

Title:

Dissolution of Marriage.

Property:

Equitable distribution. Fault is not considered. Separate property is property acquired by one party as inheritance or gift. Marital property divided considering: (1) length of marriage; (2) property brought into the marriage; (3) each party's contribution to the marriage; (4) each party's age, physical and emotional health; (5) either party's contribution to the other's education, training, and increased earning power; and (6) each party's earning capacity, including educational background, training, employment skills, work experience, length of absence from job market, child custodial responsibilities, and time and expense needed to acquire education and training to become self-supporting at the standard of living established during the marriage; (7) desirability of custodial party remaining in marital home; (8) amount and duration of alimony, and whether property division should be in lieu of or in addition to alimony; (9) each party's other economic circumstances, including pension benefits; (10) tax consequences; (11) any written agreements of the parties; and (12) any other relevant factor. (I.C.A., Sec. 598.21.)

Alimony:

Called *support.* Factors: (1) length of marriage; (2) age and physical and emotional health of the parties; (3) property distribution; (4) educational level of each party at time of marriage and at time petition is filed; (5) earning capacity of party seeking alimony, including educational background, training, employment skills, work experience, length of absence from job market, child custodial responsibilities, and time and expense needed to acquire education and training to find appropriate employment; (6) the feasibility of the party seeking alimony becoming self-supporting at a standard of living reasonably comparable to that during marriage, and length of time needed to do so; (7) tax consequences; (8) any agreements between the parties; and (9) any other relevant factors. (I.C.A., Secs. 598.21.)

KANSAS

THE LAW

In General:

Kansas Statutes Annotated, Section 23-801 (K.S.A., Sec. 23-801). [Look for the set of books titled "Kansas Statutes Annotated, Official."] Any recent changes can be found in a soft-cover separate volume supplement. Avoid the set titled "Vernon's Kansas Statutes Annotated," or ask the librarian for assistance if this is all you can find. Both sets have very poor indexing systems. If using statutes from the website, you may either enter the statute number or search by keyword.

UPAA:

K.S.A., Sec. 23-801.

Probate:

K.S.A., Sec. 59-6a213. Standard UPC-type waiver.

Divorce:

None.

PROBATE LAWS

In General:

K.S.A., Sec. 59-101.

Elective Share:

3% to 50%, based on length of marriage. Supplemental amount for less than one year. K.S.A., Sec. 59-6a202. Elective share provisions are fairly complicated; for details see K.S.A., Secs. 59-6a201 through 59-6a211. In addition to elective share, spouse is entitled to the homestead or a "homestead allowance" of $35,000. (K.S.A., Sec. 59-6a215.)

Intestate Share:

$^1/_2$ to all. (K.S.A., Sec. 59-504.)

DIVORCE LAWS

Title:

Divorce.

Property:

Equitable distribution. All property is marital property. Factors for division: (1) age of parties; (2) duration of marriage; (3) property owned by the parties; (4) each party's present and future earning capacity; (5) time, source, and manner of acquisition of the property; (6) family ties and obligations; (7) any award of alimony or lack thereof; (8) any dissipation of assets; (9) tax consequences of property division; and (10) any other relevant factor. (K.S.A., Sec. 60-1610(b)(1).)

Alimony:

Called *maintenance*. Limited to 121 months, with one application for up to a 121 month extension. Fault not considered. No statutory factors other than "in an amount the court finds to be fair, just and equitable under all of the circumstances." Payment must be through court clerk or court trustee. (K.S.A., Sec. 60-1610(b)(2).)

KENTUCKY

THE LAW

In General:
Kentucky Revised Statutes, Section 371.010(5) (K.R.S., Secs. 371.010(5).

UPAA:
No.

Misc:
K.R.S., Secs. 371.010(5) and 382.080. These statutes simply refer to "agreements in consideration of marriage," thereby implying that they are acceptable in Kentucky.

Probate:
None.

Divorce:
None.

PROBATE LAWS

In General:
K.R.S., Secs. 391.010 to 397.080.

Elective Share:
$^1/_3$ to $^1/_2$. (K.R.S., Secs. 392.020 and 392.080.)

Intestate Share:
$7,500 in personal property; to all real and personal property. (K.R.S., Secs. 391.010 to 391.030.)

DIVORCE LAWS

Title:
Dissolution of Marriage.

Property:
Equitable distribution. nonmarital property is property acquired (1) before marriage; (2) by gift or inheritance; (3) in exchange for such property; (4) after a legal separation; (5) property set forth as nonmarital in a written agreement; and (6) the increase in value of premarriage property, unless the increase in value is due to the efforts of the other party. Also, if one party's retirement benefits are nonmarital, so are the other's. Marital misconduct not considered. Division of marital property is determined by the following factors: (1) contribution of each party to the acquisition; (2) value of separate property; (3) duration of the marriage; and (4) economic circumstances of the parties, including whether the custodial parent should remain in the marital home. (K.R.S., Sec. 403.190.)

Alimony:
Called *maintenance.* Fault is not considered. Alimony is only permitted if the person seeking alimony (1) lacks sufficient property to provide for his or her needs; and (2) is unable to be self-supporting through employment, or is custodian of a child whose condition or circumstances make it appropriate not to seek outside employment. Once eligible, the amount is determined by considering the following factors: (1) financial resources of the person seeking alimony; (2) time needed to acquire education and training to become employable; (3) standard of living established during the marriage; (4) duration of the marriage; (5) age, and physical and emotional condition of the person seeking alimony; and (6) the ability of the payor to meet his or her own needs while paying alimony. (K.R.S., Sec. 403.200.)

LOUISIANA

THE LAW

In General:

West's LSA, Civil Code, Article 2328 (L.S.A., Civil Code, Art. 2328). "L.S.A." stands for "Louisiana Statutes Annotated." These are divided into sets of volumes titled "Revised Statutes," "Civil Code," "Civil Procedure," and "Criminal Procedure," so be sure you locate the correct set. If using statutes from website, you will need to enter the "Law Body," which is "CC" for "Civil Code"; then enter the article number.

UPAA:

No.

Probate:

L.S.A., Civil Code, Art. 1734.

Divorce:

None.

Misc.:

L.S.A., Civil Code, Art. 2328, which provides: "A matrimonial agreement is a contract establishing a regime of separation of property or modifying or terminating the legal regime. Spouses are free to establish by matrimonial agreement a regime of separation of property or modify the legal regime as provided by law. The provisions of the legal regime that have not been excluded or modified by agreement retain their force and effect." See also L.S.A., Civil Code, Art. 1734 through 1742 regarding "donations by marriage contract."

PROBATE LAWS

In General:

L.S.A., Civil Code, Art. 1467.

Elective Share:

None (but survivor gets $1/2$ of community property estate and all of his or her separate estate).

Intestate Share:

Use of (called *usufruct*) community property, to all. L.S.A., Civil Code, Art. 888 through 894.

DIVORCE LAWS

Title:

Divorce.

Property:

Community property. No factors in statute. Although not considered a part of the marital property, it is possible to obtain an award for financial contributions to a spouse's education and training that increased the spouse's earning power, "to the extent that the claimant did not benefit during the marriage from the increased earning power." (C.C., Art. 121.)

Alimony:

Permanent alimony may only be awarded to a spouse without fault. Limited to one-third of the payor's net income. Factors for entitlement, amount, and duration: (1) needs of the parties; (2) each party's income and means, including the liquidity of means; (3) each party's financial obligations; (4) each party's earning capacity; (5) the effect of child custody on earning capacity; (6) time needed for party seeking alimony to acquire education, training, or employment; (7) each party's health and age; (8) duration of the marriage; and (9) tax consequences. (L.S.A., Civil Code, Art. 111 and Art. 112.)

MAINE

THE LAW

In General:

Maine Revised Statutes Annotated, Title 19-A, Section 601 (19-A M.R.S.A., Sec. 601).

UPAA:

19-A M.R.S.A., Sec. 601.

Probate:

18-A M.R.S.A., Sec. 2-204. Standard UPC-type waiver.

Divorce:

None.

PROBATE LAWS

In General:

UPC: 18A M.R.S.A., Sec. 1-101. Known as the "Probate Code."

Elective share:

$1/3$ to all. 18A M.R.S.A., Secs. 2-201 and 2-301. Also, homestead of $5,000 (18-A M.R.S.A., Sec. 2-401); $3,500 exempt property (18-A M.R.S.A., Sec. 2-402); and family allowance of a "reasonable allowance in money" for up to one year (18-A M.R.S.A., Sec. 2-403).

Intestate Share:

$1/2$ to all. (18A M.R.S.A., Sec. 2-102.)

DIVORCE LAWS

Title:

Divorce.

Property:

Equitable distribution. Fault not considered. Separate property is property: (1) acquired before marriage; (2) acquired by gift or inheritance; (3) acquired in exchange for separate property; (4) acquired after a decree of legal separation; (5) designated separate by agreement of the parties; or (6) increased value of separate property. Marital property is divided considering: (1) each party's contribution to acquisition; (2) the value of each party's separate property; and (3) the parties' economic circumstances at the time of division, including whether the child custodian should remain in the marital home. (M.R.S.A., Title 19-A, Sec. 953.)

Alimony:

Called *spousal support.* There are three types of spousal support: (1) *General support* may be awarded to "a spouse with substantially less income potential than the other spouse." There is a rebuttable presumption that general support may not be awarded if marriage was for less than ten years, and may not be awarded for more than one half the length of the marriage if parties were married more than ten but less than twenty years. (2) *Transitional support* may be awarded "to provide for a spouse's transitional needs." (3) *Reimbursement support* may be awarded "to achieve an equitable result in the overall dissolution of the parties' financial relationship in response to exceptional circumstances," such as for economic misconduct of a spouse, or substantial contributions made by one spouse toward the other's "educational or occupational advancement." Factors: (1) length of the marriage; (2) each party's ability to pay; (3) age of each party; (4) each party's employment history and potential; (5) each party's income history and potential; (6) education and training of each party; (7) provisions for retirement and health insurance benefits; (8) tax consequences of property division; (9) health and disabilities of each party; (10) tax consequences of spousal support; (11) contributions of either party as homemaker; (12) contributions of either party to the other's education or earning potential; (13) any economic misconduct by either party resulting in the diminution of marital property or income; (14) standard of living during the marriage; (15) ability of party seeking support to become self-supporting within a reasonable period of time; (16) the effect of actual or potential income from property, or child support, on either party's need or ability to pay; or (17) any other appropriate factor. (19-A M.R.S.A., Sec. 951-A.)

MARYLAND

THE LAW

In General:

Annotated Code of Maryland, Estates and Trusts, Section 3-205 (A.C.M., Estates & Trusts, Sec. 3-205). [These volumes are arranged by subject, so be sure you have the volume marked for the subject you want, such as "Estates and Trusts," or "Family Law."] If using statutes from the website, first enter the "article" (e.g., "Estates and Trusts" or "Family Law"); then enter the section number.

UPAA:

No.

Probate:

A.C.M., Estates & Trusts, Sec. 3-205). [Be sure you have the volume marked "Estates and Trusts."] Similar to the standard UPC-type waiver provision.

Divorce:

A.C.M., Family Law, Secs. 4-204 and 8-101. [Be sure you have the volume marked "Family Law."] Section 4-204 merely states that a wife may enter into contracts with her husband. Section 8-101 states: "(a) A husband and wife may make a valid and enforceable deed or agreement that relates to alimony, support, property rights, or personal rights. (b) A husband and wife may make a valid and enforceable settlement of alimony, support, property rights, or personal rights."

PROBATE LAWS

In General:

A.C.M., Estates & Trusts, Sec. 1-101.

Elective Share:

$^1/_3$ to $^1/_2$. A.C.M., Estates & Trusts, Sec. 3-203. Also, spouse is entitled to an "allowance of $5,000 for personal use." (A.C.M., Estates & Trusts, Sec. 3-201.)

Intestate Share:

$^1/_2$ to all. (A.C.M., Estates & Trusts, Sec. 3-102.)

DIVORCE LAWS

Title:

Divorce.

Property:

Equitable distribution. Marital property does not include property: (1) acquired before marriage; (2) acquired by gift or inheritance; (3) excluded by a valid agreement; or (4) directly traceable to any of these sources. Marital property divided considering the following factors: (1) contributions of each party to the well-being of the family; (2) value of all property interests; (3) economic circumstances of each; (4) circumstances contributing to the divorce; (5) duration of the marriage; (6) ages of the parties; (7) physical and mental condition of the parties; (8) how and when property was acquired, and the efforts of each party to acquire the property; (9) contribution by either party of nonmarital property to the acquisition of real property held as tenants by the entirety; (10) any award of alimony or use of marital home; or (11) any other factor the judge considers proper.

Alimony:

Factors: (1) ability of the person seeking alimony to be self-supporting; (2) time needed to gain sufficient education and training; (3) standard of living established during the marriage; (4) duration of the marriage; (5) contributions of each to the well-being of the family; (6) circumstances contributing to the divorce; (7) age of the parties; (8) physical and mental condition of the parties; (9) ability of the payor to meet his or her own needs while paying alimony; (10) any agreement of the parties; (11) financial needs of the parties, including income and assets, property award, nature and amount of financial obligations, and rights to retirement benefits; and (12) if the payor is in certain types of health care facilities, whether an award of support would cause the payor to become eligible for medical assistance earlier than otherwise. Generally limited to rehabilitative period, but indefinite alimony may be awarded if (1) it is not reasonable to expect progress due to age, illness, infirmity or disability; or (2) after all progress has been made, the standard of living of the parties will be unconscionably disparate. (A.C.M., Family Law Sec. 11-106.)

MASSACHUSETTS

THE LAW

In General:
Annotated Laws of Massachusetts, Chapter 209, Section 3 (A.L.M., C.209 Sec. 3).

UPAA:
No.

Probate:
None.

Divorce:
None.

Misc.:
A.L.M., C.209 Sec. 3, which provides: "Transfers of real and personal property between husband and wife shall be valid to the same extent as if they were sole." A.L.M., C.209 Secs. 25 and 26, which provide that a premarital agreement is void as to third parties unless it is recorded before, or within 90 days after, the marriage.

PROBATE LAWS

In General:
A.L.M, Chapters 190 through 206.

Elective Share:
$1/3$ to $25,000 plus $1/3$ the residue. (A.L.M., C.191 Sec. 15.)

Intestate Share:
$1/2$ to all. (A.L.M., C.190 Sec. 1.)

Misc.:
Massachusetts residents can adopt the standard will under the "Massachusetts Uniform Statutory Will Act," which gives a surviving spouse $1/2$ to all. (A.L.M., C.191B Sec. 5.)

DIVORCE LAWS

Title:
Divorce.

Property:
Equitable distribution. Factors: (1) length of marriage; (2) conduct of parties during the marriage; (3) age, health, station, occupation, amount and sources of income, vocational skills, employability, estate, liabilities, and needs of each; (4) opportunity for future acquisition of capital assets and income; (5) present and future needs of dependent children; (6) contribution of each to acquisition, preservation, or appreciation of the property; and (7) contribution of each as homemaker. (A.L.M., C. 208 Secs. 1A & 34.)

Alimony:
Same factors as for property. (A.L.M., C. 208 Secs. 1A & 34.)

MICHIGAN

THE LAW

In General:

Michigan has two official sets of laws, each from a different publisher. One set is Michigan Statutes Annotated (abbreviated "M.S.A."), and the other is Michigan Compiled Laws Annotated (abbreviated "M.C.L.A.") Each has a completely different numbering system, although the wording of the laws will be the same. References are given to both sets as most libraries will only have one set. Ignore the volume and chapter numbers, and look for the section numbers. The website is based on M.C.L.A., although it may contain a cross-reference to the M.S.A.

UPAA:

No.

Misc:

Laws relating to premarital agreements are found in: Michigan Statutes Annotated, Section 26.244 (M.S.A., Sec. 26.244); and Michigan Compiled Laws Annotated, Sections 557.28 (M.C.L.A., Sec. 557.28). This section states: "A contract relating to property made between persons in contemplation of marriage shall remain in full force after marriage takes place."

Probate:

M.S.A., Sec. 27.12205; M.C.L.A., Sec. 700.2205. Standard UPC-type waiver provision.

Divorce:

None.

PROBATE LAWS

In General:

The probate laws in Michigan have recently been rewritten. At the time this book went to press, only the M.C.L.A. section numbers were available. The law dealing with the distribution of property upon death is called the "Estate and Protected Individuals Code." (M.S.A., Sec. 27.11101; M.C.L.A., Sec. 700.1101.)

Elective Share:

$1/2$ of what would have been received if the spouse had died intestate, reduced by $1/2$ of what was derived from the spouse by means other than will or intestate laws. If the surviving spouse is a woman, she may instead choose her rights to dower under M.S.A., Secs. 26.221-26.245; M.C.L.A., Secs. 558.1-558.29. M.S.A., Sec. 27.12202; M.C.L.A., Sec. 700.2202. Also, spouse is entitled to a homestead of $15,000 (plus a cost of living allowance, or COLA, as provided in M.S.A., Sec. 27.11210; M.C.L.A., Sec. 700.1210 (M.S.A., Sec. 27.12401; M.C.L.A., Sec. 700.2401)); exempt property of $10,000 (plus COLA) (M.S.A., Sec. 27.12404; M.C.L.A., Sec. 700.2404); and a "reasonable family allowance" for up to one year during the pendency of the probate case (M.S.A., Sec. 27.12403; M.C.L.A., Sec. 700.2403).

Intestate Share:

First $100,000 (plus COLA) plus $1/2$ the balance of the estate; to all. (M.S.A., Sec. 27.12102; M.C.L.A., Sec. 700.2102.)

DIVORCE LAWS

Title:

Divorce.

Property:

Equitable distribution. Vested pension benefits accumulated during the marriage are marital assets. M.S.A., Sec. 25.98; M.C.L.A., Sec. 552.18 No specific criteria are listed in the statute; only that the property will be divided as the judge "shall deem just and reasonable." (M.S.A., Sec. 25.99; M.C.L.A., Secs. 552.19.)

Alimony:

Alimony may be awarded if "the estate and effects awarded . . . are insufficient for the suitable support and maintenance of either party and any children of the marriage as are committed to the care and custody of either party." The amount will be determined "as the court considers just and reasonable, after considering the ability of either to pay and the character and situation of the parties, and all the other circumstances of the case." (M.S.A., Sec. 25.103; M.C.L.A., Sec. 552.23.)

MINNESOTA

THE LAW

In General:

Minnesota Statutes Annotated, Section 519.11 (M.S.A., Sec. 519.11). If using the website, you have several options for searches and to bring up a particular section or and entire chapter.

UPAA:

No.

Misc:

M.S.A., Sec. 519.11. Provides for prenuptial and postnuptial agreements. For a prenuptial agreement, the law requires full and fair disclosure of the earnings and property of each party, and that the parties have had an opportunity to consult with legal counsel of their own choice; and that the agreement be signed prior to the day of the marriage. For a postnuptial agreement, both parties must be represented by separate attorneys and other requirements must be met. For either, two witnesses are required, as well as signature before a notary.

Probate:

M.S.A., Sec. 524.2-213. Standard UPC-type waiver provision. Any waiver prior to marriage must comply with M.S.A., Sec. 519.11.

Divorce:

None.

PROBATE LAWS

In General:

UPC: M.S.A., Sec. 524.1-101.

Elective Share:

3% to 50%, based on length of marriage. Supplemental amount for less than one year. M.S.A., Sec. 524.2-201. In addition, spouse gets the homestead if there are no children, or a life estate in homestead if there are children (M.S.A., Sec. 524.2-402); exempt property of $10,000 and one automobile of any value (M.S.A., Sec. 524.2-403); and a "reasonable family allowance" of up to $1,500 per month for up to 18 months. (M.S.A., Sec. 524.2-404).

Intestate Share:

First $150,000 plus $1/2$ of the balance of the estate; to all. (M.S.A., Sec. 524.2-102.)

DIVORCE LAWS

Title:

Dissolution of Marriage.

Property:

Equitable distribution. Fault not considered. Nonmarital property is property: (1) acquired before marriage; (2) acquired by gift or inheritance; (3) acquired in exchange for or increase in value of nonmarital property; (4) acquired after the valuation date (date of the prehearing settlement conference); or (5) designated in prenuptial agreement. (M.S.A., Sec. 518.54.) Factors for dividing marital property: (1) length of marriage; (2) prior marriages; (3) each party's age, health, station, occupation, amount and sources of income, vocational skills, employability, estate, liabilities, and needs; (4) each party's opportunity for future acquisition of capital assets; (5) each party's income; (6) each party's contribution to acquisition, preservation, depreciation, or appreciation of assets; and (7) contribution of a spouse as homemaker. There is a conclusive presumption that both parties contributed substantially to the acquisition of property and income during the time they lived together as husband and wife. (M.S.A., Sec. 518.58.)

Alimony:

Called *maintenance.* Fault not considered. Either party may be awarded if he or she: (1) lacks sufficient property to meet own needs; or (2) is unable to be self-supporting through employment, or is not required to seek employment due to responsibilities as child custodian. Amount and duration of alimony determined by: (1) financial resources of party seeking alimony; (2) time needed for education and training to find appropriate employment; (3) standard of living established during the marriage; (4) duration of the marriage, and, for a homemaker, the length of absence from employment and the extent education, skills, or experience have become outmoded and earning capacity permanently diminished; (5) any loss of earnings, seniority, retirement benefits, or other employment opportunities foregone; (6) age, and physical and emotional condition of the party seeking alimony; (7) ability of the other party to meet own needs while paying alimony; and (8) either party's contribution to acquisition, preservation, depreciation, or appreciation of marital property, and in furtherance of the other's employment or business. (M.S.A., Sec. 518.552.)

MISSISSIPPI

THE LAW

In General:

Mississippi Code 1972 Annotated, Section 91-1-1 (M.C., Sec. 91-1-1). There are no laws relating to premarital agreements in Mississippi. If using statutes from the website: (1) click on either "HTML Version" or "Java Version"; (2) on the left side of the screen, under the heading "Contents," click on folder for "Mississippi"; (3) click on folder for "Title 91" for probate sections or folder for "Title 93" for divorce sections. To get to probate sections, click on "Chapter 1" or "Chapter 5." AUTHOR'S NOTE: The Mississippi Code is so devoid of substance in the area of divorce that it basically allows a judge to do anything he or she wants, so a prenuptial agreement is especially recommended.

UPAA:

No.

Probate:

None.

Divorce:

None.

PROBATE LAWS

In General:

M.C., Sec. 91-1-1.

Elective Share:

Spouse gets the same share as intestate share, but only up to $\frac{1}{2}$ of the estate. (M.C., Secs. 91-5-25 and 91-5-27.) This amount may be reduced if surviving spouse has separate property. (M.C., Sec. 91-5-29.)

Intestate Share:

If no children of decedent, spouse gets all; if there are children, spouse and children get equal shares (i.e., if one child, spouse gets $\frac{1}{2}$, if two children, spouse gets $\frac{1}{3}$). (M.C., Sec. 91-1-7.)

DIVORCE LAWS

Title:

Divorce.

Property:

There are no statutory provisions for property division, which leaves the matter up to the judge interpreting prior appellate court decisions. These are mostly based on the concept of "title," in which each party keeps what is titled in his or her name. Jointly titled property will be divided by the judge. This system has a history of favoring the husband. Judges have offset an otherwise unfair result by liberally awarding lump-sum alimony, or by considering the wife's contributions to acquiring the property.

Alimony:

There are no statutory factors. Either party may be awarded alimony "having regard to the circumstances of the parties and the nature of the case." (M.C., Sec. 93-5-23.)

MISSOURI

THE LAW

In General:

Vernon's Annotated Missouri Statutes, Chapter 474, Section 474.120 (A.M.S., Sec. 474.120). If using statutes from the website, for probate laws click on "Title XXXI, TRUSTS AND ESTATES OF DECEDENTS AND PERSONS UNDER DISABILITY," for divorce laws click on "Title XXX, DOMESTIC RELATIONS."

UPAA:

No.

Probate:

Waiver provided for in A.M.S., Secs. 474.220 and 474.120. Similar to standard UPC waiver provision.

Divorce:

A.M.S., Secs. 451.220 to 451.240. Agreement must be in writing and acknowledged or proved by at least one witness.

PROBATE LAWS

In General:

A.M.S., Sec. 474.010.

Elective share:

$1/3$ to $1/2$. A.M.S., Sec. 474.160. In addition, spouse is entitled to a homestead allowance of up to the lesser of $1/2$ the estate or $15,000 (A.M.S., Sec. 474.290); a "reasonable allowance" for support during administration of the estate for up to one year (A.M.S., Sec. 474.260); and an automobile and various household and person items specified in the statute as exempt property (A.M.S., Sec. 474.250).

Intestate Share:

$1/2$ to all. (A.M.S., Sec. 474.010.)

DIVORCE LAWS

Title:

Dissolution of Marriage.

Property:

Equitable distribution. Nonmarital property is property: (1) acquired before marriage; (2) acquired by gift or inheritance; (3) acquired in exchange for (1) or (2); (4) acquired after a decree of legal separation; (5) designated by agreement; or (6) increased in value, except due to marital labor or assets. Factors for dividing marital property: (1) economic circumstances of the parties, including whether custodian should remain in marital home; (2) each party's contribution to acquisition of property and as homemaker; (3) value of nonmarital property; (4) each party's conduct during marriage; (5) custody arrangements; and (6) any other relevant factor. (A.M.S., Sec. 452.330.)

Alimony:

Called *maintenance*. Either party may be awarded if he or she: (1) lacks sufficient property to meet own needs; and (2) is unable to be self-supporting through appropriate employment. Amount and duration determined by: (1) financial resources of party seeking alimony; (2) time needed for education and training to obtain appropriate employment; (3) parties' comparative earning capacities; (4) standard of living established during marriage; (5) each party's obligations and assets; (6) duration of marriage; (7) age, and physical and emotional condition of party seeking alimony; (8) ability of other party to meet own expenses while paying alimony; (9) each party's conduct during the marriage; and (10) any other relevant factor. Decree must state whether alimony may be modified. (A.M.S., Sec. 452.335.)

MONTANA

THE LAW

In General:

Montana Code Annotated 1997, Title 40, Chapter 2, Section 40-2-601 (M.C.A., Sec. 40-2-601). The Montana Code Annotated is a set of black, soft-cover volumes. The annotations are in a separate set of loose-leaf binders. If using the website, use the table of contents on the left side of the screen.

UPAA:

M.C.A., Sec. 40-2-601.

Probate:

M.C.A., Sec. 72-2-224. Standard UPC waiver provision.

Divorce:

None.

PROBATE LAWS

In General:

UPC: M.C.A., Sec. 72-1-101.

Elective Share:

3% to 50%, based on length of marriage. Supplemental amount for less than one year. (M.C.A., Sec. 72-2-221.)

Intestate Share:

First $100,000 plus $1/2$ of the balance; to all. (M.C.A., Sec. 72-2-112.)

DIVORCE LAWS

Title:

Dissolution of Marriage.

Property:

Equitable distribution. All property is marital property. Factors: (1) duration of the marriage, and any prior marriages; (2) each party's age, health, station, occupation, amount and sources of income, vocational skills, employa-bility, estate, liabilities, and needs; (3) child custody provisions; (4) whether property division is in lieu of or in addition to alimony; (5) each party's opportunity for future acquisition of capital assets and income; and (6) each party's contribution to or dissipation of the value of property. If property was acquired prior to marriage, by gift or inheritance, in exchange for such property, or increased value of such property, or acquired after a decree of legal separation, the following factors are considered: (1) any nonmonetary contributions of a homemaker; (2) the extent such contribution facilitated maintenance of the property; and (3) whether property division is an alternative to alimony. (M.C.A., Sec. 40-4-202.)

Alimony:

Called *maintenance*. Fault not considered. Either party may be awarded alimony if he or she: (1) lacks sufficient property to meet own needs; and (2) is unable to be self-supporting through appropriate employment. Amount and duration determined by: (1) financial resources of the party seeking alimony; (2) time needed for education and training to obtain appropriate employment; (3) standard of living established during marriage; (4) duration of the marriage; (5) age, and physical and emotional condition of the party seeking alimony; and (6) the other party's ability to meet own expenses while paying alimony. (M.C.A., Sec. 40-4-203.)

NEBRASKA

THE LAW

In General:

Revised Statutes of Nebraska, Chapter 42, Article 10, Section 42-1001 (R.S.N., Sec. 42-1001).

UPAA:

R.S.N., Sec. 42-1001.

Probate:

R.S.N., Sec. 30-2316. Standard UPC waiver provision.

Divorce:

R.S.N., Sec. 42-205, which provides: "Nothing contained in section 42-201 to 42-205 shall invalidate any marriage settlement or contract."

PROBATE LAWS

In General:

UPC: R.S.N., Sec. 30-2201 [Nebraska Probate Code.]

Elective Share:

$^1/_2$. R.S.N., Sec. 30-2313. Also, spouse is entitled to a homestead of $7,500 (R.S.N., Sec. 30-2322); exempt property of $5,000 in car and household and personal items (R.S.N., Sec. 30-2323); and a "reasonable allowance" during administration of the estate, up to one year (R.S.N., Sec. 30-2324).

Intestate Share:

$^1/_2$ to all. (R.S.N., Sec. 30-2302.)

DIVORCE LAWS

Title:

Dissolution of Marriage.

Property:

Equitable distribution. All property is marital, although fact that property was acquired before marriage, or by gift or inheritance, is considered as part of the circumstances of the parties. Case of *Lord v. Lord*, 213 Neb. 557, 330 N.W.2d 492 (1983). Factors: (1) circumstances of the parties; (2) duration of the marriage; (3) each party's contributions to the marriage, including the care and education of the children and any interruption of personal careers or educational opportunities; and (4) the ability of the party seeking alimony to engage in gainful employment without interfering with the interests of a child in that party's custody. (R.S.N., Sec. 42-365.)

Alimony:

Fault not considered. Factors: (1) circumstances of the parties; (2) duration of the marriage; (3) each party's contributions to the marriage, including the care and education of the children and any interruption of personal careers or educational opportunities; and (4) the ability of the party seeking alimony to engage in gainful employment without interfering with the interests of a child in that party's custody. (R.S.N., Sec. 42-365.)

NEVADA

THE LAW

In General:
Nevada Revised Statutes Annotated, Chapter 123A, Section 123A.010 (N.R.S.A., Sec. 123A.010).

UPAA:
N.R.S.A., Sec. 123A.010.

Probate:
N.R.S.A., Sec. 146.005 provides that the terms of a premarital agreement under N.R.S.A., Sec. 123A.010 overrides the provisions of the probate code.

Divorce:
N.R.S.A., Sec. 125.150 provides that the terms of a premarital agreement under N.R.S.A., Sec. 123A.010 overrides the statutory provisions for alimony and property division in divorce cases.

PROBATE LAWS

In General:
N.R.S.A., Sec. 132.010.

Elective Share:
Homestead, wearing apparel, household furniture, and "a reasonable provision" for support. (N.R.S.A., Sec. 146.010.)

Intestate Share:
$^1/_3$ to all. (N.R.S.A., Secs. 134.040 and 134.050.)

DIVORCE LAWS

Title:
Divorce.

Property:
Community property. Separate property is property: (1) acquired before marriage; (2) acquired by gift or inheritance; (3) acquired as personal injury damages; (4) income or prof-its from (1), (2), or (3) above, [N.R.S.A., Sec. 123.130]; as well as (5) designated separate by written agreement; (6) acquired as separate pursuant to or after a decree of separate maintenance; and (7) acquired pursuant to a decree under N.R.S.A., Sec. 123.259, if one spouse is institutionalized [N.R.S.A., Sec. 123.220]. Community property is divided equally, unless the judge "finds a compelling reason" for unequal division and states the reason in writing. (N.R.S.A., Sec. 125.150.)

Alimony:
Fault not considered. May be granted to either party "…as appears just and equitable." Alimony for training or education may be awarded upon consideration of: (1) whether the party to pay alimony has obtained greater job skills or education during the marriage; and (2) whether the party seeking alimony provided financial support while the other party obtained job skills or education. If ordered, the decree must state the time within which the training or education must begin. (N.R.S.A., Sec. 125.150.)

NEW HAMPSHIRE

THE LAW

In General:
New Hampshire Revised Statutes Annotated, Chapter 560, Section 560:14 (N.H.R.S.A., Sec. 560:14).

UPAA:
No.

Probate:
N.H.R.S.A., Secs. 560:14; 560:15; and 560:16. These sections only provide for waiver of the elective share, and that any agreement between the spouses is to be enforced by the probate court.

Divorce:
None.

PROBATE LAWS

In General:
N.H.R.S.A., Chapters 547 through 567-A.

Elective Share:
$10,000 plus $2,000 for each full year of marriage plus $1/2$ the balance of real property and $1/2$ balance of personal property; if total estate is less than $10,000, spouse gets all. N.H.R.S.A., Sec. 560:10. If premarital agreement gives spouse a specified settlement in lieu of distributive share, it will be enforced. (N.H.R.S.A., Secs. 560:15 and 560:16.)

Intestate Share:
$1/2$ to all. (N.H.R.S.A., Sec. 561:1.)

DIVORCE LAWS

Title:
Divorce.

Property:
Equitable distribution. Fault is a factor. Separate property is property acquired (1) before marriage or in exchange for such property; and (2) by gift or inheritance. Equal division of marital property, unless inequal division is justified considering: (1) duration of the marriage; (2) age, health, social or economic status, occupation, vocational skills, employability, separate property, amount and sources of income, needs, and liabilities of the parties; (3) each party's opportunity for future acquisition of capital assets and income; (4) ability of custodial parent to engage in gainful employment without substantially interfering with the interests of the child; (5) custodial parent's need to remain in the marital home; (6) action during the marriage which contributed to the growth or diminution in value of any property; (7) any significant disparity between the parties in relation to contribution to the marriage; (8) any contribution to help educate or develop the career or employability of the other, and any interruption in one party's education or career opportunities for the benefit of the other's career, the marriage, or the children; (9) any expectation of pension or retirement rights acquired prior to or during the marriage; (10) tax consequences; (11) value of property allocated in a premarital agreement; (12) either party's fault for the breakdown of the marriage if fault was the cause and either (a) it caused substantial physical or mental pain and suffering, or (b) it resulted in substantial economic loss to the marital estate or to the injured party; (13) value of each parties' separate property; and (14) any other relevant factor. If division is not equal, the reasons must be stated in the decree. (N.H.R.S.A., Sec. 458:16-a.)

Alimony:
Either party may be awarded if that party: (1) lacks income or property to maintain a standard of living similar to that during the marriage; and (2) is unable to support self through

employment, or has child custody duties making it inadvisable to be employed; and (3) the party to pay has the ability to pay and meet his or her own needs. Amount and duration of alimony to be determined considering: (1) length of marriage; (2) age, health, social or economic status, occupation, amount and sources of income, property awarded, vocational skills, employability, estate, liabilities, and needs of each party; (3) each party's opportunity for future acquisition of capital assets and income; (4) fault; (5) federal tax consequences; (6) each party's contribution to the acquisition, preservation or appreciation in value of assets and to the family unit. The decree must state the reasons for granting or denying alimony. (N.H.R.S.A., Sec. 458:19.) See N.H.R.S.A., Sec. 458:16-a, II (1) regarding fault.

NEW JERSEY

THE LAW

In General:

NJSA (for New Jersey Statutes Annotated), Title 37, Chapter 2, Section 37:2-31 (N.J.S.A., Sec. 37:2-31). If using website, use the Table of Contents. Website instructions say you can enter the section number in quotations, however, this results in an error message.

UPAA:

N.J.S.A., Sec. 37:2-31.

Probate:

N.J.S.A., Sec. 3B:8-10. Standard UPC-type waiver provision.

Divorce:

None.

PROBATE LAWS

In General:

N.J.S.A., Sec. 3B:1-1.

Elective Share:

$^1/_3$. (N.J.S.A., Sec. 3B:8-1.)

Intestate Share:

$^1/_2$ to all. (N.J.S.A., Sec. 3B:5-3.)

DIVORCE LAWS

Title:

Divorce.

Property:

Equitable distribution. Each party keeps property acquired before marriage or by gift or inheritance. Factors: (1) duration of marriage; (2) age, and physical and emotional condition of parties; (3) property or income prior to marriage; (4) standard of living established during marriage; (5) any written agreement as to property division; (6) economic circumstances of each; (7) income and earning capacity of each; (8) contribution to the other party's education, training or earning power; (9) contribution to acquisition, dissipation, preservation, depreciation or appreciation of marital property; (10) tax consequences; (11) present value of property; (12) need of custodial parent to remain in the marital home; (13) debts and liabilities of each; (14) need for trust fund to secure foreseeable medical or educational costs for a child or spouse; (15) any other relevant factor. (N.J.S.A., Sec. 2A:34-23.1.)

Alimony:

Fault not considered. Factors: (1) actual need and ability of parties to pay; (2) duration of the marriage; and age, physical and emotional condition of the parties; (4) standard of living established during the marriage, and the likelihood each can maintain that standard; (5) earning capacity, educational level, vocational skills and employability of the parties; (6) length of absence from the job market and child custodial responsibilities of the party seeking alimony; (7) time and expense needed for education and training; availability of training and employment; and the opportunity for future acquisition of capital assets and income; (8) contribution of each to the marriage; (9) property division; and (10) any other relevant factor. (N.J.S.A., Sec. 2A:34-23.)

NEW MEXICO

THE LAW

In General:
New Mexico Statutes 1978 Annotated, Chapter 40, Section 40-3A-1 (N.M.S.A., Sec. 40-3A-1). Supplement is found at the end of each chapter.

UPAA:
N.M.S.A., Sec. 40-3A-1.

Probate:
N.M.S.A., Sec. 45-2-407. Standard UPC-type waiver, plus specific application to family allowance and personal property allowance.

Divorce:
N.M.S.A., Secs. 40-2-1 to 40-2-9. Section 40-2-4 provides: "All contracts for marriage settlements and contracts for separation, must be in writing, and executed and acknowledged or proved in like manner as a grant of land is required to be executed and acknowledged or proved."

PROBATE LAWS

In General:
UPC: N.M.S.A., Sec. 45-1-101 [Probate Code.]

Elective Share:
No statutory provision for elective share, but surviving spouse gets ¹/₂ of the community property estate.

Intestate Share:
Decedent's half of community property plus ¹/₂ to all of decedent's separate property. N.M.S.A., Sec. 45-2-102. In addition, a family allowance of $30,000 (N.M.S.A., Sec. 45-2-402); and a personal property allowance of $15,000 (N.M.S.A., Sec. 45-2-403).

DIVORCE LAWS

Title:
Dissolution of Marriage.

Property:
Community property. Separate property is property: (1) acquired before marriage; (2) acquired after a decree of legal separation; (3) designated separate by court order or written agreement of the parties; or (4) acquired by gift or inheritance. (N.M.S.A., Sec. 40-3-8.) Fault not considered. No statutory factors. (N.M.S.A., Sec. 40-4-7.)

Alimony:
Fault not considered. Factors: (1) each party's age, health, and means of support; (2) current and future earnings and earning capacity; (3) good-faith efforts to maintain employment or to become self-supporting; (4) needs; (5) duration of the marriage; (6) property division; (7) type and nature of assets; (8) type and nature of liabilities; (9) income produced by property; and (10) any agreements of the parties. (N.M.S.A., Sec. 40-4-7.)

NEW YORK

THE LAW

In General:

McKinney's Consolidated Laws of New York Annotated, General Obligations, Section 3-303 (C.L.N.Y., Gen.O. Sec. 3-303). New York's laws are divided into subjects, so be sure you have the correctly titled volume. For premarital agreement forms specifically for New York, see a separate set of books called West's McKinney's Forms, Secs. 4:13 to 4:19A.

UPAA:

No.

Misc:

C.L.N.Y., General Obligations Sec. 3-303, which provides: "A contract made between persons in contemplation of marriage, remains in full force after the marriage takes place."

Probate:

C.L.N.Y., Estates, Powers and Trusts Law Sec. 5-1.3, which makes reference to "ante nuptial agreement" as it relates to a waiver of the elective share when the deceased person's will predates the marriage.

Divorce:

C.L.N.Y., Domestic Relations Sec. 236 – Part B.1.d (4) and Part B.3.

PROBATE LAWS

In General:

C.L.N.Y., 4 volumes designated 17B, titled "Estates, Powers and Trusts Law," and volume 58A, titled "Surrogate's Court Procedure Act."

Elective Share:

$1/3$ to $1/2$, although this is a lengthy section which needs to be fully considered. (C.L.N.Y., Estates, Powers and Trusts Law Sec. 5-1.1.)

Intestate Share:

First \$50,000 plus $1/2$ of the balance; to all. (C.L.N.Y., Estates, Powers & Trusts Law Sec. 4-1.1.)

DIVORCE LAWS

Title:

Divorce.

Property:

Equitable distribution. Separate property is: (1) property acquired before marriage; (2) property acquired by gift or inheritance; (3) compensation for personal injuries; (4) property acquired in exchange for, or increase in value of, (1) or (2), unless due to the efforts of the other party; and (5) property designated as separate in a written agreement of the parties. C.L.N.Y., Domestic Relations Law, Sec. 236, Part B.1.d. Marital property is divided according to the following factors: (1) income and property at time of marriage and at the commencement of the divorce; (2) duration of marriage, and age and health of the parties; (3) need of party with child custody to remain in the marital home; (4) loss of inheritance or pension rights; (5) alimony award, if any; (6) contribution of each to the acquisition of the property; (7) liquidity of the marital property; (8) probable future financial circumstances of each party; (9) difficulty in evaluating an asset or business entity; (10) tax consequences; (11) either party's wasteful dissipation of assets; (12) any transfer or encumbrance in contemplation of divorce without fair consideration; and (13) any other relevant factor. (C.L.N.Y., Domestic Relations Law Sec. 236-Part B.5.)

Alimony:

Called *maintenance.* Fault not considered. Factors: (1) income and property distribution; (2) duration of marriage, and the age and health of the parties; (3) present and future earning capacity of each; (4) ability of the party seeking alimony to become self-supporting, and the training and time needed; (5) the reduced earning capacity due to career building of the other party; (6) child custody arrangement; (7) tax consequences; (8) contribution to the career of the other party; (9) either party's wasteful dissipation of marital property; (10) any transfer or encumbrance in contemplation of divorce without fair consideration; and (11) any other relevant factor. (C.L.N.Y., Domestic Relations Law Sec. 236-Part B.)

NORTH CAROLINA

THE LAW

In General:
General Statutes of North Carolina, Chapter 52B, Section 52B-1 (G.S.N.C., Sec. 52B-1).

UPAA:
G.S.N.C., Sec. 52B-1.

Probate:
G.S.N.C., Sec. 30-3.6. Provides for waiver of elective share.

Divorce:
None.

PROBATE LAWS

In General:
G.S.N.C., Chapters 28A through 31C.

Elective Share:
$1/6$ to all. (G.S.N.C., Sec. 30-3.1.) Also a "year's allowance" of $10,000. (G.S.N.C., Sec. 30-15.)

Intestate Share:
$1/3$ to all of real property; $30,000 3to all of personal property. (G.S.N.C., Sec. 29-14.)

DIVORCE LAWS

Title:
Divorce.

Property:
Equitable distribution. Fault not considered. Separate property is property: (1) acquired before marriage or by gift or inheritance; (2) acquired in exchange for such property; (3) any increase in value of, or income from, separate property; (4) nontransferable professional or business licenses; and (5) any non-vested retirement benefits. Division of marital property is to be equal, unless the judge decides this would not be equitable, considering: (1) income, property, and liabilities of each party; (2) any obligation of support from a prior marriage; (3) duration of the marriage, and the age, physical and mental health of the parties; (4) need of the child custodian to occupy the marital home; (5) any expectation of non-vested retirement benefits; (6) each party's contribution to the acquisition of property; (7) the contribution of either party to the other's education or career development; (8) any direct contribution to the increase in value of the other's separate property; (9) liquidity of marital assets; (10) difficulty in evaluating any assets or business interest, and the economic desirability of retaining such an asset or business interest free of the other's intervention; (11) tax consequences; and (12) acts of either party to maintain, preserve, develop, expand, waste, neglect, devalue, or convert marital property after separation; and (13) any other relevant factor. (G.S.N.C., Sec. 50-20.)

Alimony:
Alimony may be awarded if the party seeking it is determined to be a "dependent spouse," the other party is determined to be a "supporting spouse," and an award of alimony is equitable. No alimony is allowed if the dependent spouse is guilty of "illicit sexual behavior." Alimony will be awarded if support spouse committed act of illicit sexual behavior. If both engaged in illicit sexual behavior, award of alimony is in the judge's discretion. Illicit sexual behavior will not be considered if it was condoned by the other spouse. Factors: (1) marital misconduct of either party; (2) relative earnings and earning capacity; (3) ages, and physical, mental, and emotional conditions of the parties; (4) amount and sources of earned and unearned income; (5) duration of the marriage; (6) contribution of one spouse to the education, training, or increased earn-

ing power of the other; (7) extent that earning power, expenses, or financial obligations of one spouse will be affected by serving as custodial of a minor child; (8) standard of living during the marriage; (9) relative education of the spouses, and time needed for spouse seeking alimony to acquire education or training to find employment to meet his or her needs; (10) relative assets and liabilities of the parties; (11) property each brought into the marriage; (12) contribution as homemaker; (13) relative needs of the parties; (14) tax ramifications; (15) any other relevant factor relating to the parties' economic circumstances; and (16) "the fact that income received by either party was previously considered by the court in determining the value of a marital or divisible asset in an equitable distribution of the parties' marital or divisible property." (G.S.N.C., Sec. 50-16.3A.)

NORTH DAKOTA

THE LAW

In General:
North Dakota Century Code Annotated, Title 14, Chapter 14-03.1, Section 14-03.1-01 (N.D.C.C., Sec. 14-03.1-01). If using website, scroll down to list of titles.

UPAA:
N.D.C.C., Sec. 14-03.1-01.

Probate:
None.

Divorce:
None.

PROBATE LAWS

Probate:
UPC: N.D.C.C., Sec. 30.1-01-01.

Elective Share:
$^1/_2$. (N.D.C.C., Sec. 30.1-05-01.) But if less than a certain amount (about $50,000), then the supplemental share. Also, homestead up to $80,000 (N.D.C.C., Sec. 47-18-01); exempt property up to $10,000 (N.D.C.C., Sec. 30.1-07-01); and a "reasonable allowance" for up to one year of $10,000 (N.D.C.C., Sec. 30.1-07-02).

Intestate Share:
First $100,000 plus $^1/_2$ of the balance; to all. (N.D.C.C., Sec. 30.1-04-02.)

DIVORCE LAWS

Title:
Divorce.

Property:
Equitable distribution. All property, regardless of how or when acquired (although this is a factor to be considered) will be divided as judge feels is just. No statutory factors. (N.D.C.C., Sec. 14-05-24.)

Alimony:
Fault is a factor. No other statutory factors. (N.D.C.C., Sec. 14-05-24.)

OHIO

THE LAW

In General:
Page's Ohio Revised Code Annotated, Title 31, Section 3103.05 (O.R.C., Sec. 3103.05). [Look for volume marked "Title 31." The first two numbers in the section number indicate the "Title" number.]

UPAA:
No.

Misc:
Page's Ohio Revised Code Annotated, Section 3103.05 (O.R.C., Sec. 3103.05), which provides: "A husband or wife may enter into any engagement or transaction with the other, or with any other person, which either might if unmarried; subject, in transactions between themselves, to the general rules which control the actions of persons occupying confidential relations with each other."

Probate:
None.

Divorce:
None.

PROBATE LAWS

In General:
O.R.C., Sec. 2101.01 through 2107.77. [Look for volume marked "Title 21."]

Elective Share:
¹/₃ to ¹/₂. O.R.C., Sec. 2106.01. Also, an "allowance for support" of $40,000.

Intestate Share:
$20,000 plus ¹/₃ residue, to all. (O.R.C., Sec. 2105.06.)

DIVORCE LAWS

Title:
Divorce (general procedure), or Dissolution of Marriage (simplified procedure if both parties sign petition and have settlement agreement).

Property:
Equitable distribution. Separate property is property: (1) acquired prior to marriage; (2) acquired by inheritance; (3) passive income and appreciation of separate property; (4) acquired after a decree of legal separation; (5) excluded by an antenuptial agreement; (6) obtained as personal injury compensation; or (7) clearly acquired as a gift to only one party. Marital property is divided considering: (1) duration of the marriage; (2) assets and liabilities of each party; (3) desirability of child custodian remaining in the marital home; (4) liquidity of property; economic desirability of retaining intact assets or business interests; (5) tax consequences; (6) costs of sale, if sale is necessary; (7) any division pursuant to a separation agreement; and (8) any other relevant factor. (O.R.C., Secs. 3105.171.)

Alimony:
Referred to as *spousal support*. Court will determine property division first. Fault not considered. Factors: (1) income; (2) earning ability; (3) age, and physical, mental and emotional condition; (4) retirement benefits; (5) duration of the marriage; (6) extent it would be inappropriate for the party with child custody to seek outside employment; (7) standard of living established during the marriage; (8) education; (9) assets and liabilities; (10) one party's contribution to the other's education, training or earning ability; (11) the time and expense to obtain education and training; (12) tax consequences; (13) income loss due to marital responsibilities; and (14) any other relevant factor. (O.R.C., Sec. 3105.18.)

OKLAHOMA

THE LAW

In General:
Oklahoma Statutes Annotated, Title 84, Section 44 (84 O.S.A., Sec. 44). If using the website, enter the Title and Section numbers (e.g., 84-44), then click on "Submit Inquiry." This will take you to a screen where you will need to click on the Title and Statute numbers after the word "Filename" (e.g., "Filename: 84-44.html").

UPAA:
No.

Probate:
84 O.S.A., Sec. 44, which provides: "Every estate in property may be disposed of by will except that a will shall be subservient to any antenuptial marriage contract in writing."

Divorce:
43 O.S.A., Sec. 121. Provides that the court may divide property "subject to a valid antenuptial contract in writing."

PROBATE LAWS

In General:
Title 84, O.S.A.

Elective share:
$1/2$. (84 O.S.A., Sec. 44.)

Intestate Share:
$1/3$ to all. (84 O.S.A., Sec. 213.)

DIVORCE LAWS

Title:
Divorce.

Property:
Equitable distribution. Separate property is property acquired (1) before marriage, or (2) after marriage "in his or her own right." Fault not considered. Marital property divided in a just and reasonable manner. (O.S.A., Sec. 43-121.)

Alimony:
Fault not considered. No statutory factors. See O.S.A., Secs. 43-121.

OREGON

THE LAW

In General:
Oregon Revised Statutes Annotated, Chapter 108, Section 108.700 (O.R.S., Sec. 108.700). If using website, scroll down to chapter number desired.

UPAA:
O.R.S., Sec. 108.700.

Probate:
None.

Divorce:
None.

PROBATE LAWS

In General:
O.R.S., Chapters 111 through 119.

Elective Share:
$^1/_2$ of community property. (O.R.S., Sec. 112.735.)

Intestate Share:
$^1/_2$ to all. (O.R.S., Secs. 112.025 and 112.035.)

DIVORCE LAWS

Title:
Dissolution of Marriage.

Property:
Equitable distribution. Fault not considered. O.R.S., Sec. 107.036. Property is divided "as may be just and proper in all the circumstances." There is a rebuttable presumption that both parties contributed equally to all property acquired during the marriage. Contributions as homemaker are considered to acquisition of property. Court is also required to consider "reasonable costs of sale of assets, taxes and any other costs reasonably anticipated by the parties." Otherwise, no factors are specified. (O.R.S., Sec. 107.105(1)(f).)

Alimony:
Called support. Fault not considered. (O.R.S., Sec. 107.036.) Party receiving alimony must make reasonable effort to become self-supporting within ten years, or alimony may be terminated. (O.R.S., Sec. 107.412.) Factors: (1) length of marriage; (2) age and physical and mental health of the parties; (3) contribution of one spouse to the education, training, or earning power of the other; (4) earning capacity of each party, including educational background, training, employment skills, and work experience; (5) need for education, training, or retraining to become self-supporting at standard of living during marriage; (6) extent to which present or future earning capacity is impaired due to the party having custody; (7) number, ages, health, and conditions of dependents of the parties and provisions of the decree relating to custody; (8) tax consequences; (9) amount of long-term financial obligation; (10) costs of health care; (11) standard of living during marriage; (12) life insurance costs; and (13) any other matters the court deems relevant. (O.R.S., Sec. 107.105(1)(d).)

PENNSYLVANIA

THE LAW

In General:
Purdon's Pennsylvania Consolidated Statutes Annotated, Title 23, Section 3104 (23 Pa. C.S.A., Sec. 3104).

UPAA:
No.

Probate:
None.

Divorce:
23 Pa. C.S.A., Sec. 3104). This section gives the court jurisdiction to determine rights created by an antenuptial agreement.

PROBATE LAWS

In General:
Title 20, Pa.C.S.A. [Title 20 is in four volumes.]

Elective share:
$1/3$. (20 Pa.C.S.A., Sec. 2203.)

Intestate Share:
$1/2$ to all. (20 Pa.C.S.A., Sec. 2102.)

DIVORCE LAWS

Title:
Divorce.

Property:
Equitable distribution. nonmarital property includes property: (1) acquired before marriage, by gift or inheritance; (2) acquired after separation, unless in exchange for marital property; (3) designated nonmarital in a valid agreement; (4) sold or mortgaged in good faith and for value before separation; (5) acquired in payment of an award or settlement for a claim accrued prior to the marriage or after separation; or (6) certain veterans benefits. (23 Pa.C.S.A., Sec. 3501.)

Marital property is divided considering: (1) length of marriage; (2) any prior marriages of the parties; (3) age, health, station, amount and sources of income, vocational skills, employability, estate, liabilities and needs of each party; (4) contribution to the education, training or increased earning power of the other; (5) opportunity of each for future acquisition of capital assets or income; (6) each party's sources of income, including medical, retirement and insurance benefits; (7) each party's contribution or dissipation to the acquisition, preservation, depreciation, or appreciation of marital property; (8) value of separate property; (9) standard of living established during the marriage; (10) economic circumstances of the parties, including tax consequences; and (11) whether either party will be custodian of any children. (23 Pa.C.S.A., Sec. 3502(a).)

Alimony:
Factors: (1) relative earnings and earning capacities of the parties; (2) ages, physical, mental and emotional condition of the parties; (3) sources of income, including medical, retirement and insurance benefits; (4) "expectancies and inheritances"; (5) duration of the marriage; (6) contribution to the education, training or increased earning power of the other party; (7) extent to which the earning power, expenses or financial obligations are affected by serving as child custodian; (8) standard of living established during the marriage; (9) the parties' relative education, and time needed to acquire education and training to become adequately employed; (10) relative assets and liabilities; (11) property brought to the marriage; (12) contribution of a spouse as homemaker; (13) the parties' relative needs; (14) any marital misconduct during the marriage, up to

separation; (15) tax ramifications; (16) whether the party seeking alimony lacks sufficient property to provide for his or her needs; and (17) whether the party seeking alimony is incapable of self-support through employment. (23 Pa.C.S.A., Sec. 3701.) Cohabitation with a non-relative member of the opposite sex terminates alimony. (23 Pa.C.S.A., Sec. 3706.)

RHODE ISLAND

THE LAW

In General:

General Laws of Rhode Island, Section 15-17-1 (G.L.R.I., Sec. 15-17-1). If using Rhode Island statute books, ignore "Title" and "Chapter" numbers. If using statutes from the website, you will need to use Title 15 for divorce laws and Title 33 for probate laws.

UPAA:

G.L.R.I., Sec. 15-17-1.

Probate:

None.

Divorce:

None.

PROBATE LAWS

In General:

G.L.R.I., Sec. 33-1-1.

Elective Share:

Life estate in the real property. (G.L.R.I., Secs. 33-1-5, 33-25-2, and 33-25-4.) Also, wearing apparel, household effects, and other property exempt by law (G.L.R.I., Sec. 33-10-1); and a "reasonable allowance" for family support for up to one year (G.L.R.I., Sec. 33-10-3).

Intestate Share:

Life estate in real property. (G.L.R.I., Sec. 33-1-5.) At court's discretion, up to $75,000 in real property. (G.L.R.I., Sec. 33-1-6.)

DIVORCE LAWS

Title:

Divorce.

Property:

Equitable distribution. Separate property is property acquired before marriage, or by gift or inheritance; but income from, and appreciation in value of, separate property may be considered marital property. Factors: (1) length of the marriage; (2) conduct of parties during marriage; (3) contribution of each in the acquisition, preservation, or appreciation in value of their respective estates; (4) contribution as homemaker; (5) health and age of the parties; (6) each party's amount and sources of income; (7) occupation and employability; (8) opportunity for future acquisition of capital assets and income; (9) contribution by one party to the education, training, licensure, business, or increased earning power of the other; (10) need of custodial party to occupy or own the marital residence and household effects, considering the best interests of the child; (11) either party's wasteful dissipation of assets or transfer or encumbrance of assets in contemplation of divorce with fair consideration; and (12) any other factor the court finds just and proper. (G.L.R.I., Sec. 15-5-16.1.)

Alimony:

Property division must be done before issue of alimony is considered. (G.L.R.I., Sec. 15-5-16.1(c).) Factors: (1) length of marriage; (2) conduct of parties during marriage; (3) each party's age, station, occupation, amount and source of income, vocational skills, and employability; (4) the state and the liabilities and needs of each party; (5) the extent to which either party is unable to be self-supporting because that party is the primary physical custodian of a child; (6) the extent to which either party is unable to be self-supporting considering: (a) the extent of absence from employment due to homemaking duties, and extent to which education, skills, or experience have become outmoded so as to diminish earning capacity; (b) time and expense required to become employable;

(c) probability, given the party's age and skills, of completing education or training; (d) standard of living during marriage; (e) opportunity of either party for future acquisition of capital assets or income; (f) the supporting spouse's ability to pay; and (g) any other factor the court finds just and proper. (G.L.R.I., Sec. 15-5-16.)

SOUTH CAROLINA

THE LAW

In General:

Code of Laws of South Carolina, Title 20, Section 20-5-50 (C.L.S.C., Sec. 20-5-50). [Look for volume 8], which provides: "All marriage contracts, deeds and settlements shall therein describe, specify and particularize the real and personal estate thereby intended to be included, comprehended, conveyed and passed or shall have a schedule thereto annexed containing a description and the particulars and articles of the real and personal estate intended to be conveyed and passed by such marriage contracts, deeds and settlements. Any such schedule shall be annexed to the contract, deed or other settlement paper, signed, executed and delivered by the parties therein interested at the time of the signing, executing and delivering the marriage contract, deed or settlement, be subscribed by the same witness who subscribed the marriage contract, deed or settlement and be recorded therewith; otherwise, and in default of such schedule and recording thereof as aforesaid, the marriage contract, deed or settlement shall be deemed and declared to be fraudulent, null and void with respect to and against creditors and bona fide purchasers or mortgagees."

UPAA:

None.

Probate:

None.

Divorce:

None.

PROBATE LAWS

In General:

UPC: C.L.S.C., Sec. 62-1-100 (Referred to as the South Carolina Probate Code.)

Elective share:

$1/3$. C.L.S.C., Sec. 62-2-201. Intestate share is $1/2$ to all. (C.L.S.C., Sec. 62-2-102.)

Intestate Share:

$1/2$ to all. (C.L.S.C., Sec. 62-2-102.)

DIVORCE LAWS

Title:

Divorce.

Property:

Equitable distribution. Nonmarital property is property: (1) acquired before marriage; (2) acquired by gift or inheritance; (3) acquired after an order in a divorce or separate maintenance action; (4) acquired after signing a settlement agreement; (5) acquired after a permanent court order regarding property; (6) acquired in exchange for any of the above property; (7) designated as such in a written agreement of the parties; and (8) any increase in value of any such property, unless due to the other's efforts. The court has no jurisdiction to award one party the other's nonmarital property. C.L. S.C., Sec. 20-7-473. Marital property divided considering: (1) duration of marriage, and the parties' ages at the time of marriage and now; (2) any marital misconduct or fault; (3) value of marital property, and each party's contribution to the acquisition, preservation, depreciation or appreciation of assets; (4) each party's income, earning potential and opportunity for future acquisition of capital assets; (5) each party's physical and emotional health; (6) each party's need for training or education; (7) each party's nonmarital property; (8) existence of any vested retirement benefits; (9) whether alimony was awarded; (10) whether the custodial party should remain in the marital home; (11) tax consequences; (12) any other support obligations; (13) any encumbrances on property, and other debt; (14) any child custody arrangements and obligations; and (15) any other relevant factor. (C.L.S.C., Sec. 20-7-472.)

Alimony:

Either party may be awarded alimony. Factors: (1) duration of marriage, and the parties' ages at the time of marriage and now; (2) each party's physical and emotional condition; (3) educational background, and need for additional training or education; (4) employment history and earning potential; (5) standard of living established during marriage; (6) current and reasonably anticipated earnings; (7) current and reasonably anticipated expenses and needs; (8) all property; (9) any child custody conditions and circumstances; (10) any marital misconduct or fault; (11) tax consequences; (12) any other support obligations; and (13) any other relevant factor. (C.L.S.C., Sec. 20-3-130.)

SOUTH DAKOTA

THE LAW

In General:

South Dakota Codified Laws, Title 25, Chapter 2, Section 25-2-16 (S.D.C.L., Sec. 25-2-16). If using statutes from website, click on "Quick Find" and you will be able to enter the statute number.

UPAA:

S.D.C.L., Sec. 25-2-16.

Probate:

S.D.C.L., Sec. 29A-2-213. Standard UPC-type waiver provision.

Divorce:

None.

PROBATE LAWS

In General:

S.D.C.L., Sec. 29A-2-101.

Elective Share:

3% to 50%, based on length of marriage. Supplemental amount for less than one year. S.D.C.L., Sec. 29A-2-202. Also, homestead (S.D.C.L., Sec. 29A-2-402); and a family allowance of either a lump sum of $18,000 or $1,500 per month for one year (S.D.C.L., Sec. 29A-2-403).

Intestate Share:

First $100,000 plus $1/2$ the balance; to all. (S.D.C.L., Sec. 29A-2-102.)

DIVORCE LAWS

Title:

Divorce.

Property:

Equitable distribution. No separate property mentioned in the Code. Fault not considered. (S.D.C.L., Sec. 25-4-45.1.) Only factor is statute is the circumstances of the parties, which courts have interpreted by using the usual factors, including the value of each party's property. See S.D.C.L., Sec. 25-4-44.

Alimony:

Only factor in statute is the "circumstances of the parties." Fault is considered. (S.D.C.L., Sec. 25-4-41.)

TENNESSEE

THE LAW

In General:

Tennessee Code Annotated, Title 66, Section 66-24-105 (T.C.A., Sec. 66-24-105). Refers to registration requirements for protection against creditors. Also T.C.A., Sec. 66-24-105.

UPAA:

No.

Probate:

None.

Divorce:

T.C.A., Sec. 36-3-501 which provides: "Notwithstanding any other provision of law to the contrary, except as provided in Sec. 36-3-502, any antenuptial or prenuptial agreement entered into by spouses concerning property owned by either spouse before the marriage which is the subject of such agreement shall be binding upon any court having jurisdiction over such spouses and/or such agreement if such agreement is determined in the discretion of such court to have been entered into by such spouses freely, knowledgeably and in good faith and without exertion of duress or undue influence upon either spouse. The terms of such agreement shall be enforceable by all remedies available for enforcement of contract terms."

PROBATE LAWS

In General:

T.C.A., Secs. 30-1-101 to 32-5-110.

Elective Share:

Percentage based upon length of marriage, from 10% for less than three years to 40% for nine years or more. (T.C.A., Sec. 31-4-101.)

Intestate Share:

$^1/_3$ to all. (T.C.A., Sec. 31-2-104.)

DIVORCE LAWS

Title:

Divorce.

Property:

Equitable distribution. Separate property is property acquired (1) before marriage; (2) in exchange for such property; (3) as income or appreciation from such property; and (4) by gift or inheritance; (5) awards for pain and suffering, crime victim compensation, and future medical expenses and wages; (6) property acquired pursuant to an order of legal separation. Marital property divided according to following factors: (1) duration of the marriage; (2) each party's age, physical and mental health, vocational skills, employability, earning capacity, estate, financial liabilities and needs; (3) either party's tangible and intangible contribution to the education, training or increased earning power of the other; (4) the parties' relative abilities for future acquisition of capital assets and income; (5) each party's contribution to the acquisition, preservation, appreciation, or dissipation of marital or separate property; (6) value of separate property; (7) estate of each at time of marriage; (8) economic circumstances at the time of property division; (9) tax consequences; (10) available Social Security benefits; and (11) any other relevant factor. (T.C.A., Sec. 36-4-121.)

Alimony:

Factors: (1) Relative earning capacity, obligations, needs and financial resources; (2) relative education and training, and opportunity to secure education and training, and necessity to secure education and training, to improve earning capacity; (3) duration of the marriage; (4) age, and physical and mental condition of each party; (5) any limitation on a party's earning capacity due to child custody responsibilities; (6) separate assets; (7) property division; (8) standard of living established during the marriage; (9) contribution to the marriage, and to the other's education, training and increased earning power; (10) relative fault of the parties; and (11) any other relevant factor, including tax consequences. (T.C.A., Sec. 36-5-101.)

TEXAS

THE LAW

In General:

Vernon's Texas Codes Annotated, Family Code, Section 5.41 (T.C.A., Family Code Sec. 5.41). The Texas laws are divided into subjects, so be sure you have the volumes marked for the correct subject, such as "Family," or "Probate Code." If using statutes from the website, scroll down to the Code you want (e.g., "Probate Code" or "Family Code"), and click on the name of the Code under the heading "Tables of Contents." This will allow you to view the Code sections without having to download them. If you want to download, note the warning not to use Netscape "Smart Download."

UPAA:

T.C.A., Family Code Sec. 4.001.

Probate:

None.

Divorce:

None.

PROBATE LAWS

In General:

Vernon's Texas Civil Statutes, Probate Code (referred to as "Texas Probate Code."). Again, be sure you have the volumes titled "Probate."

Elective Share:

There is no specific statute for an elective share, but the surviving spouse is entitled to $^1/_2$ of the community property estate. There is also a homestead (T.C.S., Probate Code Secs. 270 and 273); a family allowance for one year in an amount "sufficient for the maintenance of such surviving spouse and minor children" (T.C.S., Probate Code Secs. 286 and 287); and exempt property as provided by Texas Constitution and law (T.C.S., Probate Code Sec. 271. In lieu of exempt property, court may grant a "reasonable allowance" of up to $15,000 for homestead and up to $5,000 for personal property. (T.C.S., Probate Code Sec. 273.)

Intestate Share:

(a) $^1/_3$ of the personal property and a life estate in $^1/_3$ of the real property if there are children, and (b) all of the personal property and $^1/_2$ of the real property if there are no children but there are parents or siblings of the deceased spouse (all of the real estate if no parents or siblings). (T.C.S., Probate Code Sec. 38(b).)

DIVORCE LAWS

Title:

Divorce.

Property:

Community property. Separate property is that acquired before marriage, by gift or inheritance, or as personal injury recovery. Community property is divided "in a manner that the court deems just and right, having due regard for the rights of each party and any children of the marriage." Various sections cover specific situations. (T.C.A., Family Code Secs. 7.001 through 7.006.)

Alimony:

Called *maintenance.* Court may order alimony if (1) payor was convicted of a crime of domestic violence, or (2) the marriage was of at least ten years and the party seeking alimony lacks the ability to provide for minimal needs. T.C.A., Family Code Sec. 8.002. Alimony can only last three years, unless spouse is incapacitated. T.C.A., Family Code Sec. 8.005. There is a presumption against awarding maintenance unless the spouse seeking it exercised diligence in (1) seeking suitable employment, or (2) developing necessary skills to become self-supporting during any period of separation and the period when the dissolution case is pending; unless that spouse has an incapacitating physical or mental disability. T.C.A., Family Code Sec. 8.004. Factors: (1) financial resources of spouse seeking maintenance, after property division; and ability to meet his or her needs independently; (2) each party's education and employment skills; and time needed for spouse seeking maintenance to acquire education or training to find appropriate employment, and the availability and feasibility of such education or training; (3) duration of the marriage; (4) the age, employment history, earning ability, and physical and emotional condition of the spouse seeking maintenance; (5) ability of the payor to meet spouse's needs and provide for child support; (6) acts of either party resulting in excessive or abnormal expenditures or destruction, concealment, or fraudulent disposition of community property or other property held jointly or in common; (7) comparative financial resources of the parties; (8) contribution of one spouse to the education, training, or increased earning power of the other; (9) property brought into the marriage by either party; (10) contribution of a spouse as homemaker; (11) any marital misconduct by spouse seeking maintenance; and (12) efforts by spouse seeking maintenance to pursue available employment counseling. (T.C.A., Family Code Sec. 8.003.)

UTAH

THE LAW

In General:
Utah Code Annotated 1953, Title 30, Section 30-2-1 (U.C.A., Sec. 30-2-1).

UPAA:
U.C.A., Sec. 30-8-1.

Probate:
U.C.A., Sec. 75-2-204. Standard UPC waiver provision.

Divorce:
U.C.A., Secs. 30-2-2 to 30-2-6. These sections provide:

Sec. 30-2-2. "Contracts may be made by a wife, and liabilities incurred and enforced by or against her, to the same extent and in the same manner as if she were unmarried."

Sec. 30-2-3. "A conveyance, transfer or lien executed by either husband or wife to or in favor of the other shall be valid to the same extent as between other persons."

Sec. 30-2-6. "Should the husband or wife obtain possession or control of property belonging to the other before or after marriage, the owner of the property may maintain an action therefor, or for any right growing out of the same, in the same manner and to the same extent as if they were unmarried."

PROBATE LAWS

In General:
UPC: U.C.A., Sec. 75-1-101.

Elective Share:
$1/3$. (U.C.A., Sec. 75-2-202.)

Intestate Share:
First $50,000 plus $1/2$ of the balance (minus any nonprobate transfer as defined in U.C.A., Sec. 75-2-206); to all. (U.C.A., Sec. 75-2-102.)

DIVORCE LAWS

Title:
Divorce.

Property:
Equitable distribution. Court has authority to make "equitable orders relating to...property...of the parties." (U.C.A., Sec. 30-3-5.)

Alimony:
Factors: (1) financial condition and needs of party seeking alimony; (2) recipient's earning capacity or ability to produce income; (3) ability of payor to pay; (4) length of the marriage; (5) whether recipient has custody of minor children; (6) whether recipient worked in a business owned or operated by the spouse; (7) whether recipient directly contributed to any increase in the payor's skill by paying for education or allowing spouse to attend school during the marriage; (8) fault; and (9) standard of living or the parties. If marriage is of short duration and there are no children, court may consider restoring each party to the condition that existed at the time of marriage. Alimony may only last for a duration equal to the number of years the parties were married, unless the court finds extenuating circumstances exist. (U.C.A., Sec. 30-3-5.)

VERMONT

THE LAW

In General:
Vermont Statutes Annotated, Title 14, Section 465 (14 V.S.A., Sec. 465). Ignore "Chapter" numbers.

UPAA:
No.

Probate:
Vermont Statutes Annotated, Title 14, Section 465 (14 V.S.A., Sec. 465). This law provides, in part: "If the widow was not the first wife of the deceased and he leaves no issue by her, and an agreement was entered into between them, previous to or after their marriage, in relation to the widow's claim on the estate of her husband in lieu of such third interest, and if, in the opinion of the court, she has a sufficient provision for her comfortable support during life, the court may deny to such widow such third part of his real estate or any provision other than such as is provided by the agreement of the parties."

Divorce:
None.

PROBATE LAWS

In General:
14 V.S.A., Sec. 1.

Elective Share:
$^1/_3$ or more. (14 V.S.A., Secs. 401 and 402.)

Intestate Share:
Minimum of $^1/_3$ of personal property. 14 V.S.A., Sec. 401. Household goods. (14 V.S.A., Sec. 403.) Reasonable support. 14 V.S.A., Sec. 404. $^1/_3$ to $^1/_2$ real property. (14.V.S.A., Secs. 461 and 474.)

DIVORCE LAWS

Title:
Divorce.

Property:
Equitable distribution. All property divided regardless of how or when acquired, but how and by whom acquired is a factor. Concept of "separate property" is recognized, but not defined in statute. Factors: (1) length of marriage; (2) age and health of parties; (3) each party's occupation, and sources and amount of income; (4) each party's vocational skills and employability; (5) either party's contribution to the education, training and increased earning power of the other; (6) value of property, liabilities, and needs of each; (7) whether property division is in lieu of or in addition to alimony; (8) each party's opportunity for future acquisition of capital assets or income; (9) desirability of the custodial parent remaining in the marital home; (10) the party through whom the property was acquired; (11) each party's contribution to the acquisition, preservation, depreciation, and appreciation of the property; and (12) the "respective merits of the parties." (15 V.S.A., Sec. 751.)

Alimony:
Fault not considered. May be awarded if (1) party seeking alimony lacks sufficient income or property to provide for his or her reasonable needs; and (2) is unable to support self through appropriate employment at the same standard of living established during the marriage, or is custodian of a child. Factors in determining amount and duration: (1) financial resources of the party seeking alimony, the property apportioned to him or her, ability to meet his or her own needs, and the extent to which child support contains an amount for him or her as custodian; (2) time and expense

needed to acquire education and training to find appropriate employment; (3) standard of living established during marriage; (4) duration of marriage; (5) age, and physical and emotional condition of the parties; (6) ability of the person to pay alimony to meet his or her own needs while paying; and (7) "inflation with relation to the cost of living." (15 V.S.A., Sec. 752.)

VIRGINIA

THE LAW

In General:
Code of Virginia 1950, Title 20, Section 20-147 (C.V., Sec. 20-147). Ignore "Chapter" numbers, and look for "Title" and "Section" numbers.

UPAA:
C.V., Sec. 20-147

Probate:
None.

Divorce:
None.

PROBATE LAWS

In General:
C.V., Sec. 64.1-1.

Elective Share:
$1/3$ to $1/2$. (C.V., Sec. 64.1-16.)

Intestate share:
$1/3$ to all. (C.V,. Sec. 64.1-1.)

DIVORCE LAWS

Title:
Divorce.

Property:
Equitable distribution. Separate property is property acquired (1) before marriage; (2) by gift or inheritance; (3) by exchange for separate property, provided it was always maintained as separate property; and (4) any income from, or increase in value of, such property, unless the income or increase was from the efforts of the spouse. Factors for dividing marital property: (1) each party's contribution to the well-being of the family; (2) each party's contribution to the acquisition and care and maintenance of marital property; (3) duration of marriage; (4) age, physical and mental condition of the parties; (5) circumstances and factors contributing to the divorce; (6) how and when property was acquired; (7) each party's debts and liabilities, and the basis for, and property securing, such debts and liabilities; (8) liquid or nonliquid character of all marital property; (9) tax consequences; and (10) any other relevant factor. (C.V., Sec. 20-107.3.)

Alimony:
In deciding whether alimony is appropriate the judge is to consider the circumstances and factors contributing to the divorce (adultery of the party seeking alimony will generally preclude alimony). Factors in determining nature, amount, and duration: (1) each party's obligations, needs, and financial resources; (2) standard of living during marriage; (3) duration of the marriage; (4) age and physical and mental condition of the parties and any special circumstances of the family; (5) extent to which age, physical and mental condition, or special circumstances of any child of the parties make it appropriate that a party not be employed outside of the home; (6) contributions of each party to the well-being of the family; (7) property interests of each party; (8) provisions for division of marital property; (9) each party's earning capacity, skills, education, training, and present employment opportunities; (10) opportunity for, ability of, and time and costs involved for a party to acquire education, training, etc., to enhance earning capacity; (11) the decisions made by the parties regarding employment, career, economics, education, and parenting arrangements, and their effect on present and future earning potential; (12) one party's contribution to the education, training, or career of the other; (13) tax consequences; and (14) any other factor "necessary to consider the equities between the parties." (C.V., Sec. 20-107.1.)

WASHINGTON

THE LAW

In General:

West's Revised Code of Washington Annotated, Title 26, Chapter 26.16, Section 26.16.120 (R.C.W.A., Sec. 26.16.120). If using website, scroll down to list of titles.

UPAA:

No.

Probate:

None.

Divorce:

R.C.W.A., Sec. 26.16.120), which provides: "Nothing contained in any of the provisions of this chapter or in any law of this state, shall prevent the husband and wife from jointly entering into any agreement concerning the status or disposition of the whole or any portion of the community property, then owned by them or afterwards to be acquired, to take effect upon the death of either. But such agreement may be made at any time by the husband and wife by the execution of an instrument in writing under their hands and seals, and to be witnessed, acknowledged and certified in the same manner as deeds to real estate are required to be, under the laws of the state, and the same may at any time thereafter be altered or amended in the same manner. Such agreement shall not derogate from the right of creditors, nor be construed to curtail the powers of the superior court to set aside or cancel such agreement for fraud or under some other recognized head of equity jurisdiction, at the suit of either party."

PROBATE LAWS

In General:

R.C.W.A., Sec. 11.02.001.

Elective Share:

No specific provision for elective share, but surviving spouse gets $1/2$ of the community property estate.

Intestate Share:

All of the community property estate, and $1/2$ of the separate property if there are children, $3/4$ if no children but there are parents or siblings, all if no children, parents or siblings. (R.C.W.A., Sec. 11.04.015.)

DIVORCE LAWS

Title:

Dissolution of Marriage.

Property:

Community property. Separate property is property acquired before marriage, or by gift or inheritance, and any income or increase in value of such property. (R.C.W.A., Secs. 26.16.010 and 26.16.020.) Factors in dividing marital property: (1) nature and extent of community property; (2) nature and extent of separate property; (3) duration of marriage; (4) each party's economic circumstances, including whether the custodial party should remain in the marital home; and (5) any other relevant factor. Sec. 26.09.080.

Alimony:

Fault not considered. Factors: (1) financial resources of the party seeking alimony; (2) time needed to acquire education and training to find employment suitable to the party's skills, interests, life style, and other circumstances of the party seeking alimony; (3) standard of living established during the marriage; (4) duration of marriage; (5) age, and physical and emotional condition, and the financial obligations of the party seeking alimony; and (6) the ability of the other party to meet his or her own needs while paying alimony. (R.C.W.A., Sec. 26.09.090.)

WEST VIRGINIA

THE LAW

In General:
West Virginia Code, Chapter 48, Article 2, Section 48-2-1(3) [W.V.C., Sec. 48-2-1(3)].

UPAA:
No.

Misc:
W.V.C., Sec. 48-2-1(3)].

Probate:
W.V.C., Sec. 42-3-3a. Waiver of elective share.

Divorce:
None.

PROBATE LAWS

In General:
W.V.C., Sec. 41-1-1 to 4-8-10.

Elective Share:
3% to 50%, depending upon the length of the marriage (must read statute for details). (W.V.C., Sec. 42-3-1.)

Intestate Share:
$1/2$ to all. (W.V.C., Sec. 42-1-3.)

DIVORCE LAWS

Title:
Divorce.

Property:
Equitable distribution. Separate property is property: (1) acquired before marriage; (2) acquired in exchange for such property; (3) designated separate by a written agreement; (4) acquired by gift or inheritance; (5) acquired after separation of the parties; and (6) increases in value of separate property not due to the efforts of the parties. Fault is not considered. Marital property to be divided equally, but this may be altered upon consideration of: (1) extent each party contributed to acquisition, preservation and maintenance, or increase in value of marital property; (2) extent each party expended efforts during the marriage which limited or decreased that party's income earning ability, or increased the other party's income earning ability; (3) conduct of either party which dissipated or depreciated value of marital property. (W.V.C., Sec. 48-2-32.)

Alimony:
Fault is a factor. Alimony is barred if party requesting (1) was adulterous, (2) was convicted of a felony during the marriage, or (3) deserted or abandoned spouse for six months. Factors: (1) length of the marriage; (2) period of time the parties actually lived together as husband and wife; (3) present employment and other recurring earnings; (4) each party's income-earning abilities; (5) property division; (6) ages, and physical, mental, and emotional condition of the parties; (7) each party's educational qualifications; (8) whether either party has forgone or postponed economic, education, or employment opportunities during the marriage; (9) standard of living during the marriage; (10) the likelihood that the party seeking alimony can substantially increase earning ability within a reasonable time by acquiring education or training; (11) any financial or other contribution made by one party to the education, training, vocational skills, career, or earning capacity of the other; (12) the anticipated expense of obtaining education and training; (13) costs of educating minor children; (14) costs of providing health care for each of the parties and any minor children; (15) tax consequences; (16) extent to which it would be inappropriate for custodial parent to seek

employment outside of the home; (17) financial needs of each party; (18) the legal obligations of each party to support any other person; (19) costs and care associated with a minor or adult child's physical or mental disabilities; and (20) any other factor the court deems appropriate. (W.V.C., Sec. 48-2-16.)

WISCONSIN

THE LAW

In General:

West's Wisconsin Statutes Annotated, Section 851.002 (W.S.A., Sec. 851.002). Ignore "Chapter" numbers. There are no references to premarital agreements in the Wisconsin Statutes.

UPAA:

None.

Probate:

None.

Divorce:

None.

PROBATE LAWS

In General:

W.S.A., Sec. 851.002.

Elective Share:

$1/2$, but be sure to read statute. W.S.A., Sec. 861.03. For elective share, homestead and other rights, see the chapter on "Family Rights," beginning at W.S.A. Sec. 861.01. There are also special provisions for the surviving spouse retaining the marital home. (W.S.A., Secs. 852.09 and 861.21.)

Intestate Share:

$1/2$ to all. (W.S.A., Sec. 852.01.)

DIVORCE LAWS

Title:

Divorce.

Property:

Community property. Separate property is property acquired: (1) before marriage; (2) by gift or inheritance; or (3) with funds obtained before marriage or by gift or inheritance. (However, these types of property may even be divided to prevent hardship to a party). Fault is not considered. Marital property divided considering: (1) length of marriage; (2) property brought to marriage by each; (3) whether one party has substantial assets not subject to division by the court; (4) contribution of each party to marriage; (5) age, physical and emotional health of each; (6) contribution of one party to the other's education, training or increased earning power; (7) earning capacity of each, custodial responsibilities, and time and expense needed to acquire education or training to become self-supporting at a standard of living reasonably comparable to that during marriage; (8) desirability of custodial party remaining in marital home; (9) amount and duration of alimony or family support, and whether property division is in lieu of such payments; (10) other economic circumstances of the parties; (11) tax consequences; (12) any written agreements; and (13) any other relevant factor. (W.S.A., Secs. 766.01 & 767.255.)

Alimony:

Called *maintenance*. Fault is not considered. Either party may be granted alimony after considering: (1) length of marriage; (2) age, physical and emotional health of the parties; (3) property division; (4) each party's educational level at the time of marriage and now; (5) earning capacity of party seeking alimony, including custodial responsibilities, and time and expense needed to acquire education or training to find appropriate employment; (6) feasibility that party seeking alimony can become self-supporting at a standard of living similar to that during marriage, and length of time needed; (7) tax consequences; (8) any agreement of the parties; (9) either party's contribution to the other's education, training, or increased earning capacity; and (10) any other relevant factor. (W.S.A., Secs. 767.26.)

WYOMING

THE LAW

In General:
Wyoming Statutes Annotated, Title 1, Chapter 23, Section 1-23-105 (W.S.A., Sec. 1-23-105).

UPAA:
No.

Misc:
W.S.A., Sec. 1-23-105 which provides that a contract in consideration of marriage must be in writing.

Probate:
W.S.A., Sec. 2-5-102. Standard UPC-type waiver provision.

Divorce:
None.

PROBATE LAWS

In General:
W.S.A., Sec. 2-1-101.

Elective Share:
$1/4$ to $1/2$. W.S.A., Sec. 2-5-101. Also entitled to homestead up to $30,000; and, if any children, to "reasonable provision" for support. (W.S.A., Secs. 2-7-501 through 2-7-509.)

Intestate Share:
$1/2$ to all. (W.S.A., Sec. 2-4-101.)

DIVORCE LAWS

Title:
Divorce.

Property:
Equitable distribution. All property is divided, regardless of how and when acquired, although this is a factor. Fault is a factor. Factors: (1) respective merits of the parties; (2) condition each party will be left in after divorce; (3) the party through whom the property was acquired; and (4) the burdens imposed on the property for the benefit of either party or their children. (W.S.A., Sec. 20-2-114.)

Alimony:
Either party may be awarded "…reasonable alimony out of the estate of the other having regard for the others ability to pay." No other statutory factors. Fault is not considered. (W.S.A., Sec. 20-2-114.)

Appendix B:
Uniform Premarital Agreement Act

This appendix contains the basic text of the *Uniform Premarital Agreement Act*. This law has been adopted by a number of states. Check the listing for your state in Appendix A to see if your state has adopted the *Uniform Premarital Agreement Act*. If so, you might find it helpful to read the law as it is written. Although this appendix contains the text of the basic Act, it may have been modified by your state. It is advisable for you to look up the Act as it has been adopted by your state. See the listing for your state in Appendix A and the information on "Legal Research" in Chapter 4 to help find the law specific to your state.

Uniform Premarital Agreement Act
Section 1. DEFINITIONS
As used in this Act:
(1) "Premarital Agreement" means an agreement between prospective spouses made in contemplation of marriage and to be effective upon marriage.
(2) "Property" means an interest, present or future, legal or equitable, vested or contingent, in real or personal property, including income and earnings.
Section 2. FORMALITIES
A premarital agreement must be in writing and signed by both spouses. It is enforceable without consideration.
Section 3. CONTENT
(a) Parties to a premarital agreement may contract with respect to:
(1) the rights and obligations of each of the parties in any of the property of either or both of them whenever and wherever acquired or located;
(2) the right to buy, sell, use, transfer, exchange, abandon, lease, consume, expend, assign, create a security interest in, mortgage, encumber, dispose of, or otherwise manage and control property;
(3) the disposition of property upon separation, marital dissolution, death, or the occurrence or nonoccurrence of

any other event;
(4) the modification or elimination of spousal support;
(5) the making of a will, trust, or other arrangement to carry out the provisions of the agreement;
(6) the ownership of rights in and disposition of the death benefit from a life insurance policy;
(7) the choice of law governing the construction of the agreement; and
(8) any other matter, including their personal rights and obligations, not in violation of public policy or a statute imposing a criminal penalty.
(b) The right of a child to support may not be adversely affected by a premarital agreement.
Section 4. EFFECT OF MARRIAGE
A premarital agreement becomes effective upon marriage.
Section 5. AMENDMENT, REVOCATION
After marriage, a premarital agreement may be amended or revoked only by a written agreement signed by the parties. The amended agreement or the revocation is enforceable without consideration.
Section 6. ENFORCEMENT
(a) A premarital agreement is not enforceable if the party against whom enforcement is sought proves that:
(1) that party did not execute the agreement voluntarily; or
(2) the agreement was unconscionable when it was exe-

cuted and, before execution of the agreement, that party:

(i) was not provided a fair and reasonable disclosure of the property or financial obligations of the other party;

(ii) did not voluntarily and expressly waive, in writing, any right to disclosure of the property or financial obligations of the other party beyond the disclosure provided; and

(iii) did not have, or reasonably could not have had, an adequate knowledge of the property or financial obligations of the other party.

(b) If a provision of a premarital agreement modifies or eliminates spousal support and that modification or elimination causes one party to the agreement to be eligible for support under a program of public assistance at the time of separation or marital dissolution, a court, notwithstanding the terms of the agreement, may require the other party to provide support to the extent necessary to avoid that eligibility.

(c) An issue of unconscionability of a premarital agreement shall be decided by the court as a matter of law.

Section 7. ENFORCEMENT: VOID MARRIAGE

If a marriage is determined to be void, an agreement that would otherwise have been a premarital agreement is enforceable to the extent necessary to avoid an inequitable result.

Section 8. LIMITATION OF ACTIONS

Any statute of limitations applicable to an action asserting a claim for relief under a premarital agreement is tolled during the marriage of the parties to the agreement. However, equitable defenses limiting the time for enforcement, including laches and estoppel, are available to either party.

Section 9. APPLICATION AND CONSTRUCTION

This Act shall be applied and construed to effectuate its general purpose to make uniform the law with respect to the subject of this Act among states enacting it.

Section 10. SHORT TITLE

This Act may be cited as the Uniform Premarital Agreement Act.

Section 11. SEVERABILITY

If any provision of this Act or its application to any person or circumstance is held invalid, the invalidity does not affect other provisions or applications of this Act which can be given effect without the invalid provision or application, and to this end the provisions of this Act are severable.

Section 12. TIME OF TAKING EFFECT

This Act takes effect _____ and applies to any premarital agreement executed on or after that date.

Appendix C:
Blank Forms

This appendix contains sample forms for your use in preparing your own prenuptial agreement. You will not need all of these forms, but will need to choose the forms best suited to your situation and what you want to accomplish. You may also modify these forms as needed to fit your circumstances.

Form 2 is not necessarily a form to be used as is. This form enables you to choose from alternative provisions and put together a prenuptial agreement suited to your specific situation. You can also use it as is by placing an "X" in the appropriate boxes.

The following forms are included in this appendix, and can be found on the pages listed.

PRENUPTIAL AGREEMENT

This Agreement is entered into on _____, _____, by and between
_____ (hereafter referred to as the Husband), and
_____ (hereafter referred to as the Wife), who agree that:

1. MARRIAGE. The parties plan to marry each other, and intend to provide in this agreement for their property and other rights that may arise because of their contemplated marriage.

2. PURPOSE OF AGREEMENT. Both parties currently own assets, and anticipate acquiring additional assets, which they wish to continue to control and they are executing this Agreement to fix and determine their respective rights and duties during the marriage, in the event of a divorce or dissolution of the marriage, or on the death of one of the parties.

3. FINANCIAL DISCLOSURE. The parties have fully revealed to each other full financial information regarding their net worth, assets, holdings, income, and liabilities; not only by their discussions with each other, but also through copies of their current financial statements, copies of which are attached hereto as Exhibits A and Exhibit B. Both parties acknowledge that they have had sufficient time to review the other's financial statement, are familiar with and understand the other's financial statement, have had any questions satisfactorily answered, and are satisfied that full and complete financial disclosure has been made by the other.

4. ADVICE OF COUNSEL. Each party has had legal and financial advice, or has the opportunity to consult independent legal and financial counsel, prior to executing this agreement. Either party's failure to so consult legal and financial counsel constitutes a waiver of such right. By signing this agreement, each party acknowledges that he or she understands the facts of this agreement, and is aware of his or her legal rights and obligations under this agreement or arising because of their contemplated marriage.

5. CONSIDERATION. The parties acknowledge that each of them would not enter into the contemplated marriage except for the execution of this agreement in its present form.

6. EFFECTIVE DATE. This Agreement shall become effective and binding upon the marriage of the parties. In the event the marriage does not take place, this agreement shall be null and void.

7. DEFINITIONS. As used in this agreement, the following terms shall have the following meanings:
    (a) "Joint Property" means property held and owned by the parties together. Such ownership shall be as tenants by the entirety in jurisdictions where such a tenancy is permitted. If such jurisdiction does not recognize or permit a tenancy by the entirety, then ownership shall be as joint tenants with rights of survivorship. The intention of the parties is to hold joint property as tenants by the entirety whenever possible.
    (b) "Joint Tenancy" means tenancy by the entirety in jurisdictions where such a tenancy is permitted, and joint tenancy with rights of survivorship if tenancy by the entirety is not recognized or permitted. The intention of the parties is to hold joint property as tenants by the entirety whenever possible.

8. HUSBAND'S SEPARATE PROPERTY. The Husband is the owner of certain property, which is set forth and described in Exhibit C attached hereto and made a part hereof, which he intends to keep as his nonmarital, separate, sole, and individual property. All income, rents, profits, interest, dividends, stock splits, gains, and appreciation in value relating to any such separate property shall also be deemed separate property.

9. **WIFE'S SEPARATE PROPERTY.** The Wife is the owner of certain property, which is set forth and described in Exhibit D attached hereto and made a part hereof, which she intends to keep as her nonmarital, separate, sole, and individual property. All income, rents, profits, interest, dividends, stock splits, gains, and appreciation in value relating to any such separate property shall also be deemed separate property.

10. **JOINT OR COMMUNITY PROPERTY.** The parties intend that certain property shall, from the beginning of the marriage, be marital, joint, or community property, which is set forth and described in Exhibit E attached hereto and made a part hereof.

11. **PROPERTY ACQUIRED DURING MARRIAGE.** The parties recognize that either or both of them may acquire property during the marriage. The parties agree that the manner in which such property is titled during the marriage shall control such property's ownership and distribution in the event of any divorce, dissolution of marriage, separation, or death of either party. Such property shall be held as provided in the instrument conveying or evidencing title to such property. If the instrument does not specify or if there is no instrument, the property shall be held as a tenancy by the entirety, or as a joint tenancy with rights of survivorship in the event tenancy by the entirety is not recognized by the court having jurisdiction over the distribution of such property. Any property acquired that does not normally have a title or ownership certificate shall be considered as joint property unless otherwise specified by the parties in writing. All wedding gifts shall be deemed joint property, unless specified as separate property in either Exhibit C or D.

12. **BANK ACCOUNTS.** Any funds deposited in either party's separate bank accounts shall be deemed that party's separate property. Any funds deposited in a bank account held by the parties jointly shall be deemed joint property.

13. **PAYMENT OF EXPENSES.** The parties agree that their expenses shall be paid as set forth in Exhibit F attached hereto and made a part hereof.

14. **DISPOSITION OF PROPERTY.** Each party retains the management and control of the property belonging to that party and may encumber, sell, or dispose of the property without the consent of the other party. Each party shall execute any instrument necessary to effectuate this paragraph on the request of the other party. If a party does not join in or execute an instrument required by this paragraph, the other party may sue for specific performance or for damages, regardless of the doctrine of spousal immunity, and the defaulting party shall be responsible for the other party's costs, expenses and attorney's fees. This paragraph shall not require a party to execute a promissory note or other evidence of debt for the other party. If a party executes a promissory note or other evidence of debt for the other party, that other party shall indemnify the party executing the note or other evidence of debt from any claims or demands arising from the execution of the instrument. Execution of an instrument shall not give the executing party any right or interest in the property or the party requesting execution.

15. **PROPERTY DIVISION UPON DIVORCE, DISSOLUTION OF MARRIAGE, OR SEPARATION.** In the event of divorce, dissolution of marriage, or separation proceedings being filed and pursued by either party, the parties agree that the terms and provisions of this agreement shall govern all of their rights as to property, alimony including permanent periodic, rehabilitative, and lump sum, property settlement, rights of community property, and equitable distribution against the other. Each party releases and waives any claims for special equity in the other party's separate property or in jointly owned property. If either party files for divorce, dissolution, alimony, or spousal support unconnected with divorce, separation, or separate maintenance, the parties agree that either shall, in the filing of said proceedings, ask the court to follow the provisions and terms of this premarital agreement and be bound by the terms of this agreement.

16. **ALIMONY.** In the event of divorce or dissolution of marriage proceedings being filed by either party in any

state or country, each party forever waives any right to claim or seek any form of alimony or spousal support, attorney's fees and costs from the other. Any rights concerning distribution of property are otherwise covered by this agreement, and any rights to community property or claims of special equity are waived and released. In the event that a final judgment or decree of divorce or dissolution of marriage is entered for whatever reason, the parties agree that the provisions of this agreement are in complete settlement of all rights to claim or seek any form of financial support, except child support for any living minor children of the parties, from the other.

17. **DISPOSITION UPON DEATH.** Each party consents that his or her estate, or the estate of the other, may be disposed of by will, codicil, or trust, or in the absence of any such instrument, according to the laws of descent and distribution and intestate succession as if the marriage of the parties had not taken place. In either event, the estate shall be free of any claim or demand of inheritance, dower, curtesy, elective share, family allowance, homestead election, right to serve as executor, administrator, or personal representative, or any spousal or other claim given by law, irrespective of the marriage and any law to the contrary. Neither party intends by this agreement to limit or restrict the right to give to, or receive from, the other an inter vivos or testamentary gift. Neither party intends by this agreement to release, waive, or relinquish any devise or bequest left to either by specific provision in the will or codicil of the other, any property voluntarily transferred by the other, any joint tenancy created by the other, or any right to serve as executor or personal representative of the other's estate if specifically nominated in the other's will or codicil.

18. **DEBTS.** Neither party shall assume or become responsible for the payment of any pre-existing debts or obligations of the other party because of the marriage. Neither party shall do anything that would cause the debt or obligation of one of them to be a claim, demand, lien, or encumbrance against the property of the other party without the other party's written consent. If a debt or obligation of one party is asserted as a claim or demand against the property of the other without such written consent, the party who is responsible for the debt or obligation shall indemnify the other from the claim or demand, including the indemnified party's costs, expenses, and attorney's fees.

19. **HOMESTEAD.** Each party releases any claim, demand, right, or interest that the party may acquire because of the marriage in any real property of the other because of the homestead property provisions of the laws of any state concerning the descent of the property as homestead.

20. **FREE AND VOLUNTARY ACT.** The parties acknowledge that executing this agreement is a free and voluntary act, and has not been entered into for any reason other than the desire for the furtherance of their relationship in marriage. Each party acknowledges that he or she has had adequate time to fully consider the consequences of signing this agreement, and has not been pressured, threatened, coerced, or unduly influenced to sign this agreement.

21. **GOVERNING LAW.** This agreement shall be governed by the laws of _____ _____.

22. **SEVERABILITY.** If any part of this agreement is adjudged invalid, illegal, or unenforceable, the remaining parts shall not be affected.

23. **FURTHER ASSURANCE.** Each party shall execute any instruments or documents at any time requested by the other party that are necessary or proper to effectuate this agreement.

24. **NO OTHER BENEFICIARY.** No person shall have a right or cause of action arising or resulting from this agreement except those who are parties to it and their successors in interest.

25. **RELEASE.** Except as otherwise provided in this agreement, each party releases all claims or demands to the property or estate of the other, however and whenever acquired, including acquisitions in the future.

26.   ENTIRE AGREEMENT. This instrument, including any attached exhibits, constitutes the entire agreement of the parties. No representations or promises have been made except those that are set out in this agreement. This agreement may not be modified or terminated except in writing signed by the parties.

27.   PARAGRAPH HEADINGS. The headings of the paragraphs contained in this agreement are for convenience only, and are not to be considered a part of this agreement or used in determining its content or context.

28.   ATTORNEYS' FEES IN ENFORCEMENT. A party who fails to comply with any provision or obligation contained in this agreement shall pay the other party's attorney's fees, costs, and other expenses reasonably incurred in enforcing this agreement and resulting from the noncompliance.

29.   SIGNATURES AND INITIALS OF PARTIES. The signatures of the parties on this document, and their initials on each page, indicate that each party has read, and agrees with, this entire Premarital Agreement, including any and all exhibits attached hereto. Any provision containing a box, ❑ , that does not contain an "X" does not apply and is not a part of the agreement of the parties.

30.   ❑ OTHER PROVISIONS. Additional provisions are contained in the Addendum to Premarital Agreement attached hereto and made a part hereof.

_____   _____
Husband   Wife

Executed in the presence of:

_____   _____
Name: _____   Name: _____
Address: _____   Address: _____
_____   _____

STATE OF   )
COUNTY OF   )

        The foregoing Prenuptial Agreement, consisting of _____ pages and Exhibits _____ through _____ was acknowledged before me this _____ day of _____, _____, b; _____, the above-named Husband, Wife, and Witnesses respectively, who are personally known to me or who have produce _____ _____as identification

_____
Signature

_____
(Typed Name of Acknowledger)
NOTARY PUBLIC
Commission Number:_____
My Commission Expires:

PRENUPTIAL AGREEMENT

This Agreement is entered into on _____ , _____ , by and between
_____ (hereafter referred to as the Husband), and
_____ (hereafter referred to as the Wife), who agree that:

1.   **MARRIAGE.** The parties plan to marry each other, and intend to provide in this agreement for their property and other rights that may arise because of their contemplated marriage.

2.   **PURPOSE OF AGREEMENT.**

    ❏ (A) Both parties currently own assets, and anticipate acquiring additional assets, which they wish to continue to control, and are executing this Agreement to establish and determine their respective rights and responsibilities during the marriage, in the event of a divorce or dissolution of the marriage, or the death of one of the parties.

    ❏ (B) The parties desire that each party having any child(ren) of a prior marriage be able to identify and maintain a separate estate so as to provide for such child(ren), and each party has the following children of a prior marriage:

        ❏ Husband: _____ .

        ❏ Wife: _____ .

3.   **FINANCIAL DISCLOSURE.**

    ❏ (A) The parties have fully disclosed to each other complete financial information regarding their net worth, assets, holdings, income, and liabilities; both by their discussions with each other, and through their current financial statements, copies of which are attached hereto as Exhibit A and Exhibit B. Both parties acknowledge that they have had sufficient time to review the other's financial statement, are familiar with and understand the other's financial statement, have had any questions satisfactorily answered, and are satisfied that full and complete financial disclosure has been made by the other.

    ❏ (B) The ❏ Husband ❏ Wife acknowledges that he/she is fully acquainted with the business and resources of the other party; that the other party is a person of substantial wealth; that the other party has answered all questions asked about his/her income and assets; that he/she understands that by entering into this agreement he/she may receive less than he/she would otherwise be entitled to under law in the event of divorce, dissolution of marriage, separation, or death of the other party; that he/she has carefully weighed all facts and circumstances; and that he/she desires to marry the other party regardless of any financial arrangements made for his/her benefit.

4.   **ADVICE OF COUNSEL.**

    ❏ (A) Each party has had advice of independent counsel prior to executing this agreement.
    The Husband received such counsel from _____ .
    The Wife received such counsel from_____ .
    As a result of such independent counsel, both parties acknowledge that they have been informed of their legal rights in the property currently owned by each of them, rights in any property which may be acquired

by either or both of them during their marriage, rights to claim interests in such property, rights to seek alimony upon divorce or dissolution of marriage, rights of inheritance and support as a surviving spouse, rights to take a certain share of the other's estate in the event the other's will makes unacceptable provisions for him or her, and has been informed of the consequences of any waivers, releases, and surrenders of such rights pursuant this agreement.

❑ (B) Each party has had sufficient opportunity to seek advice of independent counsel prior to executing this agreement.

The ❑ Husband ❑ Wife has received the advice of independent counsel from _____ _____, prior to executing this agreement.

The ❑ Husband ❑ Wife has not sought the advice of independent counsel, despite urging by the other party to do so, and despite being given sufficient time in which to seek such advice. Such party's failure to consult independent counsel constitutes a waiver of such right. By signing this agreement, each party acknowledges that he or she understands the terms of this agreement, is aware of his or her legal rights and obligations under this agreement or arising because of their contemplated marriage, and understands the consequences of his or her waivers, releases and surrenders of such rights pursuant to this agreement.

❑ (C) Each party has had legal and financial advice, or has had the opportunity to consult independent legal and financial counsel, prior to executing this agreement. Either party's failure to consult legal and financial counsel constitutes a waiver of such right. By signing this agreement, each party acknowledges that he or she understands the terms of this agreement, is aware of his or her legal rights and obligations under this agreement or arising because of their contemplated marriage, and understands the consequences of his or her waivers, releases and surrenders of such rights under this agreement.

5. CONSIDERATION. The parties acknowledge that each of them would not enter into the contemplated marriage except for the execution of this agreement.

6. EFFECTIVE DATE. This Agreement shall become effective and binding upon the marriage of the parties. In the event the marriage does not take place, this agreement shall be null and void.

7. DEFINITIONS. As used in this agreement, the following terms shall have the following meanings:
(a) "Joint Property" means property held and owned by the parties together. Such ownership shall be as tenants by the entirety in jurisdictions where such a tenancy is permitted. If such jurisdiction does not recognize or permit a tenancy by the entirety, then ownership shall be as joint tenants with rights of survivorship. The intention of the parties is to hold joint property as tenants by the entirety whenever possible. "Joint property" also means community property as to any property which may be subject to community property laws.
(b) "Joint Tenancy" means tenancy by the entirety in jurisdictions where such a tenancy is permitted, and joint tenancy with rights of survivorship if tenancy by the entirety is not recognized or permitted. The intention of the parties is to hold joint property as tenants by the entirety whenever possible." Joint property" also refers to community property as to any property which may be subject to community property laws.
(c) "Separate Property" means property owned by either party which is and will remain, or may be acquired, as that party's individual property, free from any claims of the other party. "Separate property" is not part of the community property estate in any state recognizing community property.

8. HUSBAND'S SEPARATE PROPERTY. The Husband is the owner of certain property, which is set forth and described in Exhibit C attached hereto and made a part hereof, which he intends to keep as his nonmarital, separate, sole, and individual property. All income, rents, profits, interest, dividends, stock splits, gains, and appreciation in value relating to any such separate property shall also be deemed separate property. All inheritances or gifts received by the Husband individually during the marriage shall also be deemed separate property.

9. WIFE'S SEPARATE PROPERTY. The Wife is the owner of certain property, which is set forth and described in Exhibit D attached hereto and made a part hereof, which she intends to keep as her nonmarital, separate, sole, and individual property. All income, rents, profits, interest, dividends, stock splits, gains, and appreciation in value relating to any such separate property shall also be deemed separate property. All inheritances or gifts received by the Wife individually during the marriage shall also be deemed separate property.

10. JOINT OR COMMUNITY PROPERTY. The parties intend that certain property shall, from the beginning of the marriage, be joint, as set forth and described in Exhibit E attached hereto and made a part hereof.

11. PROPERTY ACQUIRED DURING MARRIAGE. The parties recognize that either or both of them may acquire property during the marriage. The parties agree that the manner in which such property is titled during the marriage shall control such property's ownership and distribution in the event of divorce, dissolution of marriage, separation, or death of either party. Such property shall be held as stated in the instrument conveying or evidencing title. If the instrument does not specify or if there is no instrument, the property shall be held as a tenancy by the entirety, or as a joint tenancy with rights of survivorship in the event tenancy by the entirety is not recognized by the state having jurisdiction over the distribution of such property. Any property acquired that does not normally have a title or ownership certificate shall be considered as joint property unless otherwise specified by the parties in writing. All Wedding gifts shall be deemed joint property, unless specified as separate property in either Exhibit C or D, or otherwise so specified in writing by the parties.

12. BANK ACCOUNTS. Any funds deposited in either party's separate bank accounts shall be deemed that party's separate property. Any funds deposited in a bank account held by the parties jointly shall be deemed joint property.

13. PAYMENT OF EXPENSES. The parties agree that their expenses shall be paid as set forth in Exhibit F attached hereto and made a part hereof.

14. INCOME FROM AND REINVESTMENT OF SEPARATE PROPERTY.

❏ (A) Any property obtained by either party due to the use, investment, reinvestment or any transfer of any portion of his or her separate property, and any income from any such property, and any appreciation in the value of such property, shall remain that party's separate property.

❏ (B) Any property obtained by either party due to the use, investment, reinvestment or any transfer of any portion of his or her separate property, and any income from any such property, shall remain that party's separate property. Any appreciation or other increase in the value of either party's separate property, shall remain that party's separate property, unless the other party has made a direct financial contribution to the increase in value, such as by investing his or her own funds, and then only to the proportion of the increase attributable to his or her investment.

15. RESIDENCE OF THE PARTIES.

❏ (A) It is expressly recognized that the Husband and Wife are joint owners of the residence to be occupied by the parties at _____.

❏ (B) It is expressly recognized that the ❏ Husband ❏ Wife is the sole owner of the residence to be occupied by the parties at _____, and that the use of any joint funds, or separate funds of the other party, for the mortgage payments, utilities, capital improvements, repair or maintenance of the residence and grounds for the joint benefit of the parties shall not create any interest in the property in the other party.

❏ (C) It is expressly recognized that the ❏ Husband ❏ Wife is the sole owner of the residence to be occupied by the parties at _____, and that the use of any joint funds, or separate funds of the other party, for the mortgage payments, utilities, repair or maintenance of the residence and grounds for the joint benefit of the parties shall not create any interest in the property in the other party. However, if joint funds or the other party's separate funds are used to make capital improvements on the property, the other party shall thereafter have a lien against the property to the extent of one-half of the total joint funds, or the full amount of the separate funds, contributed, which lien shall be paid upon the sale of the property, the termination of the marriage, or the death of the Husband or Wife, whichever occurs first.

16. DISPOSITION OF PROPERTY.

Each party retains the ownership, management, and control of his or her separate property, and may encumber, sell, or dispose of the property without the other party's consent. Each party shall, on the request of the other, execute any instrument necessary to effectuate this paragraph. The failure or refusal of a party to join in or execute an instrument required by this paragraph shall entitle the other party to sue for specific performance or for damages, regardless of the doctrine of spousal immunity, and the defaulting party shall pay the other party's costs, expenses, and attorney's fees. This paragraph shall not require a party to execute a promissory note or other evidence of debt for the other party; but if a party executes a promissory note or other evidence of debt for the other party, that other party shall indemnify the party executing the note or other evidence of debt from any claims or demands arising from the execution of the instrument. Execution of an instrument shall not give the executing party any right or interest in the property of the party requesting execution.

17. PROPERTY DIVISION UPON DIVORCE, DISSOLUTION OF MARRIAGE, OR SEPARATION.

In the event of divorce, dissolution of marriage, or separation proceedings being filed and pursued by either party, the parties agree that the terms and provisions of this agreement shall govern all of their rights as to property; alimony including permanent periodic, rehabilitative, and lump sum; property settlement; rights of community property; and, equitable distribution against the other. Each party releases and waives any claims for special equity in the other party's separate property or in jointly owned property. If either party files for alimony, or spousal support unconnected with divorce, dissolution of marriage, separation, or separate maintenance, the parties agree that the party filing said proceedings shall ask the court to follow the provisions and terms of this premarital agreement.

18. ALIMONY.

❏ (A) In the event of divorce or dissolution of marriage proceedings being filed by either party in any state or country, each party forever waives any right to claim or seek any form of alimony or spousal support, and attorneys' fees and costs from the other. Any rights regarding distribution of property are otherwise covered by this agreement, and any rights to community property or claims of special equity are waived and released. In the event that a final judgment or decree of divorce or dissolution of marriage is entered, the parties agree that the provisions of this agreement are in complete settlement of all rights to claim or seek any form of financial support, except child support for any living minor children of the parties, from the other.

❑ (B) In the event divorce, dissolution of marriage, separation, or similar proceedings are filed by either party in any state or country, the parties agree that neither party will request or receive alimony or support, whether temporary, rehabilitative, permanent, or lump sum. In consideration for not requesting alimony, the ❑ Husband   ❑ Wife   shall pay to the other party a sum equal to $_____ for each full year of marriage up to the date a divorce, dissolution of marriage, separation, or similar action is filed. Said sum shall be paid regardless of which party files, and shall terminate on either the death or remarriage of the payee, or on the death of the payor, whichever occurs first.

❑ (C) In the event of divorce or dissolution of marriage proceedings being filed by either party in any state or country, the   ❑ Husband ❑ Wife   agrees to pay to the other party temporary and rehabilitative alimony in the sum of $_____ per _____, for a period of _____ years after the date a divorce, dissolution of marriage, or separation action is filed. Said sum shall be paid regardless of which party files, and shall terminate at the end of the period stated above, or on either the death or remarriage of the payee, or on the death of the payor, whichever occurs first.

❑ (D) In the event of divorce or dissolution of marriage proceedings being filed by either party in any state or country, the   ❑ Husband ❑ Wife   agrees to pay to the other party temporary and permanent periodic alimony in the sum of $_____ per _____. Said sum shall be paid regardless of which party files, and shall terminate on either the death or remarriage of the payee, or on the death of the payor, whichever occurs first.

19.   CHILD SUPPORT.

❑ (A) In the event of divorce, dissolution of marriage, or separation, and if there are any minor children of the parties' marriage, the parties agree that each shall contribute to the support of any such children in the following proportions:

_____% from the Husband.

_____% from the Wife.

❑ (B) The amount of support shall be determined by agreement of the parties. If the parties cannot agree, the amount of support shall be determined by the court.

Such child support shall continue until:
❑   Age 18.
❑   Age 18, or graduation from high school, whichever occurs last, provided any such child is enrolled as a full-time student and is making a good faith effort to graduate.
❑   Graduation from college or trade school, provided any such child is enrolled as a full time student and is making a good faith effort to graduate.

Both parties acknowledge that they are aware that the court has the ultimate authority to determine child support, taking into consideration the needs of the children and any other factors required by law to be considered.

20.   DISPOSITION UPON DEATH.

❑ (A) Each party consents that his or her estate, or the estate of the other, may be disposed of by will, codicil, or trust, or in the absence of any such instrument, according to the laws of descent and distribution and intestate succession as if the marriage of the parties had not taken place. In either event, the estate shall be free of any claim or demand of inheritance, dower, curtesy, elective share, family allowance, homestead election, right to serve as executor, administrator, or personal representative, or any spousal or other claim given by law, irrespective of the marriage and any law to the contrary. Neither party intends by this agreement to limit or restrict the right to give to, or receive from, the other an inter vivos or testamentary gift. Neither party intends by this agreement to release, waive, or relinquish any devise or bequest left to either by specific provision in the will or codicil of the other, any property voluntarily transferred by the other, any joint tenancy created by the other, or any right to serve as executor or personal representative of the other's estate if specifically nominated in the other's will or codicil.

❑ (B) Subject to the conditions set forth in this paragraph, the ❑ Husband ❑ Wife shall receive and accept from the other party after his/her death, the sum of $_____, free of any and all inheritance and estate taxes, in place of, and in full and final settlement and satisfaction of, any and all rights and claims which he/she might otherwise have in the other party's estate and property under any law now or hereafter in force in this or any other jurisdiction, whether by way of a right of election to take against the other party's will, as a share of the estate in intestacy, or otherwise. The ❑ Husband ❑ Wife shall only be entitled to receive said amount if all of the following conditions are met: (1) the parties were married at the time of death, (2) he/she survives the decedent, (3) the parties were not separated at the time of death, and (4) no divorce, dissolution of marriage, or separation proceedings were in progress at the time of death. If any of the above conditions are not met, then he/she shall not be entitled to any sums from the other party's estate.

21. **LIFE INSURANCE.** The parties shall maintain the following life insurance policies payable to the other party on death in the face amounts of at least:

Life insurance on the life of the Husband payable to the Wife or a person she designates of at least $_____.

Life insurance on the life of the Wife payable to the Husband or a person he designates of at least $_____.

22. **DEBTS.** Neither party shall assume or become responsible for the payment of any preexisting debts or obligations of the other party because of the marriage. Neither party shall do anything that would cause the debt or obligation of one of them to become a claim, demand, lien, or encumbrance on the other's property without the other party's written consent. If a debt or obligation of one party is asserted as a claim or demand against the other's separate property without such written consent, the party who is responsible for the debt or obligation shall indemnify the other from the claim or demand, including the payment of the other party's costs, expenses, and attorney's fees.

23. **HOMESTEAD.** Each party releases any claim, demand, right, or interest that the party may acquire because of the marriage in any real property of the other because of the homestead property provisions of the laws of any state concerning the descent of the property as homestead.

24. **COMMINGLING OF INCOME AND ASSETS.** The parties recognize that it is possible for their income or assets to become, or appear to become, commingled. It is the parties' intention that any commingling of income or assets shall not be interpreted to imply any abandonment of the terms and provisions of this agreement, that the provisions contained herein regarding the parties' interests in jointly held property be applied, and that in other instances each party's interest be determined by each party's proportionate contribution toward the total funds or value of assets in question.

25.   TAX RETURNS/GIFTS/LEGAL PROCEEDINGS. The fact that the parties may file joint local, state, or federal income tax returns, or any other joint tax papers or documents, or make gifts of property or cash to each other or not account to each other with regard to the expenditure of income shall not be interpreted to imply any abandonment of the terms and provisions of this agreement. The filing of a divorce, dissolution of marriage, separation, or other legal action or proceeding shall not be deemed as any abandonment of the terms and provisions of this agreement.

26.   FREE AND VOLUNTARY ACT. The parties acknowledge that executing this agreement is a free and voluntary act, and has not been entered into for any reason other than the desire for the furtherance of their relationship in marriage. Each party acknowledges that he or she has had adequate time to fully consider the consequences of signing this agreement, and has not been pressured, threatened, coerced, or unduly influenced to sign this agreement.

27.   GOVERNING LAW. This agreement shall be governed by the laws of _____.

28.   SEVERABILITY. If any part of this agreement is adjudged invalid, illegal, or unenforceable, the remaining parts shall not be affected.

29.   FURTHER ASSURANCE. Each party shall execute any instruments or documents at any time requested by the other party that are necessary or proper to effectuate this agreement.

30.   BINDING AGREEMENT/NO OTHER BENEFICIARY. This agreement shall be binding upon the parties, and upon their heirs, executors, personal representatives, administrators, and assigns. No person shall have a right or cause of action arising or resulting from this agreement except those who are parties to it and their successors in interest.

31.   RELEASE. Except as otherwise provided in this agreement, each party releases all claims or demands to the property or estate of the other, however and whenever acquired, including acquisitions in the future.

32.   ENTIRE AGREEMENT. This instrument, including any attached exhibits, constitutes the entire agreement of the parties. No representations or promises have been made except those that are set out in this agreement. This agreement may not be modified or terminated except in writing signed by the parties.

33.   PARAGRAPH HEADINGS. The headings of the paragraphs contained in this agreement are for convenience only, and are not to be considered a part of this agreement or used in determining its content or context.

34.   ATTORNEYS' FEES IN ENFORCEMENT. A party who fails to comply with any provision or obligation contained in this agreement shall pay the other party's attorney's fees, costs, and other expenses reasonably incurred in enforcing this agreement and resulting from the noncompliance.

35.   SIGNATURES AND INITIALS OF PARTIES. The signatures of the parties on this document, and their initials on each page, indicate that each party has read, and agrees with, this entire Premarital Agreement, including any and all exhibits attached hereto. Any provision containing a box, ❏, that does not contain an "X" does not apply and is not a part of the agreement of the parties.

36.   ❏   OTHER PROVISIONS. Additional provisions are contained in the Addendum to Premarital Agreement attached hereto and made a part hereof.

_____   _____
Husband   Wife

Executed in the presence of:

Name: _____   Name: _____

Name: _____   Name: _____
Address: _____   Address: _____

_____   _____

STATE OF   )
COUNTY OF   )

    The foregoing Prenuptial Agreement, consisting of _____ pages and Exhibits _____ through _____, was acknowledged before me this _____ day of _____, _____, by _____, the above-named Husband, Wife, and Witnesses respectively, who are personally known to me or who have produced _____ _____ as identification.

_____
Signature

_____
(Typed Name of Acknowledger)

NOTARY PUBLIC

Commission Number: _____
My Commission Expires:

HUSBAND'S FINANCIAL STATEMENT

I, _____, hereby certify that the following financial information is true and correct according to the best of my knowledge and belief:

ITEM 1: EMPLOYMENT AND INCOME

OCCUPATION: _____

EMPLOYED BY: _____

ADDRESS: _____

_____

SOC. SEC. #: _____

PAY PERIOD: _____

RATE OF PAY: _____

AVERAGE GROSS MONTHLY INCOME FROM EMPLOYMENT	$_____
Bonuses, commissions, allowances, overtime, tips, and similar payments	_____
Business income from sources such as self-employment, partnerships, close corporations, and/or independent contracts (gross receipts minus ordinary and necessary expenses required to produce income)	_____
Disability benefits	_____
Workers' compensation	_____
Unemployment compensation	_____
Pension, retirement, or annuity payments	_____
Social Security benefits	_____
Spousal support received from previous marriage	_____
Interest and dividends	_____
Rental income (gross receipts minus ordinary and necessary expenses required to produce income)	_____
Income from royalties, trusts, or estates	_____
Other income of a recurring nature:	
_____	_____
_____	_____
_____	_____
TOTAL GROSS MONTHLY INCOME	$_____

LESS DEDUCTIONS:

Federal, state, and local income taxes	$_____	
FICA or self-employment tax (annualized)	_____	
Mandatory union dues	_____	
Mandatory retirement	_____	
Health insurance payments	_____	
Court-ordered child support payments (actually paid)	_____	
Other deductions:		
_____	_____	
_____	_____	
TOTAL DEDUCTIONS		$_____

TOTAL NET MONTHLY INCOME: $_____

EXHIBIT A

ITEM 2: ASSETS

Description	Value
Cash (on hand or in banks)	$_____

Stocks/bonds/notes/annuities/other investments:

_____   _____
_____   _____
_____   _____
_____   _____
_____   _____
_____   _____

Real estate:

_____   _____
_____   _____
_____   _____

Automobiles:

_____   _____
_____   _____
_____   _____

Boats or other vehicles:

_____   _____
_____   _____
_____   _____

Other personal property:

     Clothing and personal items   _____
     Contents of home   _____
     Jewelry   _____
     Collections (art, coins, stamps, etc.)   _____
     Recreation/sports equipment   _____
     Trade tools/equipment   _____
     Life insurance (cash surrender value)   _____

Business ownership/Interest:

_____   _____
_____   _____
_____   _____

Other assets:

_____   _____
_____   _____
_____   _____
_____   _____
_____   _____
_____   _____

TOTAL ASSETS: $_____

ITEM 3: LIABILITIES

Creditor	Security	Balance
_____	_____	$_____
_____	_____	_____
_____	_____	_____
_____	_____	_____
_____	_____	_____
_____	_____	_____
_____	_____	_____
_____	_____	_____
_____	_____	_____
_____	_____	_____
_____	_____	_____
_____	_____	_____
_____	_____	_____
_____	_____	_____
_____	_____	_____
_____	_____	_____
_____	_____	_____
_____	_____	_____
_____	_____	_____
_____	_____	_____

TOTAL LIABILITIES: $_____

The above information is true and accurate to the best of my knowledge, and is based upon information currently available to me. This information is being provided in connection with a Prenuptial Agreement, and this statement shall be attached to said Prenuptial Agreement.

DATED:_____   _____
                                            Signature of Husband

ACKNOWLEDGMENT OF RECEIPT

I, _____, hereby acknowledge receiving a copy of the foregoing Husband's Financial Statement on _____, _____.

DATED:_____   _____
                                            Signature of Wife

This page intentionally left blank.

WIFE'S FINANCIAL STATEMENT

I, _____, hereby certify that the following financial information is true and correct according to the best of my knowledge and belief:

ITEM 1: EMPLOYMENT AND INCOME

OCCUPATION: _____

EMPLOYED BY: _____

ADDRESS: _____

_____

SOC. SEC. #: _____

PAY PERIOD: _____

RATE OF PAY: _____

AVERAGE GROSS MONTHLY INCOME FROM EMPLOYMENT $_____

Bonuses, commissions, allowances, overtime, tips, and similar payments   _____

Business income from sources such as self-employment, partnerships,
         close corporations, and/or independent contracts (gross receipts
         minus ordinary and necessary expenses required to produce income)   _____

Disability benefits   _____

Workers' compensation   _____

Unemployment compensation   _____

Pension, retirement, or annuity payments   _____

Social Security benefits   _____

Spousal support received from previous marriage   _____

Interest and dividends   _____

Rental income (gross receipts minus ordinary and necessary expenses
         required to produce income)   _____

Income from royalties, trusts, or estates   _____

Other income of a recurring nature:

_____   _____

_____   _____

_____   _____

     TOTAL GROSS MONTHLY INCOME $_____

LESS DEDUCTIONS:

Federal, state, and local income taxes $_____

FICA or self-employment tax (annualized)   _____

Mandatory union dues   _____

Mandatory retirement   _____

Health insurance payments   _____

Court-ordered child support payments (actually paid)   _____

Other deductions:

_____   _____

_____   _____

     TOTAL DEDUCTIONS $_____

TOTAL NET MONTHLY INCOME: $_____

EXHIBIT B

ITEM 2: ASSETS

Description	Value
Cash (on hand or in banks)	$_____
Stocks/bonds/notes/annuities/other investments:	
_____	_____
_____	_____
_____	_____
_____	_____
_____	_____
_____	_____
Real estate:	
_____	_____
_____	_____
_____	_____
_____	_____
Automobiles:	
_____	_____
_____	_____
_____	_____
Boats or other vehicles:	
_____	_____
_____	_____
_____	_____
Other personal property:	
Clothing and personal items	_____
Contents of home	_____
Jewelry	_____
Collections (art, coins, stamps, etc.)	_____
Recreation/sports equipment	_____
Trade tools/equipment	_____
Life insurance (cash surrender value)	_____
Business ownership/Interest:	
_____	_____
_____	_____
_____	_____
Other assets:	
_____	_____
_____	_____
_____	_____
_____	_____
_____	_____
_____	_____
TOTAL ASSETS:	$_____

ITEM 3: LIABILITIES

Creditor	Security	Balance
_____	_____	$_____
_____	_____	_____
_____	_____	_____
_____	_____	_____
_____	_____	_____
_____	_____	_____
_____	_____	_____
_____	_____	_____
_____	_____	_____
_____	_____	_____
_____	_____	_____
_____	_____	_____
_____	_____	_____
_____	_____	_____
_____	_____	_____
_____	_____	_____
_____	_____	_____
_____	_____	_____
_____	_____	_____

TOTAL LIABILITIES: $_____

The above information is true and accurate to the best of my knowledge, and is based upon information currently available to me. This information is being provided in connection with a Prenuptial Agreement, and this statement shall be attached to said Prenuptial Agreement.

DATED:_____   _____
                                                Signature of Wife

ACKNOWLEDGMENT OF RECEIPT

I, _____, hereby acknowledge receiving a copy of the foregoing Wife's Financial Statement on _____, _____.

DATED:_____   _____
                                                Signature of Husband

This page intentionally left blank.

HUSBAND'S SCHEDULE OF SEPARATE PROPERTY

This schedule is hereby made a part of the parties' _____
_____ dated _____, _____. The following items of
property shall be the separate property of the Husband:

EXHIBIT C

This page intentionally left blank.

WIFE'S SCHEDULE OF SEPARATE PROPERTY

This schedule is hereby made a part of the parties' _____

_____ dated _____, _____. The following items of

property shall be the separate property of the Wife:

EXHIBIT D

This page intentionally left blank.

SCHEDULE OF JOINT PROPERTY

This schedule is hereby made a part of the parties' _____

_____ dated _____, _____. The following items of

property shall be the joint property of the parties:

EXHIBIT E

This page intentionally left blank.

EXPENSE PAYMENT SCHEDULE

In connection with the parties' _____ dated
_____, _____, the parties agree to the following schedule for the manner in which they shall
pay for their living expenses:

	HUSBAND	**WIFE**
HOUSEHOLD:		
Mortgage or rent payments	_____	_____
Property taxes	_____	_____
Homeowners/renters insurance	_____	_____
Electricity	_____	_____
Water & sewer	_____	_____
Garbage collection	_____	_____
Telephone	_____	_____
Fuel oil or natural gas	_____	_____
Repairs and maintenance	_____	_____
Lawn care	_____	_____
Pool care	_____	_____
Pest control	_____	_____
Food and grocery items	_____	_____
Other:		
_____	_____	_____
_____	_____	_____
_____	_____	_____
AUTOMOBILE:		
Gasoline and oil	_____	
Repairs	_____	_____
Auto tags and license	_____	_____
Insurance	_____	_____
Other:		
_____	_____	_____
_____	_____	_____
INSURANCE:		
Health	_____	
Life	_____	_____
Other:		
_____	_____	_____
_____	_____	_____

EXHIBIT F

	HUSBAND	WIFE

OTHER EXPENSES:

Entertainment	_____	_____
Vacations	_____	_____
Pets (veterinarian & grooming, etc.)	_____	_____
Charities	_____	_____
Religious organizations	_____	_____
Other:		
_____	_____	_____
_____	_____	_____
_____	_____	_____
_____	_____	_____
_____	_____	_____

CHILDREN'S EXPENSES:

Nursery or babysitting	_____	_____
School tuition	_____	_____
School supplies	_____	_____
Lunch money	_____	_____
Allowance	_____	_____
Clothing	_____	_____
Medical, dental, prescriptions	_____	_____
Vitamins	_____	_____
Barber/beauty parlor	_____	_____
Cosmetics/toiletries	_____	_____
Gifts for special holidays	_____	_____
Other:		
_____	_____	_____
_____	_____	_____
_____	_____	_____
_____	_____	_____

Unless otherwise noted above, each party shall be responsible for the payment of the expenses relating to his or her own automobile; children of prior marriages; clothing, personal effects, and grooming expenses; and employment or other career and income-producing expenses.

ADDENDUM TO MARITAL AGREEMENT

The parties agree to the following terms and conditions, which are in addition to those set forth in their
_____ dated _____, _____:

_____   _____
Husband   Wife

Executed in the presence of:

_____   _____
Name: _____   Name: _____
Address:_____   Address:_____
      _____   _____

STATE OF   )
COUNTY OF   )

The foregoing Addendum to Marital Agreement was acknowledged before me this _____ day of
_____, _____, by _____
_____, the above-
named Husband, Wife, and Witnesses respectively, who are personally known to me or who have produced
_____ as identification.

_____
Signature

_____
(Typed Name of Acknowledger)

NOTARY PUBLIC

Commission Number: _____
My Commission Expires:

This page intentionally left blank.

AMENDMENT TO MARITAL AGREEMENT

This Amendment to Marital Agreement is entered into on _____, _____, by and between _____ (hereafter referred to as the "Husband"), and _____ (hereafter referred to as the "Wife"), who agree that they wish to amend their _____ dated _____, _____, as follows:

1. The parties' _____ shall be amended to provide:

2. In all other respects not referred to herein, said _____ is ratified and confirmed, and shall remain in full force and effect.

3. The parties agree and acknowledge that there has been full and complete disclosure in all respects as if this had been an original _____, and that the parties have each had sufficient opportunity to obtain legal and financial advice from independent counsel prior to signing this Amendment to Marital Agreement.

_____

Husband   Wife

Executed in the presence of:

_____   _____
Name: _____   Name: _____
Address:_____   Address: _____
_____   _____

STATE OF   )
COUNTY OF   )

The foregoing Amendment to Marital Agreement was acknowledged before me this _____ day of _____, _____, by _____ _____, the above-named Husband, Wife, and Witnesses respectively, who are personally known to me or who have produced _____ _____ as identification.

_____

Signature

_____

(Typed Name of Acknowledger)

NOTARY PUBLIC

Commission Number:_____
My Commission Expires:

RELEASE OF MARITAL AGREEMENT

This Release of Marital Agreement is entered into on _____, _____, by and between _____ (hereafter referred to as the "Husband"), and _____ (hereafter referred to as the "Wife"), who agree that:

1. The parties hereby release, cancel, terminate, and set aside in its entirety their _____ _____ dated _____, _____, a copy of which is attached hereto.

2. Any prior transfers of property or rights in property of the parties shall not be affected in any manner by this Release of Marital Agreement. However, the parties may act separately and independently of this Release of Marital Agreement to reverse or negate any such prior transfers.

3. Each party agrees and acknowledges that he or she has had sufficient opportunity to obtain legal and financial advice from independent counsel, and to consider the consequences of this agreement, prior to signing this Release of Marital Agreement. Each party further acknowledges and represents that no promises have been made in connection with this Release of Marital Agreement, except (state any promises, or if none, state "None"):

4. The parties agree and acknowledge that there has been full and complete disclosure in all respects as if this had been an original _____.

5. This Release of Marital Agreement states the entire agreement between the parties, and may not be modified except in writing signed by both parties before two witnesses and acknowledged by a notary public.

_____
Husband

_____
Wife

Executed in the presence of:

_____

Name: _____
Address:_____
_____

_____

Name:_____
Address:_____
_____

STATE OF   )
COUNTY OF   )

The foregoing Amendment to Marital Agreement was acknowledged before me this _____ day of __ _____, _____, by _____ ___ _____, the above-named Husband, Wife, and Witnesses respectively, who are personally known to me or who have produced ____ _____ ____ _____ as identification.

_____ _____
Signature

_____ _____
(Typed Name of Acknowledger)

NOTARY PUBLIC

Commission Number _____
My Commission Expires:

POSTNUPTIAL AGREEMENT

This Agreement is entered into on _____, _____, by and between
_____ (hereafter referred to as the Husband), and
_____ (hereafter referred to as the Wife), who agree that:

1. PURPOSE OF AGREEMENT.

❏ (A) Both parties currently own assets, and anticipate acquiring additional assets, which they wish to continue to control, and are executing this agreement to establish and determine their respective rights and responsibilities during the marriage, in the event of a divorce or dissolution of the marriage, or the death of one of the parties.

❏ (B) The parties desire that each party having any child(ren) of a prior marriage be able to identify and maintain a separate estate so as to provide for such child(ren), and each party has the following children of a prior marriage:

Husband: _____.
Wife: _____.

2. FINANCIAL DISCLOSURE.

❏ (A) The parties have fully disclosed to each other complete financial information regarding their net worth, assets, holdings, income, and liabilities; both by their discussions with each other, and through their current financial statements, copies of which are attached hereto as Exhibit A and Exhibit B. Both parties acknowledge that they have had sufficient time to review the other's financial statement, are familiar with and understand the other's financial statement, have had any questions satisfactorily answered, and are satisfied that full and complete financial disclosure has been made by the other.

❏ (B) The ❏ Husband ❏ Wife acknowledges that he/she is fully acquainted with the business and resources of the other party; that the other party is a person of substantial wealth; that the other party has answered all questions asked about his/her income and assets; that he/she understands that by entering into this agreement he/she may receive less than he/she would otherwise be entitled to under law in the event of divorce, dissolution of marriage, separation, or death of the other party; that he/she has carefully weighed all facts and circumstances; and that he/she desires to enter into this agreement regardless of any financial arrangements made for his/her benefit.

3. ADVICE OF COUNSEL.

❏ (A) Each party has had advice of independent counsel prior to executing this agreement.

The Husband received such counsel from _____.

The Wife received such counsel from_____.

As a result of such independent counsel, both parties acknowledge that they have been informed of their legal rights in the property currently owned by each of them, rights in any property which may be acquired by either or both of them during their marriage, rights to claim interests in such property, rights to seek alimony upon divorce or dissolution of marriage, rights of inheritance and support as a surviving spouse, rights to take a certain share of the other's estate in the event the other's will makes unacceptable provisions for him or her, and has been informed of the consequences of any waivers, releases, and surrenders of such rights pursuant this agreement.

❑) Each party has had sufficient opportunity to seek advice of independent counsel prior to executing this agreement.

Th ❑ Husband ❑ Wife has received the advice of independent counsel from _____ _____ _____, prior to executing this agreement.

The ❑ Husband ❑ Wife has not sought the advice of independent counsel, despite urging by the other party to so, and despite being given sufficient time in which to seek such advice. Such party's failure to consult independent counsel constitutes a waiver of such right. By signing this agreement, each party acknowledges that he or she understands the terms of this agreement, is aware of his or her legal rights and obligations under this agreement or arising because of their marriage, and understands the consequences of his or her waivers, releases, and surrenders of such rights pursuant to this agreement.

❑ (C) Each party has had legal and financial advice, or has had the opportunity to consult independent legal and financial counsel, prior to executing this agreement. Either party's failure to consult legal and financial counsel constitutes waiver of such right. By signing this agreement, each party acknowledges that he or she understands the terms of this agreement, is aware of his or her legal rights and obligations under this agreement or arising because of their marriage, and understands the consequences of his or her waivers, releases, and surrenders of such rights under this agreement.

4. EFFECTIVE DATE. This agreement shall become effective and binding upon the execution of this agreement by both of the parties.

5. DEFINITIONS. As used in this agreement, the following terms shall have the following meanings:
   (a) "Joint Property" means property held and owned by the parties together. Such ownership shall be as tenants by the entirety in jurisdictions where such a tenancy is permitted. If such jurisdiction does not recognize or permit a tenancy by the entirety, then ownership shall be as joint tenants with rights of survivorship. The intention of the parties is to hold joint property as tenants by the entirety whenever possible. "Joint property" also means community property as to any property which may be subject to community property laws.
   (b) "Joint Tenancy" means tenancy by the entirety in jurisdictions where such a tenancy is permitted, and joint tenancy with rights of survivorship if tenancy by the entirety is not recognized or permitted. The intention of the parties is to hold joint property as tenants by the entirety whenever possible. "Joint property" also refers to community property as to any property which may be subject to community property laws.
   (c) "Separate Property" means property owned by either party which is and will remain, or may be acquired, as that party's individual property free from any claims of the other party. "Separate property" is not part of the community property estate in any state recognizing community property.

6. HUSBAND'S SEPARATE PROPERTY. The Husband is the owner of certain property, which is set forth and described in Exhibit C attached hereto and made a part hereof, which he intends to keep as his nonmarital, separate, sole, and individual property. All income, rents, profits, interest, dividends, stock splits, gains, and appreciation in value, relating to any such separate property shall also be deemed separate property. All inheritances or gifts received by the Husband individually during the marriage shall also be deemed separate property.

7.   WIFE'S SEPARATE PROPERTY. The Wife is the owner of certain property, which is set forth and described in Exhibit D attached hereto and made a part hereof, which she intends to keep as her nonmarital, separate, sole, and individual property. All income, rents, profits, interest, dividends, stock splits, gains, and appreciation in value, relating to any such separate property shall also be deemed separate property. All inheritances or gifts received by the Wife individually during the marriage shall also be deemed separate property.

8.   JOINT OR COMMUNITY PROPERTY. The parties intend that certain property shall, from the beginning of the marriage, be joint, as set forth and described in Exhibit E attached hereto and made a part hereof.

9.   PROPERTY ACQUIRED DURING MARRIAGE. The parties recognize that either or both of them may acquire property during the marriage. The parties agree that the manner in which such property is titled during the marriage shall control such property's ownership and distribution in the event of divorce, dissolution of marriage, separation, or death of either party. Such property shall be held as stated in the instrument conveying or evidencing title. If the instrument does not specify or if there is no instrument, the property shall be held as a tenancy by the entirety, or as a joint tenancy with rights of survivorship in the event tenancy by the entirety is not recognized by the state having jurisdiction over the distribution of such property. Any property acquired that does not normally have a title or ownership certificate shall be considered as joint property unless otherwise specified by the parties in writing. All wedding gifts shall be deemed joint property, unless specified as separate property in either Exhibit C or D, or otherwise so specified in writing by the parties.

10.   BANK ACCOUNTS. Any funds deposited in either party's separate bank accounts shall be deemed that party's separate property. Any funds deposited in a bank account held by the parties jointly shall be deemed joint property.

11.   PAYMENT OF EXPENSES. The parties agree that their expenses shall be paid as set forth in Exhibit F attached hereto and made a part hereof.

12.   INCOME FROM AND REINVESTMENT OF SEPARATE PROPERTY.

❑ (A) Any property obtained by either party due to the use, investment, reinvestment or any transfer of any portion of his or her separate property, and any income from any such property, and any appreciation in the value of such property, shall remain that party's separate property.

❑ (B) Any property obtained by either party due to the use, investment, reinvestment or any transfer of any portion of his or her separate property, and any income from any such property, shall remain that party's separate property. Any appreciation or other increase in the value of either party's separate property, shall remain that party's separate property, unless the other party has made a direct financial contribution to the increase in value, such as by investing his or her own funds, and then only to the proportion of the increase attributable to his or her investment.

13.   RESIDENCE OF THE PARTIES.

❑ (A) It is expressly recognized that the Husband and Wife are joint owners of the residence occupied by the parties at _____.

❏ (B) It is expressly recognized that the ❏ Husband ❏ Wife is the sole owner of the residence occupied by the parties at _____ and that the use of any joint funds, or separate funds of the other party, for the mortgage payments, utilities, capital improvements, repair or maintenance of the residence and grounds for the joint benefit of the parties shall not create any interest in the property in the other party.

❏ (C) It is expressly recognized that the ❏ Husband ❏ Wife is the sole owner of the residence occupied by the parties at _____ and that the use of any joint funds, or separate funds of the other party, for the mortgage payments, utilities, repair or maintenance of the residence and grounds for the joint benefit of the parties shall not create any interest in the property in the other party. However, if joint funds or the other party's separate funds are used to make capital improvements on the property, the other party shall thereafter have a lien against the property to the extent of one-half of the total joint funds, or the full amount of the separate funds, contributed, which lien shall be paid upon the sale of the property, the termination of the marriage, or the death of the Husband or Wife, whichever occurs first.

14.   **DISPOSITION OF PROPERTY.** Each party retains the ownership, management and control of his or her separate property, and may encumber, sell, or dispose of the property without the other party's consent. Each party shall, on the request of the other, execute any instrument necessary to effectuate this paragraph. The failure ore refusal of a party to join in or execute an instrument required by this paragraph shall entitle the other party to sue for specific performance or for damages, regardless of the doctrine of spousal immunity, and the defaulting party shall pay the other party's costs, expenses, and attorney's fees. This paragraph shall not require a party to execute a promissory note or other evidence of debt for the other party; but if a party executes a promissory note or other evidence of debt for the other party, that other party shall indemnify the party executing the note or other evidence of debt from any claims or demands arising from the execution of the instrument. Execution of an instrument shall not give the executing party any right or interest in the property of the party requesting execution.

15.   **PROPERTY DIVISION UPON DIVORCE, DISSOLUTION OF MARRIAGE, OR SEPARATION.** In the event of divorce, dissolution of marriage, or separation proceedings being filed and pursued by either party, the parties agree that the terms and provisions of this agreement shall govern all of their rights as to property; alimony including permanent, periodic, rehabilitative, and lump sum; property settlement; rights of community property; and equitable distribution against the other. Each party releases and waives any claims for special equity in the other party's separate property or in jointly owned property. If either party files for alimony, or spousal support unconnected with divorce, dissolution of marriage, separation, or separate maintenance, the parties agree that the party filing said proceedings shall ask the court to follow the provisions and terms of this postmarital agreement.

16.   **ALIMONY.**

❏ (A) In the event of divorce or dissolution of marriage proceedings being filed by either party in any state or country, each party forever waives any right to claim or seek any form of alimony or spousal support, and attorneys' fees and costs from the other. Any rights regarding distribution of property are otherwise covered by this agreement, and any rights to community property or claims of special equity are waived and released. In the event that a final judgment or decree of divorce or dissolution of marriage is entered, the parties agree that the provisions of this agreement are in complete settlement of all rights to claim or seek any form of financial support, except child support for any living minor children of the parties, from the other.

❏ (B) In the event divorce, dissolution of marriage, separation, or similar proceedings are filed by either party in any state or country, the parties agree that neither party will request or receive alimony or support, whether temporary, rehabilitative, permanent, or lump sum. In consideration for not requesting alimony, the ❏ Husband ❏ Wife shall pay to the other party a sum equal to $_____ for each full year of marriage up to the date a divorce, dissolution of marriage, separation, or similar action is filed. Said sum shall be paid regardless of which party files, and shall terminate on either the death or remarriage of the payee, or on the death of the payor, whichever occurs first.

❏ (C) In the event of divorce or dissolution of marriage proceedings being filed by either party in any state or country, the ❏ Husband ❏ Wife agrees to pay to the other party temporary and rehabilitative alimony in the sum of $_____ per _____, for a period of _____ years after the date a divorce, dissolution of marriage, or separation action is filed. Said sum shall be paid regardless of which party files, and shall terminate at the end of the period stated above, or on either the death or remarriage of the payee, or on the death of the payor, whichever occurs first.

❏ (D) In the event of divorce or dissolution of marriage proceedings being filed by either party in any state or country, the ❏ Husband ❏ Wife agrees to pay to the other party temporary and permanent periodic alimony in the sum of $_____ per _____. Said sum shall be paid regardless of which party files, and shall terminate on either the death or remarriage of the payee, or on the death of the payor, whichever occurs first.

17.   **CHILD SUPPORT.**

❏ (A) In the event of divorce, dissolution of marriage, or separation, and there are any minor children of the parties' marriage, the parties agree that each shall contribute to the support of any such children in the following proportions:

_____% from the Husband.

_____% from the Wife.

❏ (B) The amount of support shall be determined by agreement of the parties. If the parties cannot agree, the amount of support shall be determined by the court.

Such child support shall continue until:
❏   Age 18.
❏   Age 18, or graduation from high school, whichever occurs last, provided any such child is enrolled as a full-time student and is making a good faith effort to graduate.
❏   Graduation from college or trade school, provided any such child is enrolled as a full-time student and is making a good faith effort to graduate.

Both parties acknowledge that they are aware that the court has the ultimate authority to determine child support, taking into consideration the needs of the children and any other factors required by law to be considered.

18.   **DISPOSITION UPON DEATH.**

❏ (A) Each party consents that his or her estate, or the estate of the other, may be disposed of by will, codicil, or trust, or in the absence of any such instrument, according to the laws of descent and distribution and intestate succession as if the marriage of the parties had not taken place. In either event, the estate shall be free of any claim or demand of inheritance, dower, curtesy, elective share, family allowance, homestead election, right to serve as executor, administrator, or personal representative, or any spousal or other claim given by law, irrespective of the marriage and any law to the contrary. Neither party intends by this agreement to limit or restrict the right to give to, or receive from, the other an inter vivos or testamentary gift. Neither party intends by this agreement to release, waive, or relinquish any devise or bequest left to either by specific provision in the will or codicil of the other, any property voluntarily transferred by the other, any joint tenancy created by the other, or any right to serve as executor or personal representative of the other's estate if specifically nominated in the other's will or codicil.

❏ (B) Subject to the conditions set forth in this paragraph, the ❏ Husband ❏ Wife shall receive and accept from the other party after his/her death, the sum of $_____, free of any and all inheritance and estate taxes, in place of, and in full and final settlement and satisfaction of, any and all rights and claims which he/she might otherwise have in the other party's estate and property under any law now or hereafter in force in this or any other jurisdiction, whether by way of a right of election to take against the other party's will, as a share of the estate in intestacy, or otherwise. The ❏ Husband ❏ Wife shall only be entitled to receive said amount if all of the following conditions are met: (1) the parties were married at the time of death, (2) he/she survives the decedent, (3) the parties were not separated at the time of death, and (4) no divorce, dissolution of marriage, or separation proceedings were in progress at the time of death. If any of the above conditions are not met, then he/she shall not be entitled to any sums from the other party's estate.

19.   LIFE INSURANCE. The parties shall maintain the following life insurance policies payable to the other party on death in the face amounts of at least:

Life insurance on the life of the Husband payable to the Wife or a person she designates of at least $_____.

Life insurance on the life of the Wife payable to the Husband or a person he designates of at least $_____.

20.   DEBTS. The parties may incur debts either individually or jointly. Neither party shall assume or become responsible for the payment of any debts or obligations of the other party because of their marriage. Neither party shall do anything that would cause any debt or obligation of one of them to become a claim, demand, lien, or encumbrance on the other's property without the other party's written consent. If a debt or obligation of one party is asserted as a claim or demand against the other's separate property without such written consent, the party who is responsible for the debt or obligation shall indemnify the other from the claim or demand, including the payment of the other party's costs, expenses, and attorney's fees.

21.   HOMESTEAD. Each party releases any claim, demand, right, or interest that the party may have acquired because of their marriage in any real property of the other because of the homestead property provisions of the laws of any state concerning the descent of the property as homestead.

22.   COMMINGLING OF INCOME AND ASSETS. The parties recognize that it is possible for their income or assets to become, or appear to become, commingled. It is the parties' intention that any commingling of income or assets shall not be interpreted to imply any abandonment of the terms and provisions of this agreement, that the provisions contained herein regarding the parties' interests in jointly held property be applied, and that in other instances each party's interest be determined by each party's proportionate contribution toward the total funds or value of assets in question.

23. TAX RETURNS/GIFTS/LEGAL PROCEEDINGS. The fact that the parties may file joint local, state, or federal income tax returns, or any other joint tax papers or documents, or make gifts of property or cash to each other or not account to each other with regard to the expenditure of income shall not be interpreted to imply any abandonment of the terms and provisions of this agreement. The filing of a divorce, dissolution of marriage, separation, or other legal action or proceeding shall not be deemed as any abandonment of the terms and provisions of this agreement.

24. FREE AND VOLUNTARY ACT. The parties acknowledge that executing this agreement is a free and voluntary act, and has not been entered into for any reason other than the desire for the furtherance of their relationship in marriage. Each party acknowledges that he or she has had adequate time to fully consider the consequences of signing this agreement, and has not been pressured, threatened, coerced, or unduly influenced to sign this agreement.

25. GOVERNING LAW. This agreement shall be governed by the laws of _____.

26. SEVERABILITY. If any part of this agreement is adjudged invalid, illegal, or unenforceable, the remaining parts shall not be affected.

27. FURTHER ASSURANCE. Each party shall execute any instruments or documents at any time requested by the other party that are necessary or proper to effectuate this agreement.

28. BINDING AGREEMENT/NO OTHER BENEFICIARY. This agreement shall be binding upon the parties, and upon their heirs, executors, personal representatives, administrators, and assigns. No person shall have a right or cause of action arising or resulting from this agreement except those who are parties to it and their successors in interest.

29. RELEASE. Except as otherwise provided in this agreement, each party releases all claims or demands to the property or estate of the other, however and whenever acquired, including acquisitions in the future.

30. ENTIRE AGREEMENT. This instrument, including any attached exhibits, constitutes the entire agreement of the parties. No representations or promises have been made except those that are set out in this agreement. This agreement may not be modified or terminated except in writing signed by the parties.

31. PARAGRAPH HEADINGS. The headings of the paragraphs contained in this agreement are for convenience only, and are not to be considered a part of this agreement or used in determining its content or context.

32. ATTORNEYS' FEES IN ENFORCEMENT. A party who fails to comply with any provision or obligation contained in this agreement shall pay the other party's attorney's fees, costs, and other expenses reasonably incurred in enforcing this agreement and resulting from the noncompliance.

33. SIGNATURES AND INITIALS OF PARTIES. The signatures of the parties on this document, and their initials on each page, indicate that each party has read, and agrees with, this entire Postmarital Agreement, including any and all exhibits attached hereto. Any provision containing a box, ❏, that does not contain an "X" does not apply and is not a part of the agreement of the parties.

34. ❏ OTHER PROVISIONS. Additional provisions are contained in the Addendum to Postmarital Agreement attached hereto and made a part hereof.

_____   _____
Husband   Wife

Executed in the presence of:

_____   _____
Name: _____   Name: _____
Address:_____   Address:_____
_____   _____

STATE OF   )
COUNTY OF   )

    The foregoing Postmarital Agreement, consisting of _____ pages and Exhibits _____ through _____, was acknowledged before me this _____ day of _____, _____, by

_____

_____,

the above-named Husband, Wife, and Witnesses respectively, who are personally known to me or who have produced _____

_____ as identification.

_____
Signature

_____
(Typed Name of Acknowledger)

NOTARY PUBLIC
Commission Number:_____
My Commission Expires:

PROPERTY OWNERSHIP AGREEMENT

The parties agree that the personal property described below shall be deemed the sole property of the ❏ Husband ❏ Wife.

Description of property (include, make, model, serial number, etc., if applicable):

Date of Purchase: _____

Place of Purchase: _____

Dated: _____ Dated: _____

_____ _____

Husband   Wife

Index

About the Author

Edward A. Haman received his law degree in 1978 from the University of Toledo College of Law. As a student, he served as coordinator of the law school's Client Counseling Competition team, and as editor of the law school's legal journal, *Discovery*. He also has a bachelor of arts degree from Western Michigan University, with a major in communication and minors in accounting and general business.

Since graduating from law school, he has practiced law in three states. In Hawaii, Mr. Haman was engaged in general private practice, initially as a sole practitioner, then with a small law firm emphasizing family law, real estate, and business law. This included trial practice, as well as criminal appellate work before the Supreme Court of Hawaii and the U.S Court of Appeals in San Francisco. In Michigan, he served as a Circuit Court domestic relations hearing officer. After moving to Florida in 1986, he spent several years as an attorney for the Florida social services agency, handling a variety of legal matters, including cases involving the abuse and neglect of children, the elderly, and the disabled; public health matters; child support enforcement; welfare fraud; and the licensing of assisted living facilities, nursing homes, and other health care facilities. Mr. Haman has also engaged in private practice in area such as real estate, family law, and probate.

Since 1987, Mr. Haman has authored and co-authored numerous self-help law books, including *The Complete Bankruptcy Guide*, *File Your Own Divorce*, and *The Complete Living Will Kit*. In connection with the self-help law books, he has been a guest on numerous radio programs, and has appeared on the Fox News Channel. He has also written several articles for *The Florida Keystone Series*, a legal publication for attorneys. Currently residing in Tampa, Florida, Mr. Haman continues to write books, and also volunteers as a support group facilitator for the Alzheimer's Association. In his spare time, he enjoys traveling, kayaking, snow skiing, hiking, and mountaineering.

How to Use the CD-ROM

Thank you for purchasing *The Complete Prenuptial Agreement Kit*. In this book, we have worked hard to compile exactly what you need to customize and complete your own prenuptial agreement. To make this material even more useful, we have included every document in the book on the CD-ROM in the back of the book.

You can use these forms just as you would the forms in the book. Print them out, fill them in, and use them however you need. You can also fill in the forms directly on your computer. Just identify the form you need, open it, click on the space where the information should go, and input your information. Customize each form for your particular needs. Use them over and over again.

The CD-ROM is compatible with both PC and Mac operating systems. (While it should work with either operating system, we cannot guarantee that it will work with your particular system and we cannot provide technical assistance.) To use the forms on your computer, you will need to use Microsoft Word or another word processing program that can read Word files. The CD-ROM does not contain any such program.

Insert the CD-ROM into your computer. Double-click on the icon representing the disc on your desktop or go through your hard drive to identify the drive that contains the disc and click on it.

Once opened, you will see the files contained on the CD-ROM listed as "Form #: [Form Title]." Open the file you need. You may print the form to fill it out manually at this point, or you can click on the appropriate line to fill it in using your computer.

* * * * *

Purchasers of this book are granted a license to use the forms contained in it for their own personal use. By purchasing this book, you have also purchased a limited license to use all forms on the accompanying CD-ROM. The license limits you to personal use only and all other copyright laws must be adhered to. No claim of copyright is made in any government form reproduced in the book or on the CD-ROM. You are free to modify the forms and tailor them to your specific situation.

The author and publisher have attempted to provide the most current and up-to-date information available. However, the courts, Congress, and your state's legislatures review, modify, and change laws on an ongoing basis, as well as create new laws from time to time. Due to the very nature of the information and the continual changes in our legal system, to be sure that you have the current and best information for your situation, you should consult a local attorney or research the current laws yourself.

This publication is designed to provide accurate and authoritative information in regard to the subject matter covered. It is sold with the understanding that the publisher is not engaged in rendering legal, accounting, or other professional service. If legal advice or other expert assistance is required, the services of a competent professional person should be sought.

> —*From a Declaration of Principles Jointly Adopted by a Committee of the American Bar Association and a Committee of Publishers and Associations*

This product is not a substitute for legal advice.
> —*Disclaimer required by Texas statutes*

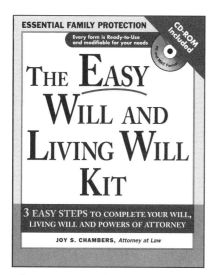
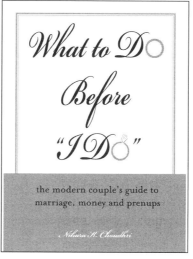
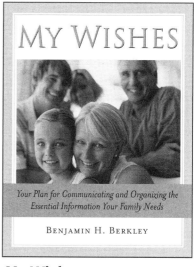

Sphinx® Publishing's National Titles
Valid in All 50 States

LEGAL SURVIVAL IN BUSINESS

The Complete Book of Corporate Forms (2E)	$29.95
The Complete Hiring and Firing Handbook	$19.95
The Complete Limited Liability Kit	$24.95
The Complete Partnership Book	$24.95
The Complete Patent Book	$26.95
The Complete Patent Kit	$39.95
The Entrepreneur's Internet Handbook	$21.95
The Entrepreneur's Legal Guide	$26.95
Financing Your Small Business	$16.95
Fired, Laid-Off or Forced Out	$14.95
Form Your Own Corporation (5E)	$29.95
The Home-Based Business Kit	$14.95
How to Buy a Franchise	$19.95
How to Form a Nonprofit Corporation (3E)	$24.95
How to Register Your Own Copyright (5E)	$24.95
HR for Small Business	$14.95
Incorporate in Delaware from Any State	$26.95
Incorporate in Nevada from Any State	$24.95
The Law (In Plain English)® for Restaurants	$16.95
The Law (In Plain English)® for Small Business	$19.95
The Law (In Plain English)® for Writers	$14.95
Making Music Your Business	$18.95
Minding Her Own Business (4E)	$14.95
Most Valuable Business Legal Forms You'll Ever Need (3E)	$21.95
Profit from Intellectual Property	$28.95
Protect Your Patent	$24.95
The Small Business Owner's Guide to Bankruptcy	$21.95
Start Your Own Law Practice	$16.95
Tax Power for the Self-Employed	$17.95
Tax Smarts for Small Business	$21.95
Your Rights at Work	$14.95

LEGAL SURVIVAL IN COURT

Attorney Responsibilities & Client Rights	$19.95
Crime Victim's Guide to Justice (2E)	$21.95
Legal Research Made Easy (4E)	$24.95
Winning Your Personal Injury Claim (3E)	$24.95

LEGAL SURVIVAL IN REAL ESTATE

The Complete Kit to Selling Your Own Home	$18.95
The Complete Book of Real Estate Contracts	$18.95
Essential Guide to Real Estate Leases	$18.95
Homeowner's Rights	$19.95
How to Buy a Condominium or Townhome (2E)	$19.95
How to Buy Your First Home (2E)	$14.95
How to Make Money on Foreclosures	$16.95
The Mortgage Answer Book	$14.95
Sell Your Own Home Without a Broker	$14.95
The Weekend Landlord	$16.95
The Weekend Real Estate Investor	$14.95
Working with Your Homeowners Association	$19.95

LEGAL SURVIVAL IN SPANISH

Cómo Comprar su Primera Casa	$8.95
Cómo Conseguir Trabajo en los Estados Unidos	$8.95
Cómo Hacer su Propio Testamento	$16.95
Cómo Iniciar su Propio Negocio	$8.95
Cómo Negociar su Crédito	$8.95
Cómo Organizar un Presupuesto	$8.95
Cómo Solicitar su Propio Divorcio	$24.95
Guía de Inmigración a Estados Unidos (4E)	$24.95
Guía de Justicia para Víctimas del Crimen	$21.95
Guía Esencial para los Contratos de Arrendamiento de Bienes Raices	$22.95
Inmigración y Ciudadanía en los EE.UU. Preguntas y Respuestas	$16.95
Inmigración a los EE.UU. Paso a Paso (2E)	$24.95
Manual de Beneficios del Seguro Social	$18.95
El Seguro Social Preguntas y Respuestas	$16.95
¡Visas! ¡Visas! ¡Visas!	$9.95

LEGAL SURVIVAL IN PERSONAL AFFAIRS

101 Complaint Letters That Get Results	$18.95
The 529 College Savings Plan (2E)	$18.95
The 529 College Savings Plan Made Simple	$7.95
The Alternative Minimum Tax	$14.95
The Antique and Art Collector's Legal Guide	$24.95
The Childcare Answer Book	$12.95
Child Support	$18.95
The Complete Book of Insurance	$18.95
The Complete Book of Personal Legal Forms	$24.95
The Complete Credit Repair Kit	$19.95
The Complete Legal Guide to Senior Care	$21.95
The Complete Personal Bankruptcy Guide	$21.95
Credit Smart	$18.95
The Easy Will and Living Will Kit	$16.95
Fathers' Rights	$19.95
File Your Own Divorce (6E)	$24.95
The Frequent Traveler's Guide	$14.95
Gay & Lesbian Rights (2E)	$21.95
Grandparents' Rights (4E)	$24.95
How to Parent with Your Ex	$12.95
How to Write Your Own Living Will (4E)	$18.95
How to Write Your Own Premarital Agreement (3E)	$24.95
The Infertility Answer Book	$16.95
Law 101	$16.95
Law School 101	$16.95
The Living Trust Kit	$21.95
Living Trusts and Other Ways to Avoid Probate (3E)	$24.95
Make Your Own Simple Will (4E)	$26.95
Mastering the MBE	$16.95
Money and Divorce	$14.95
My Wishes	$21.95
Nursing Homes and Assisted Living Facilities	$19.95
Power of Attorney Handbook (6E)	$24.95
Quick Cash	$14.95
Seniors' Rights	$19.95
Sexual Harassment in the Workplace	$18.95
Sexual Harassment: Your Guide to Legal Action	$18.95
Sisters-in-Law	$16.95
The Social Security Benefits Handbook (4E)	$18.95
Social Security Q&A	$12.95
Starting Out or Starting Over	$14.95
Teen Rights (and Responsibilities) (2E)	$14.95
Unmarried Parents' Rights (and Responsibilities)(3E)	$16.95
U.S. Immigration and Citizenship Q&A	$18.95
U.S. Immigration Step by Step (2E)	$24.95
U.S.A. Immigration Guide (5E)	$26.95
What They Don't Teach You in College	$12.95
What to Do—Before "I DO"	$14.95
The Wills and Trusts Kit (2E)	$29.95
Win Your Unemployment Compensation Claim (2E)	$21.95
Your Right to Child Custody, Visitation and Support (3E)	$24.95